CONSTRUCTION PROFIT MANAGEMENT

THE SECRETS OF SUCCESSFUL CONTRACTING

LEONARD BRUNOTTE

Prentice-Hall, Inc.
Englewood Cliffs, New Jersey

Prentice-Hall International, Inc., *London*
Prentice-Hall of Australia, Pty. Ltd., *Sydney*
Prentice-Hall Canada, Inc., *Toronto*
Prentice-Hall of India Private Ltd., *New Delhi*
Prentice-Hall of Japan, Inc., *Tokyo*
Prentice-Hall of Southeast Asia Pte. Ltd., *Singapore*
Editora Prentice-Hall do Brasil Ltda., *Rio de Janeiro*
Prentice-Hall Hispanoamericana, S.A., *Mexico*

© 1987 by

Leonard Brunotte

10   9   8   7   6   5   4   3   2   1

Library of Congress Cataloging-in-Publication Data

Brunotte, Leonard.
  Construction profit management.

  Includes index.
  1. Construction industry—Management. 2. Building—
Contracts and specifications. I. Title.
HD9715.A2B78   1987   692'.8   87-1168

ISBN 0-13-168980-0

Printed in the United States of America

To my family...
and to the one who directed
and edited this work...
my son, Leonard Michael

About the Author

LEONARD BRUNOTTE has more than twenty-five years of technical construction, business management, and management consulting experience in the construction industry. He is president of Deerfield Consultants and Associates, Inc., and president of Industrial Environmental Controls, Inc.

Deerfield Consultants and Associates, Inc. is a management consulting company whose objective is to provide solutions to profit management problems in the construction industry. It focuses on developing technical research and implementing positive practical CONSTRUCTION PROFIT MANAGEMENT solutions for both project and company management problems of risk, bid, money, and collection management.

Industrial Environmental Controls, Inc. (electrical constructors) emphasizes design and construction of air pollution projects for utilities and solid waste disposal facilities for government municipalities. IEC has performed construction projects for many major companies, such as Revere Copper and Brass, Commonwealth Edison Company, Dairyland Power Co-Op, Mechanical Nuclear Division of General Electric, American Boiler and Tank Company, and the Reilly Stoker Corporation.

Mr. Brunotte has demonstrated his expertise in a wide range of technical construction areas—including engineering, project management, purchasing, scheduling, field supervision, start-up, and acceptance—as well as the business management areas of risk, bid, money, and collection management. He has worked on government, utility, industrial, and commercial construction projects, and he has extensive experience working closely with developers, architects, consulting engineers, manufacturers, and contractors.

Mr. Brunotte held positions of vice-president and general manager at Industrial Environmental Controls, Inc.; as project manager of governmental municipal projects at Plibrico Company, a $150 million a year international manufacturing/construction company; and at Frank R. Valvoda and Associates, consulting engineers, as assistant to the president. While at Valvoda, 1,500 construction projects for industrial and commercial clients were completed, valued in excess of $250 million.

Mr. Brunotte was awarded the keys to two U.S. cities, Buffalo, New York, and New Orleans, Louisiana, in recognition of his work on their major solid waste disposal facilities. Moreover, one of his projects in Dade County, Florida, received a national recognition award by the National Society of Professional Engineers.

Mr. Brunotte has an M.B.A. degree from Loyola University of Chicago, where he concentrated in the additional areas of international business, marketing, and finance, and a bachelor's degree from Northeastern Illinois University.

Who Can Benefit by Using *Construction Profit Management?*

This book is uniquely written for the construction industry and provides "educated communication" for everyone involved in the construction process. Its content is extremely valuable to contractors, architects and engineers, attorneys, accountants, insurers, financiers, manufacturers and suppliers, owners, and developers alike.

Contractors just starting in business and those already established in business will find CONSTRUCTION PROFIT MANAGEMENT vital to their success—those fighting for survival and those already established. The ones who need and want the secrets of big profit and fast company growth are provided immediate project and company management answers that they can use today.

Architects and Engineers will find the project management information invaluable, as it will provide administrative and negotiating information and ideas for developing new and improved services for their clients. They will be given in-depth insight into how to get the project they designed, built the way they designed it, in the time they scheduled, and constructed for the dollars they estimated.

Attorneys will be provided immediate in-depth insight into construction problems, and contractors will gain insight into the legal problems and their solutions that the attorneys face. The result of this book will bring improved communication between attorney and client. It will enable the attorney to determine what is fair and equitable for everyone, and it also provides practical ways to substantiate entitlement and quantum of construction losses.

Accountants will also be given in-depth insight into construction problems, and contractors will acquire insights into the cost accounting problems and solutions that accountants face. Also, if the accountant is working for someone other than a contractor on a particular construction project, this book will be helpful in providing ideas for negotiating support and mitigation of damages.

Insurers will find immediate insight into many facets of construction technical and profit management vital to their ability to accurately underwrite construction risks, upgrade claims management, and improve sales. Underwriters and safety engineers will gain a complete understanding of the scope and extent of construction risks so important to their areas of responsibility. Claims managers will learn how claims emerge and how many not heretofore quantifiable can be determined. Sales managers and agents will discover a treasure house of information and ideas upon which to build strong, accurate, and competitive sales approaches. Bonding companies are provided information enabling them to more thoroughly underwrite coverages and to determine and defend claims for those involved in the construction process.

Financiers will learn new elements for maximizing profits— what projects and what companies will be successful. They will find the information invaluable when evaluating construction loan applications. And for the contractor: insights into the concerns of those financing the construction project as well as the contracting company that will enhance their financing proposals.

Manufacturers and Suppliers will find this book extremely useful, whether they do construction installation as a profit center or whether they do not. Manufacturers will find an improved common base of knowledge relative to the construction process for more profitable results. In addition, both manufacturers and suppliers will discover what affects their liability and what does not.

Owners and Developers will learn many new project management ideas for maximizing profits—whether performing one construction project, many construction projects, or for selling what has been built. They will find the information invaluable to build the highest quality project, in the shortest possible time, at the lowest possible cost. This will assist them to successfully calculate and negotiate the correct amount of financial resources needed for their construction project(s). In addition, developers will acquire knowledge to calculate and competitively price their project. Therefore, this information should enable the owners and developers to pursue success in their primary business activities. The contractor will gain the information he needs to successfully "quarter back" the whole team involved in the construction process.

How This Book Will Help You Dramatically Improve Your Construction Profits

CONSTRUCTION PROFIT MANAGEMENT: THE SECRETS OF SUCCESSFUL CONTRACTING is the first and only comprehensive, carefully organized, and fully illustrated book that guides you step-by-step to successful and profitable construction. In a single volume, you'll find all the techniques of profit management through easy-to-understand language, research data, graphs, diagrams, charts, and cases that add up to a proven system for making big profits.

CONSTRUCTION PROFIT MANAGEMENT: THE SECRETS OF SUCCESSFUL CONTRACTING provides all the tools for producing maximum profit at minimum risk in the shortest possible time and at the lowest possible cost. Here are just a few of the profit-making techniques this *Guide* shows you:

- *How to* decrease administration time and increase construction management efficiency and leadership performance.
- *How to* get the project built the way it was designed, in the time scheduled and for the amount estimated.

- *How to* quickly read and easily evaluate your legal contract, finding those items of big profit or huge loss.
- *How to* map your potential for growth and profit and make sure big profit contracts do not slip by unnoticed.
- *How to* ask "What if...?" questions before a loss instead of "I should have...?" afterward.
- *How to* establish communication between all principals in the construction process—make sure everyone understands and is correctly executing your instructions.
- *How to* determine the best method of collection and the optimum method of payment for you and your client.
- *How to* "outbid" your competition—increase your profit and lower your bid price—and how to calculate and make sure what percentage should be used in the project bid for overhead and for profit.
- *How to* identify contract risks, how they can be controlled, and how to take action to effectively control the risks.
- *How to* negotiate and win the next big contract from the one you are working on now.
- *How to* determine strategies to carry out company goals and implement cost effective tactics to actualize the strategies.
- *How to* ensure that you will have the money you need when you need it.
- *How to* "crunch" vexing balance sheet and income statement numbers to make them useful in Construction Profit Management.
- *How to* determine the real dollar cost of construction delays.
- *How to* track profit—but of most importance how to make sure you keep the profit by tracking profit losses.
- *How to* determine if your profit losses are your fault or someone else's—how to recover your profit losses that are someone else's fault, with profit—and how to stop the profit losses that are your fault.
- *How to* identify and win the contracts you need and want—the most "bang for your buck."
- *How to* maximize the use of all cash received for growth and profit at the lowest risk to the owners.

- *How to* "set up" for super market penetration.
- *How to* create the time to find the best source of financing, time to "cut the best deal."
- *How to* chop down the mountains of financial data to only the few critical numbers needed for profitable action management of exceptions.
- *How to* schedule the project so everyone will understand the schedule: workman, foreman, superintendent, project manager, engineer, architect, manufacturer, and owner. The sequence and amount of men, material, and equipment.
- *How to* have the contract visually managed on a daily, weekly, or monthly basis to guarantee the project is built on time, with documentation.
- *How to* make sure your "extras" (including contract "extras") do not cost you profit.
- *How to* calculate your true "man-hour" insurance rate in dollars and in percentage of man-hour cost.
- *How to* set up your own internal insurance audit system.
- *How to* determine when you should rent construction equipment and when you should buy.
- *How to* prove if you need a computer—in dollars and cents—and if you do, what you need before you buy.
- *How to* collect ALL your hard-earned profits.

What Construction Profit Management Is and Why It Will Help You

CONSTRUCTION PROFIT MANAGEMENT is a comprehensive, highly organized management system that yields maximum *pre-planned* company profit and growth with minimum downside risk. This system is composed of four major elements: Risk Management, Bid Management, Money Management, and Collection Management, which execute the goals set by the predetermined company business plan or project schedule which are governed by a "watch-dog" Information and Control System.

CONSTRUCTION PROFIT MANAGEMENT increases profit while simultaneously decreasing construction costs by enhancing the total operating performance and leadership effectiveness of those involved in the construction process.

CONSTRUCTION PROFIT MANAGEMENT provides the construction industry with a system of educated communication, establishing a "common language of business" between every principal in the construction process: contractor, field supervisor, architect, engineer, attorney, accountant, insurer, financier, manufacturer, supplier, developer, and building owner.

CONSTRUCTION PROFIT MANAGEMENT has one primary objective: to receive full payment for constructing the highest quality project in the shortest possible time at the lowest possible cost.

It is an entirely new and proven system that you can use to devise a profit management program uniquely tailored to your needs. Here are just a few of the ways this *Guide* can help you:

Tools of profit management. Construction projects lose money because of the crippling lack of profit management. To prevent this from happening to you, this *Guide* illustrates the difference between technical management and profit management and explains why you need to master both areas to be successful. You'll discover the importance of knowing the profit equation, how to use break-even, and how to identify impacted damages. The difference between *new time* and *float time* and their effects on *how* and *when* you perform your contract are also explained (Chapter 1).

Guidelines for project control and big profits. Risk management means knowing what the risks are, knowing how they can be controlled, and taking action to control them effectively. In addition, explanations of possible profit effects are provided for 111 sources of profit losses (Chapter 2).

Ways to invoice for more than the original contract value. This is the secret of how to invoice the costs of those losses caused by others. It provides a working model to prepare your own invoice that can be used immediately. It clearly demonstrates the major sections and the intricacies of the substantiating report. It provides the format that will substantiate your losses and will completely overwhelm all opposition, receiving full payment in the shortest possible time, with a minimum of difficulty (Chapter 3).

Secrets of how to identify and win the contracts you need and want. Bid management is what you must know and do to win each project contract relative to the total profit and growth impact of all contracts won by your company. Bid management is the determination of strategies to carry out company goals and objectives and the development and implementation of tactics to actualize the strategies. You will learn how to map out internal and external company potential for growth and profits. This *Guide* also demonstrates the secret of how you can reduce your selling price to increase your profit (Chapter 4).

Techniques for project control, company growth and big profits. Money management is the management of all assets and liabilities for maximum owner benefits. With money management you are able to ask "What if...?" questions before a loss instead of "I should have ... " afterward. You will see how to maximize the use of all cash received for growth and profit at the lowest risk to the owners (Chapter 5).

Secrets for collecting big profits. Collection management determines the method of collection, the conditions of collection, and the optimum method of payment for you and your client. You are given the techniques to collect *all* your hard-earned profits...and how to get the next big contract from the one you are now working on (Chapter 6).

The method to guarantee fast growth and big profits. The information and control system is a comprehensive management action plan...a network of channels of communication and a system of checks and balances that manages the entire project schedule or business plan. It is a closed-loop system that ensures that instructions have been understood and are being carried out correctly. You'll learn about action management of exceptions— what you have to know and do to concentrate on those items that can cost you the most profit. You will find a system whereby management takes positive action to exceptions to *preplanned* profit and growth. You will be shown how to identify the problem, determine corrective action, ensure that effective corrective action has been taken, and the effectiveness of the action in guaranteeing preplanned profit. The information and control system also helps you know when to buy a computer, what you need before you buy, and how to know when you can afford a computer. It shows how to calculate in dollars whether or not you need a computer (Chapter 7).

MODEL FORMS, TABLES, CHARTS, AND GRAPHS

CONSTRUCTION PROFIT MANAGEMENT: THE SECRETS OF SUCCESSFUL CONTRACTING also provides you with a number of model forms, tables, charts, and graphs.

For example, the *Insurance Coverage Chart* in Chapter 5 is a powerful tool for evaluating commercial and self-insurance coverage presented in a comprehensive format that you can use immediately. The *Confidential Foreman's Cost Report* in Chapter 7 organizes each workman's jobsite activity, which allows everyone to know what is occurring and provides the information to make everyone involved in the construction process aware of it as soon as possible. The *Company Break-even Schedule* in Chapter 1 discloses the method to outbid the competition at a profit. It is a vital bidding and negotiating tool to win the contracts you need and want. The *Trend Chart* in Chapter 5 provides a quick and easy method to "crunch" the vexatious numbers of both balance sheet and income statement. It provides management a real tool for making operating decisions. The *Cash Flow Projection Chart* in Chapter 5 provides a time calendar to plan in advance when and how much money you will need, to ensure that you have the money you need when you need it. It creates sufficient time to "cut the best deal" and find the optimum source of financing. This is just a sample of the more than 250 "hands on" construction management tools you will find.

HOW TO USE THIS BOOK

CONSTRUCTION PROFIT MANAGEMENT shares the secrets of successful construction, providing you with the information you need to earn big profits by implementing your own personalized construction profit management program.

Each chapter clearly and concisely explains each element of construction profit management with practical, easy-to-understand language and gives special profit guides, profit aids, profit opportunity examples, and profit losses.

PROFIT GUIDES are written in bold type and appear interspersed throughout the book. These are helpful ideas or "catch-phrases" that are easy to remember.

PROFIT AIDS are graphs, tables, calculations, and forms that elaborate or illustrate concepts presented in the book. They provide models to use immediately or to help in designing your own system to guarantee big profits.

PROFIT OPPORTUNITY EXAMPLES are accounts of actual cases, which further explain the information presented with a "real world" application.

PROFIT LOSSES are a detailed listing of 111 precise sources of impacted damages that turn big profits into huge losses.

CONSTRUCTION PROFIT MANAGEMENT is a system whereby each chapter builds on the information from the preceding chapter(s) to develop a comprehensive profit management program. By reading each chapter consecutively you will gain a maximum amount of understanding in a minimum amount of time. By the time you have completed the final chapter, you will have a complete working knowledge of profit management. You will know how to use construction profit management to guarantee big profits.

To help you work more efficiently, a Directory that compiles all the profit guides, profit aids, and profit opportunity examples is provided. You are encouraged to use the Directory (located immediately following the text at the back of the book) before you read each chapter to help fix in your mind the profit secrets that you will discover in each chapter. Then by reading through the Directory at the conclusion of a chapter it will serve as a review of the secrets you have just learned. Chapter summaries are also provided for your review.

The Glossary compiles the terms used throughout the book. Because of the quantity and "newness" of most of these terms, you are encouraged to use the Glossary while reading the book.

The Directory, Glossary, and Index have been provided to give you a quick, easy way to find what you need, when you need it, to win your profits.

Preface

There are approximately 4 million businesses in the United States with roughly 25 percent in one way or another involved in the construction industry. This industry directly earns over $400 billion a year, which is over 9 percent of the gross national product.* With this tremendous volume of work and number of companies that find the construction industry important enough to serve, it is of no surprise that there are large profits to be made in construction. In fact, of the 25 percent of the companies involved, over 500,000 of them are contractors. However, it is astounding to learn that despite the great profit potential to be realized, the national business turnover rate for contractors is exceedingly high, often surpassing 20 percent a year.* Research shows that the majority of contractors manage to stay in business for only five years. Obviously, something is wrong.

To many contractors this paradox—of substantial amounts of work and potential profit versus a high risk of business failure—appears unmanageable. They find themselves in the dilemma of virtually working alone in the dark without sufficient business information or advice to cope with the situation. They feel the available material and advice is not especially applicable to construction and often find it impossible to explain the urgency and uniqueness of the problems they encounter to those professionals that provide them advice. It was not until I began doing management consulting work and had the opportunity of witnessing the tragedy of suffering contractors and builders firsthand, that I realized how widespread and serious the problem is in the industry.

*Council of Economic Advisors, *Economic Indicators* (Washington, D.C.: United States Government Printing Office, 1985).

While working with one of my clients who was having difficulty with a particular concept, he asked me for a book on the subject to study on his own. That night I stopped by the local book store, assuming my problem would be choosing which book was best. Much to my astonishment I could not find one. It is not surprising why these contractors lack the basic tools essential for success and why successful contractors and builders watch their bulging profits dwindle to enormous debt. These are tragedies that can be prevented! It was based on the need for this information that I wrote this book.

Leonard Brunotte

Acknowledgments

This book was made possible by the educational opportunities and patience of the faculty at the Graduate School of Business of Loyola University of Chicago for solidifying my marriage of theoretical business research with construction management problems. I would also like to express my gratitude to the many people and organizations who have provided experience, ideas, suggestions, and critical review of this work.

My appreciation begins with John Brunotte Sr., Birch Bruce, Ray Dixon, Esco Harrison, Marvin Hughes, Richy Hunter, Ron Kitchen, Bill Partain, Fred Roper, and Bill Smith, who have provided many valuable jobsite lessons which have been used in the text.

I am also indebted to Pat Barnett, Art Bennett, Earl Berry, Tony Cazolas, Ron Cook, Floyd Fernau, Ira Fogg, Roger Herre, Allan Horst, Allan Giesen, Art Kleinrath, Tom Malone, Bob Ormond, Burt Reilly, Joe Rockleman, Lou Ross, Paul Stevens, Frank Valvoda, Don Wahlen, Roy Will, Tom Wood, and Fred Wysk, whom I have worked with through the years and who have provided many critical and practical construction business lessons, often serving like laboratory experimenters developing the entire concept of *Construction Profit Management*.

I am grateful to Dr. Oscar Bedrosian, Dr. Ralph Brill, Norm Kozy, Ed Nicewick, Leonard March, Charles McWaters, Virginia McWaters, and Chuck Reed, colleagues who have directly contributed to the technical development and refinement of *Construction Profit Management* through their experience and friendship which they provided in overgenerous amounts.

In addition, I wish to thank Andrew Alpern of Coopers & Lybrand Co., Roger Burns of Hayden/Wegman Engineering Co., Jeff

Farr of Peat, Marwick, Mitchell & Co., Colonel F. H. Griffis of the U.S. Army Corps of Engineers, Mike Kelly of the First Bank of Oak Park, Dr. A. G. Malliaris of the Graduate School of Business at Loyola University of Chicago, Mike Marinelli of Inter County Construction Co., Donald Miller of the Frank B. Hall Insurance Co., Ed Nicewick of the Law Firm Nisen, Elliott & Meier, Don Scott of The Associated General Contractors of America, Mike Shirley of Morrison-Knudsen Construction Co., Denis Slavich of the Bechtel Group Inc., and Daniel Walter of The National Electrical Contractors Association, for their tremendous personal effort and time to provide their critical review of this book. I also would like to thank their companies or organizations for graciously providing these reviews.

Finally, I would like to express my special gratitude to my loving wife, Jane Mary, and my son, Leonard Michael Brunotte, for their support and long hours at the PC; and the staff at Prentice-Hall: acquisitions editor Olivia Lane and senior production editor Catherine Johnson, who so conscientiously worked with me to see this book to its final form. I couldn't have done it without you.

To my readers, I welcome your construction management insight. I sincerely believe *Construction Profit Management* is a dynamic program that can certainly benefit and only improve from the experience of everyone involved in the construction process.

Contents

————————————————

How to Succeed with a Profit Management Program— And Why Contractors Lose Money

WHY TECHNICAL "KNOW-HOW" ISN'T ENOUGH TO BE SUCCESSFUL

A contractor is literally out of business every time he completes a project. By definition, a contractor is only "in business" when he is performing a particular contract. Since the completion of a project is the contractor's sole source of income, *each* project often involves gut-twisting personal financial risk and requires unique and careful consideration.

Why, then, do contractors lose money? The answer is simple. Contractors lose money because they are *construction experts*. A construction expert is a technical expert in his field. However, technical know-how is not enough. Sure it's important. Your clients expect you to be an expert in the field. But to be successful you must also be a *profit management expert*.

A contractor who is a profit management expert knows the secrets that allow him to guarantee and to collect *all* of his profits. He utilizes a system that identifies his profits and ensures that his profit is collected on *every* project.

As you read the following chapters, the secrets of profit management will become obvious to you. But don't let their simplicity fool you. If these secrets are so simple, then why do the majority of contractors limp along with profit-losing jobs and then, after many years of backbreaking work, go out of business and close their doors forever?

THE PROFIT EQUATION:
KEY TO UNDERSTANDING HOW TO MAKE MONEY

The secret key to success is understanding the profit equation and knowing the secrets of profit management. Very few contractors understand the profit equation, which is why very few consistently make money.

The profit equation states that

$$\boxed{\text{PROFIT} = \text{FULL PAYMENT}}$$

Without full payment, there is no profit. A contractor must collect *all* of his profits. Not half, not 80 percent, but all of his profits. Figure 1.1 is a diagram that illustrates the major compo-

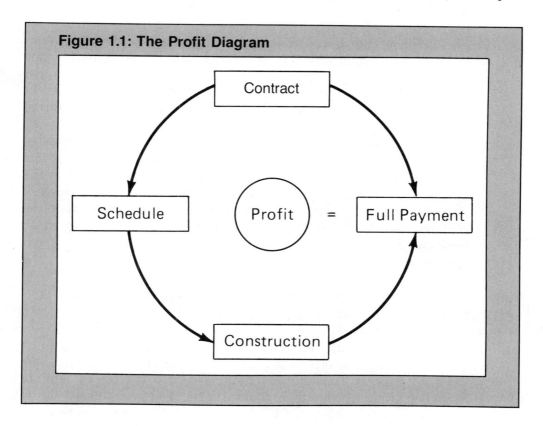

Figure 1.1: The Profit Diagram

nents that make up a project. Consider the areas in which you may be losing profits. Can you identify which area is losing you the most profit?

To begin to understand the dynamics of the profit equation and the profit diagram, the distinct difference between a contractor and a contracting company must be clearly understood. It is the basis for developing the knowledge you need to sucessfully manage either a contract or a contracting company.

The Difference Between a Contractor and a Contracting Company

A *contract* is a promise to perform a specified task. A *contractor* earns income by performing a contract. A *contracting company* is a firm that performs more than one contract over an extended period of time. Time and the number of contracts performed are the determining factors in understanding the difference between a contractor and a contracting company.

Being a successful contractor and being successful in contracting are often thought to be the same, but actually they represent two separate ideas. To be a successful contractor, you must have successfully performed a *single* contract. To be successful in contracting, you must have a successful contracting company that performs *many* contracts.

Similar knowledge must be used to manage both a successful contract and a successful contracting company, but a contract requires management of only the defined conditions stated in the contract documents, while the contracting company requires not only the management of the contract conditions, but also the management of internal and external variables affecting daily business operations. These variables include pricing, costs, expenses, profits, and market timing.

WHAT YOU NEED TO ESTABLISH A COMPREHENSIVE CONSTRUCTION MANAGEMENT SYSTEM

Both the individual contractor and the contracting company must have a system that efficiently manages their contract or firm. We refer to this as *construction management*. Contractors tend to overspecialize in the technical aspects of the industry while ignoring profit managing skills. A comprehensive construction management system that consists of both *technical management* and *profit management* is therefore essential.

The Role of Technical and Profit Management

Technical management refers to estimating and engineering capabilities applied to labor, material installation techniques, and cost control.

Profit management refers to risk management, bid management, money management, and collection management. Profit management is based on the knowledge and control of the dynamics of the profit equation and how risk, bid, money, and collection management positively or negatively impact profit. This book will focus your attention and efforts on understanding profit management and its essential role in guaranteeing *preplanned* profits on every project and in building a successful contracting company.

Let's take a look at Figure 1.2, which illustrates the Construction Management Model and the role of technical and profit management.

The Controlling Factor:
The Project Schedule or Business Plan

As you can see, technical management and profit management are represented as equal and balancing factors. A successful contractor will utilize both these factors of construction management efficiently. You cannot have one without the other. Take note of the "controlling factor," labeled the *Project Schedule or Business Plan*. The project schedule and the business plan are the guiding forces of any project or company, respectively. All management (technical and profit) must conform to the project schedule and to the business plan.

The *project schedule* allows you to complete a project by charting its progress and seeing that it is completed according to the original contract documents. In other words, a project schedule is the game plan for completing an individual project on time and on budget.

The *business plan* is the overall organizational strategy of a contracting firm. The plan consists of the basic goals and objectives of the organization, the major programs of actions, and the allocation of resources needed to achieve these goals.

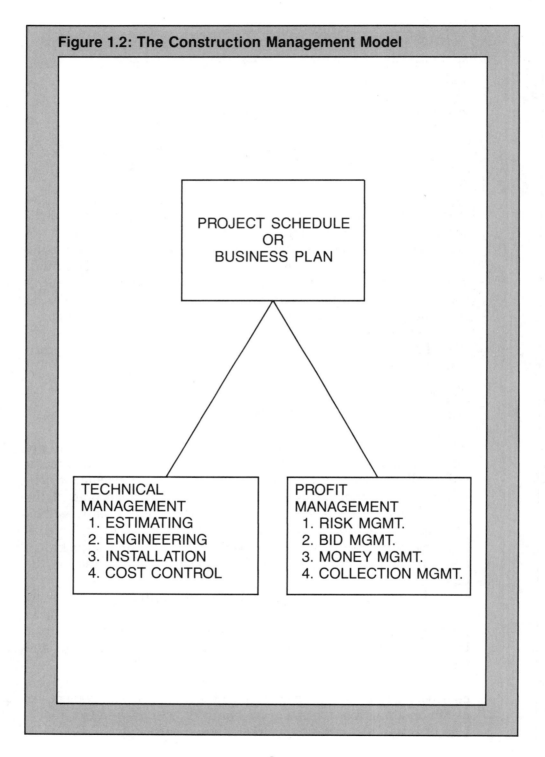

Figure 1.2: The Construction Management Model

PROJECT SCHEDULE
OR
BUSINESS PLAN

TECHNICAL
MANAGEMENT
  1. ESTIMATING
  2. ENGINEERING
  3. INSTALLATION
  4. COST CONTROL

PROFIT
MANAGEMENT
  1. RISK MGMT.
  2. BID MGMT.
  3. MONEY MGMT.
  4. COLLECTION MGMT.

Figure 1.2 demonstrates the important balance between technical management and profit management. If you apply the profit equation to technical management only, ignoring profit management, your overall construction management plan will suffer. This is why contractors lose money.

How to Keep a Workable Balance Between Technical Management and Profit Management

The construction company must keep a balance between technical management and profit management; otherwise, the company will not experience any real growth or realize its full profit potential. A company that emphasizes only technical management often suffers from such characteristics as (1) 80 percent of its work being received from only 20 percent of its clients and (2) 90 percent of the total work being minimum profit negotiated contracts, leaving only 10 percent in high profit fixed-price contracts. It is easy, therefore, to see the dangerous position in which many contractors find themselves. If only one or two clients stop giving them work, they are literally "out of business" overnight. Real growth is impossible under these conditions, and the struggle for survival becomes their only business plan.

On the other hand, a company with a strong technical *and* profit management system has the ability to develop and implement a plan for real growth and profit. Thus (1) no single client provides more than 10 percent of total sales revenue and (2) a realistic balance between high-profit, fixed-price contracts and low-profit, negotiated contracts results. This balance is a benefit that automatically leads companies into newly developing high-profit areas of construction. This is accomplished through a realistic bidding plan (see Chapter 4, which discusses bid management). Such a plan will almost automatically win contracts in new emerging areas, allowing for the development of expertise that increases the company's competitive position in a timely fashion.

THE PROFIT EQUATION: THE CORNERSTONE OF PROFIT MANAGEMENT

Technical management and profit management are equal factors that work together to make up a comprehensive construction management plan. However, it is the focus of this book to concentrate on the role of profit management as it applies to the profit equation relative to the project and the contracting company, leaving the physical "technique" of construction to other books.

The profit equation is the foundation of profit management. However, in order to increase the power of this formula, let's add to our previously given profit equation (which set profit equal to full payment). It now becomes the *project profit equation*.

Thus

$$\boxed{\text{PROFIT} = \text{FULL PAYMENT}}$$

is expanded to read

Project Profit = (Break-even Project Payment)

+

(Change Order Payment)

+

(Contract Payment)

The project profit equation states that profit is the same as full payment, which is equal to break-even project payment plus change order payment plus contract payment. In other words, if you do not receive full payment, you receive dollar losses (which are by no means of nominal amounts). These losses often run from tens of thousands to hundreds of thousands of dollars. However, it is crucial that you realize that these dollar losses are unnecessary and controllable. What these losses are and the secrets of how you can control them will be illustrated for you in the following chapters. Why suffer losses when they can just as easily be profit in your pocket?

As you have just seen, the project profit equation introduces the break-even project payment. As you will see, the profit equation relies heavily on *break-even analysis*, which includes the break-even point, break-even scheduling, and break-even schedule analysis.

BREAK-EVEN ANALYSIS

Break-even analysis is a numerical evaluation of profit and loss that determines the amount of existing profit or loss at a specific point in time relative to known fixed expenses.

Since the profit equation relies on this analysis, each of its component parts of (1) the break-even point, (2) the break-even schedule, and (3) the break-even schedule analysis shall be thoroughly explained and pragmatically illustrated.

To understand why contractors lose money by not controlling the dynamics of the profit equation, you must understand the concept of the *break-even* point, the various types of *break-even points* that operate in the construction industry, and how to use the correct type of break-even.

The Concept of the Break-even Point

The break-even point is a point in time, money, or sales where all fixed expenses have been paid. It is the point of "breaking even." When the break-even point is reached, fixed expense is zero and profit can be realized. After break-even, with each dollar now received, you must subtract only *variable cost* (for example, labor, materials, and so forth). The rest is all profit. The break-even point is measured in both dollars and in time.

How to Calculate the Break-even Point

Figure 1.3 shows a company's profit and loss statement represented as a pie chart, which is separated into categories of profit, variable cost, semivariable costs, and fixed expenses. Take note of "semivariable expense" shown in the pie chart. Semivariable expense includes items that have both variable cost and fixed expense

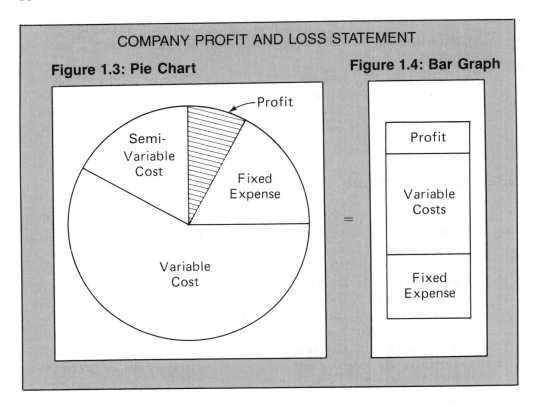

COMPANY PROFIT AND LOSS STATEMENT

Figure 1.3: Pie Chart   Figure 1.4: Bar Graph

amounts (for example, telephone bills). As semivariable expenses are both "variable" and "fixed," these costs have been separated and applied to the appropriate variable cost and fixed expense sections of the bar graph in Figure 1.4. By separating semivariable costs into only variable cost and fixed expense, you can simplify your break-even point calculations.

Now let us consider the factor of "time." If "time" is added to the bar graph of the company's profit and loss statement, you can develop a graph as shown in Figure 1.5. By drawing a line representing sales volume and another line representing costs (starting above fixed expense), the break-even point is found at the point of intersection of these two lines.

Either the graph or the general break-even equation (shown following) can be used to determine the break-even point.[1]

[1]Ray H. Garrison, *Managerial Accounting*, fourth ed. (Dallas: Business Publications, Inc., 1985), p. 209.

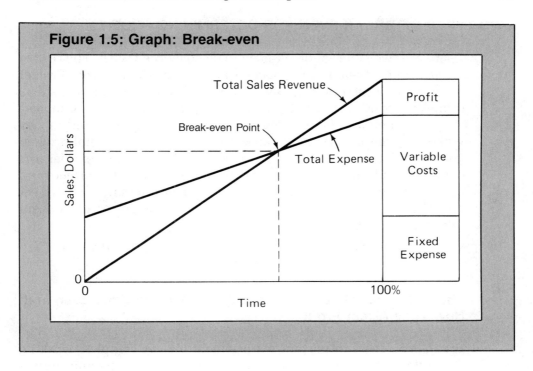

Figure 1.5: Graph: Break-even

The general break-even equation states that

TOTAL SALES = VARIABLE COSTS + FIXED EXPENSE
+ PROFIT

Since profit equals zero, it becomes

BREAK-EVEN SALES = VARIABLE COSTS + FIXED
EXPENSE + ZERO PROFIT

If you are confused by mathematical equations and graphs, just keep in mind that break-even is the point (in time and money) where profit is made because all fixed expenses have been paid.

TWO TYPES OF BREAK-EVEN FOR DETERMINING PROFIT

There are two types of break-even to be concerned with. The first is *project break-even* and the second is *company break-even*. *Project break-even* is the point in time and money where the project starts to make money, or the point where the project stops losing money.

The *company break-even point* is a point in time and money where all company fixed expenses are paid for. It is the point when you start making money in terms of *all* the projects that the company undertakes. The major difference between the project and company break-even points is that the former refers to *each* project and the latter refers to *all* projects. This is a powerful concept understood by few.

**PROFIT GUIDE: YOU MUST BE ABLE TO IDENTIFY
BREAK-EVEN**

The Difference Between Company and Project Break-even and How They Affect Profit

Break-even is an important management tool. A complete working understanding of the uses and differences of company and project break-even is essential and is one of the secrets to success. For example, if company and project break-even are treated as being the same, the industry average profits of 2 to 4 percent would appear to be the realistic profit that should be realized on each individual project. This could not be further from the truth!

The industry average profits "average out" all work done by the worst and best companies in a year's time, not what is made or lost on each individual project. To further understand the uses and differences of company and project break-even, compare the following company profit equation in Figure 1.6, with the project profit equation.

Margin Versus Profit

Figure 1.6 illustrates that the profit from an individual project is quite different from the profits earned by a company from several different projects that span an extended period of time. Accountants often refer to individual project profits as *margin*, in order to avoid confusion between project and company profit. Margin is the

---

Figure 1.6: Project and Company Profit Equation

THE PROJECT PROFIT EQUATION	THE COMPANY PROFIT EQUATION
PROFIT = FULL PAYMENT	PROFIT = FULL PAYMENT
PROFIT = (BREAK-EVEN PROJECT PAYMENT)	PROFIT = (BREAK-EVEN COMPANY PAYMENT)
+	+
(CHANGE ORDER PAYMENT)	(PROFIT PAYMENT)
+	
(CONTRACT PAYMENT)	

---

amount of money earned above break-even on an individual project. Likewise, company *profit* is earnings above break-even realized by a company at the end of its fiscal year. In other words, there is no actual "profit" realized on an individual project for a contracting company, only "margin."

Profits are only applicable to companies. They are the equalizing effect of staying in business for an entire year. This averages out the margins of all projects for a year's time. The decision to do more than one project and to stay in business is a decision that only the company owner can make.

This decision has no legitimate legal or financial bearing on the performance (or margin) of an individual project (as some owners would like to assume for their benefit and as we shall see in Chapter 2). The decision to do more than one contract does not change the break-even point or the risks of any particular project.

Why Identifying Break-even Is Important

It is important to recognize the difference between the two break-even points. This difference becomes important when formulating legal and financial reasoning for project control and profit and when learning how to control and collect impacted damages. It is also extremely important in developing risk, bid, money, and collection management strategies to realize company goals of growth and profit.

Since the person offering the contract has no legal reason to assume that the contractor accepting the contract intends to continue in business after the contract is completed, or that the contractor will be working on any other contracts during that time, it is vital that the appropriate break-even point is used to determine profits. As you shall soon see, calculating and controlling profits on a project can be very different from calculating and controlling company profits.

Further, when you consider the common industry practice that requires the contractor to "bond" a project (which is nothing more than insurance to ensure that the contractor will complete the contract), you can see that a **contractor** is only promising to perform one contract. And the person offering the contract is ensuring that the contractor will stay in business long enough to complete that person's contract. Therefore, the correct *break-even schedule analysis* must be used (by all principals involved in the construction process) for either project control and profit or for company growth and profit decisions.

HOW TO SCHEDULE BREAK-EVEN

To understand the tremendous importance of the *Break-even Schedule* and its analysis (how it is used), let's begin by considering the dynamics of the company break-even point using three time periods and three projects. The *Company Break-even Schedule* is a financial chart of the company's break-even position relative to fiscal year time periods and sales volume, and it demonstrates in Figure 1.7 company break-even and its dramatic effects on company profits.

Figure 1.7 shows a company during time periods 1, 2, and 3, with three projects going on simultaneously. Assume that the company break-even point for each time period is $30,000. The chart shows that unless the company receives $10,000 in time period 2, it will lose $10,000. Therefore, the company should consider taking a project that at least covers its remaining fixed company expense of $10,000 for period 2 or should consider shifting $10,000 of cash flow from time period 1 to time period 2. Either way will stop a $10,000 loss in time period 2.

Alternatively, suppose there is an opportunity for the company to take an additional contract in time period 1 or 3 for $5,000 over variable cost. This means that the new contract will produce $5,000 in profit for the company, but if it is done in time period 2, it will reduce the loss in that period by only $5,000.

Sound simple? It is. However, many businessmen do not understand break-even and do not know how to apply the concept to their daily lives.

Figure 1.7: Company Break-even Schedule

PROFIT AND COMPANY BREAK-EVEN SCHEDULE ANALYSIS

(Company Break-even Point = $30,000)

Time Period	1	2	3
Project 1	$10k	—	—
Project 2	$10k	$10k	—
Project 3	$20k	$10k	$30k
Total Cash Flow	$40,000	$20,000	$30,000

PROFIT GUIDE: YOU MUST SCHEDULE COMPANY
BREAK-EVEN

Once the dynamics of break-even are better understood and used in the construction industry for bid, risk, money, and collection management, the more profitable and efficient the construction industry will become. With the proper use of break-even, the percentages used for overhead and profit can be substantially reduced when calculating bids. This will produce lower construction costs, more profit, and more work, benefiting the owner, manufacturer, architect-engineer, supplier, and contractor alike. Quite simply, dollars "earmarked" for capital improvements will then buy more capital improvements (for example, buildings and process equipment). This will lead to the manufacturing of more product, which in turn creates more profit, motivating more capital improvements, and so on.

By enabling the construction company to reduce percentage overhead applications, business plans can be implemented and realized to create faster growth and greater profits. When overhead expense and job costs are controlled, profits increase and one's competitive position is enhanced.

Many contractors complain that they are consistently "outbid" by their competitor contract after contract, which forces them to take low-profit negotiated work to keep crews together. An understanding of break-even company scheduling is essential in preventing such losses.

COMPANY BREAK-EVEN SCHEDULING: A CASE EXAMPLE OF HOW TO OUTBID YOUR COMPETITION WITH BREAK-EVEN ANALYSIS

Contractor A came to me for consultation. He was distraught because he had just lost another project to his competitor, Johnny Jones. My client was convinced that Johnny Jones was consistently winning projects by bidding too low and losing money. Sound familiar?

Contractor A could not understand how Johnny Jones could stay in business. As I asked questions, I found that Jones had been in business for quite a long time and was apparently doing quite well.

I suspected that Contractor A's pricing and bidding procedures were the culprit. In almost all cases like this one I find a bid summary that looks something like the following:

Figure 1.8: Typical "Cost Plus" Pricing

CONTRACTOR A's BID:

Labor	$50,000
Supervision	5,000
Tools	1,000
	56,000
Overhead 15%	8,400
	64,400
Profit 5%	3,230
	$67,630
Material $30,000	
10% $ 3,000	$33,000
Selling Price........................	$100,630

According to Contractor A, Johnny Jones was bidding 10 percent lower than he could possibly bid and taking all the work he wanted. Contractor A was convinced that Jones was not only foregoing his 5 percent profit but also losing 5 percent of his overhead. Was he? Let's see.

Figure 1.9 shows Contractor A's bid reformatted. Note that profit has been included in fixed expense to give us a clear and simple picture to easily compare the bids.

Figure 1.9: Contractor A's Cost Plus Bid

CONTRACTOR A's BID (reformatted):

Labor	$50,000
Supervision	5,000
Tools	1,000
Material	30,000
Variable Costs	$86,000
Fixed Expense.........................	14,630
Selling Price	$100,630

Now let's look at Figure 1.10, which shows Johnny Jones's cost plus bid, which was 10 percent less than Contractor A's.

Was Johnny Jones making a profit? He sure was! Now, let's see how. Refer to the "Profit and Company Break-even Schedule" (which is a reprint of Figure 1.7). Assume Johnny Jones's break-even is the same as in Figure 1.7 (which was $30,000 per time period).

Figure 1.10: Johnny Jones's Cost Plus Bid

JOHNNY JONES's BID

Labor	$50,000
Supervision	5,000
Tools	1,000
Material	30,000
Variable Costs	$86,000
Fixed Expense...........................	4,567
Selling Price	$90,567

PROFIT AND COMPANY BREAK-EVEN SCHEDULE ANALYSIS

(Company Break-even Point = $30,000)

Time Period	1	2	3
Project 1	$10k	—	—
Project 2	$10k	$10k	—
Project 3	$20k	$10k	$30k
Total Cash Flow	$40,000	$20,000	$30,000

If Johnny Jones schedules his project to be completed in time period 1 or 3, his fixed expense of $4,567 (which is illustrated in Figure 1.10) becomes a *profit* of $4,567. The reason for this is that in time period 1 and 3, fixed expense has been paid by the other work already being done. Here Johnny Jones is already at or above break-even. Therefore, he can get all the work he wants by bidding lower than his competition and **STILL EARN A PROFIT.** You can bet that Johnny Jones understands company break-even.

PROJECT BREAK-EVEN SCHEDULING: THE IMPACT OF TIME ON PROFIT

To better understand the difference between company and project break-even and how delays or risks dramatically affect profit by creating new time periods, consider project break-even by analyzing the following project break-even schedule. The *project break-even schedule* is a financial chart of the project's break-even position relative to contract time periods and contract dollar amount.

Figure 1.11 shows contract time periods 1, 2, 3, and 4 with three tasks or jobs to be performed on a single project and a project break-even of $30,000 for each time period.

If something causes any one of these tasks to be broken up and extended into time period 4, you will not make break-even in the original time period it was taken out of and you will not make break-even in the new time period where it was moved into (time period 4). Time period 4 is called *new time*. Quite simply, *new time* is a time period into which the project schedule fills into. If the project is going "over schedule," the additional time periods into which the project spills is the new time. New time does not exist in the "original" project schedule. It is the time that is added to the original project schedule when extended.

One reason that break-even will not be realized in the original time period is that all originally scheduled work will not be performed within that time period. Therefore, the total $30,000 cash flow will not be paid or received in the original time period

Figure 1.11: Project Break-even Schedule and Time

PROJECT BREAK-EVEN ANALYSIS OF DELAYS

(Project Break-even Point = $30,000)

Time Period	1	2	3	4
Task 1 -------	$10k	—	—	—
Task 2 -------	$20k	$20k	—	—
Task 3 -------	—	$10k	$30k	$0
Total Cash Flow	$30,000	$30,000	$30,000	$0

even though the required break-even point of $30,000 will remain unchanged. Losses will result.

In the new time period, one reason break-even will not be accomplished is that the amount of work shifted from the original time period to the new time period is not enough to produce the required $30,000 time period break-even cash flow. Losses will result.

New Time Profits:
The Multiplying Loss Impact of New Time

In other words, you are going to lose money in both time periods, which means money will be lost *twice*. This doubling effect is unknown to many contractors. In fact, if this trend is continued by shifting tasks into new time periods 5 and 6, money is now lost in six time periods (the three original time periods tasks have been moved from and the three new time periods tasks have been moved into), thus *multiplying losses to six times!*

Not only must these losses be identified and controlled but profit must be added to all costs and expenses to complete a project in a time period beyond the completion date specified in the original construction schedule. This is called the *profit of new time*.

Float Time Profits:
The Importance of Controlling Ahead-of-Schedule Time

To continue with the analysis shown in Figure 1.11, if you were to reduce the total time from three periods to two periods (completing the project ahead of schedule), $30,000 in additional profit would be realized. The difference between the budgeted completion time and the actual ahead of schedule completion time is called *float time*. The concept of float time is often the subject of many heated discussions (particularly on government contracts) which hinges on the question, "Who owns float?"

If a contractor completes a project ahead of schedule, he earns a profit and, therefore, "owns the float." However, what happens when a contractor realizes that he can complete the project ahead of schedule, thus cutting expenses and earning a bigger profit (from the float), but is suddenly prevented from doing so because of a scheduling difficulty on the job site (for example, another sub-

---

Figure 1.12: Float Time

$$\text{FLOAT TIME} = T_s - T_e$$

$T_s = \text{Time Scheduled}$
$T_e = \text{Time Used Ahead of Schedule}$

---

contractor being in the same place at the same time)? Under a fixed-price contract, the owner claims he "owns the float." From the owner's point of view, why should he pay more to the contractor because the contractor claims he was prevented from completing the project ahead of schedule? That's just too bad. As a result of this attitude, the contractor cannot collect the profits from his float time because he was not allowed to shorten his own contract time, believing that he was bound to the time in his original contract. Thus, he did not claim ownership of the "float," and therefore did not realize any gains.

To further illustrate float time, consider a project with multiple tasks to be performed by a single contractor. Going back to the example in Figure 1.11, assume that the contractor must perform several tasks within the three periods shown. Assume one task takes nine days and must be completed before all tasks can continue. A second task must be performed and completed at the same time, but it takes only seven days. Therefore, the float time is two days, which is the difference between the longest task of nine days and the shortest task of seven. The seven-day task can be delayed two days and still be completed at the same time as the nine-day task, thus ensuring the on-time completion of the overall project. But *when* the seven-day task is performed within the alloted nine days can make a big difference to the contractor's profit.

Many owners do not realize that *when* the seven-day task is performed is critical to the contractor's profit and can significantly change *how* the tasks will be performed. Arbitrarily shifting tasks around without considering the physical reaction on crew size, required equipment and tools, sequence of work, and so on can clearly have a negative impact on the contractor's break-even point by increasing expenses. *When* a task is performed (within a series of tasks) can cause an increase in expenses due to losses in labor and equipment productivity.

> **PROFIT GUIDE: "WHEN" DETERMINES "HOW" WORK IS DONE**

This is precisely the cause of the heated arguments between contractors and owners. It is difficult for owners to see this negative profit impact when broken down into simple task delays, even when they occur numerous times throughout the schedule and particularly when the overall project is on time within the time allocated by the "owner's" schedule. Most important, it is often the **contractor** himself who fails to properly recognize and identify these delays as profit losses.

To maximize the profit available on every job, the contractor must realize when he is entitled to the gains from his own "float time." Therefore, should his ahead-of-schedule completion date be "pushed off" until the budgeted completion date due to outside circumstances, the *contractor is entitled to compensation for his float time.* Simply put, you are entitled to profits you create!

You are entitled to the "profit of float time," which is the amount of money saved by reducing the original scheduled construction time.

WHY YOU SHOULD IDENTIFY AND TRACK PROFIT LOSSES

Almost every contractor intuitively knows that if he comes in ahead of schedule he makes more money than when he doesn't. He beats the schedule. This is simple common sense. Many express this by saying, "Get the men and material in the same place at the same time and you will make money; if not, you will lose." However, the true secret lies in being able to guarantee big profits *every* time. This means knowing and controlling *when* and *how* tasks are performed, or losses are sure to result.

In order to guarantee those big profits you need a system that identifies, tracks, and stops your *losses*, as you will be shown in Chapter 7.

Every contractor keeps track of profits. Simple cost accounting procedures record profits as they increase and decrease. But what about losses? The contractor who watches his profits but fails to monitor his losses will simply watch his profits grow for a while but then dwindle to nothing. When I consult with contractors, I ask them, "Where have your profits gone?" I generally get no reason or fifty reasons why money is lost. I then ask the contractor with the long list of reasons, "How much does each one of these reasons cost you?" The silence is deafening. How can you stop losses if you do not know what they are and how big they are?

In order to stop profit losses you must be able to identify the source and the extent of these losses. Without this information you can easily spend all of your time working to correct a $500 problem while ignoring a $50,000 one. How can this happen? Simple. If you do not know which problem is costing you more, you will naturally spend your time on the problem causing the most personal aggravation. You have no doubt heard the adage, "The squeaking wheel gets the grease first." Well, when all four wheels are squeaking, you need a system to show which wheel to grease first.

HOW IMPACTED DAMAGES CONVERT PROFITS TO HUGE LOSSES

It is common for losses from impacted damages to exceed original contract values. What starts out to be a small contract quickly escalates into a huge one by the effect of time working on the number of separate tasks to be performed.

Impacted damages are the losses from the original time period in which the task should have been completed and the additional losses incurred as the task is extended into and completed in a new time period or periods. These losses include those caused as a result of the "when" and "how" the tasks could have been performed in accordance with the original documents versus "when" and "how" the tasks were performed.

Using new time periods to complete a project is the same as starting a new company all over again or being forced to stay in business when you could have closed your doors. The new time period or periods that the project completion is extended into will have a multiplying effect on losses (relevant to the number of time periods). This was illustrated in Figure 1.11.

In other words, impacted damages are determined as follows: all dollar losses caused from (1) items or occurrences that negatively affect "when" and "how" tasks are to be performed by using **Float Time,** and (2) items or occurrences that affect "when" and "how" tasks are performed by using **New Time.**

Figure 1.13: Impacted Damages

IMPACTED DAMAGES = FLOAT TIME LOSSES
                  + NEW TIME LOSSES

Are these losses real? You bet they are! But are they collectible? Only if you know they exist, know what they are, and know how to collect them!

It is not only critical to know what these losses are and that they diminish the profit of the original contract but that impacted damages if not collected or stopped carry an additional loss, which is the "profit of impacted damages." This is the amount of money for profit that must be added to the costs of float time and new time losses. As you have seen, this is separate and in addition to the profit of the original contract.

The Two Classifications of Impacted Damages

There are two ways to classify impacted damages. Impacted damages that produce lost profits can be found to be either *internally caused* or *externally caused. Internally caused damages* are damages caused by the contractor himself. These are self-inflicted wounds that must be immediately corrected to stop current losses and to guarantee future profits. These losses can be the result of forgetting to order a wrench or as serious as ordering an 80-ton crane too late. Internally caused damages can be avoided. But to do this, you must first identify your losses!

Externally caused damages are those damages caused by outside factors. If the lost profits have come from external causes, the contractor may be entitled to recover these losses. The question now becomes, "Are they contracted or noncontracted risks?"

In the previous illustration with the recovery of float time, the contractor was entitled to recover the lost profits of float time from the owner. In order to recover and receive break-even payment, it is necessary to know (1) the contract risks, (2) your project break-even point, and (3) all the factors that affect profits of float time and new time. These factors increase or decrease profit in direct proportion to their costs.

Checklist of 111 Sources of Impacted Damages

The following is a list of items that can negatively affect a project and a contractor's profits. These items are the sources of impacted damages (SIDs) which directly affect your break-even point.[2]

[2]This list of the sources of impacted damages is a compilation of concepts that are commonly used in the trade. I have noted the following sources to give credit to the efforts of NECA for documenting many of these common jargon terms: National Electrical Contractor's Association, *Guide to Electrical Contractors' Claims Management*, Volumes I and II (Washington, D.C.: NECA, 1976 and 1978, respectively) and National Electrical Contractor's Association, *Change Orders in Electrical Construction*, Parts I and II (Washington, D.C.: NECA, 1970 and 1978, respectively).

1. **DELAYED COMPLETION:** The extension of the original contract time schedule, requiring work to be performed in "new time."

2. **ENVIRONMENTAL CONDITIONS:** The effects on worker productivity of temperature, humidity, wind, rain, snow and sleet, freezing rain, temperature extremes, dense fog, ground freeze, drying conditions, temperature inversions, and flooding.

3. **UNFORESEEABLE DELAYS:** All project delays beyond the contractor's control.

4. **SITE ACCESS:** Security regulations necessary to obtain clearances for workers or other special conditions required to enter the work area.

5. **SITE OBSTRUCTIONS:** Anything that physically prohibits workers from proceeding with their work.

6. **OUT-OF-SEQUENCE WORK:** Work that does not follow a logical path to produce maximum productivity.

7. **REASSIGNMENT OF MANPOWER:** The changing of the job assignments of the crew or individual workers once they have been hired, trained, and scheduled.

8. **MANPOWER UNAVAILABILITY:** The unavailability of qualified and productive workers, which necessitates retaining less productive workers in order to maintain sufficient manpower to meet the original schedule.

9. **LEARNING CURVE:** The time required to become familiar with the work, supervision, other workers' habits and abilities, types of tools available, where tools are stored, procedures regarding working, and safety are all factors of the learning curve.

10. **STACKING OF TRADES:** Multiple crews of different trades working in a confined area, thus reducing the ability of working in an orderly and efficient manner.

11. **INTERRUPTED UTILITIES:** The unplanned interruption of utilities at the project site, which are required for the productive execution of the contract work. These utilities include electricity, heat, light, compressed air, and water.

12. **ATTITUDE AND MORALE:** The general perception of workers and supervisors on the project relevant to whether they believe it is a well-run project and one they are proud to be working on.

13. **SABOTAGE:** Intentional damage done to jobsite material and equipment.

14. **EQUIPMENT THEFT AND VANDALISM:** Unauthorized removal or destruction of equipment and tools stored on the project site.

15. **UNAVAILABILITY OF ADEQUATE TOOLS AND EQUIPMENT:** Unforeseen tools and equipment that are required at a project site.

16. **MATERIAL THEFT AND VANDALISM:** Unauthorized removal or destruction of material stored at the project site.

17. **VANDALISM TO STRUCTURES:** Intentional damage done to material and work already performed and installed at the project site.

18. **NEW WORK DAMAGE:** The costs incurred to restore completed work to its original condition because of unintentional damage done by others.

19. **DILUTION OF SUPERVISION:** The decrease of supervision productivity due to a diversion of supervision from the original contract work to other matters.

20. **JOINT OCCUPANCY:** When work area is occupied by another organization performing tasks not stipulated in the original bid documents.

21. **BENEFICIAL OCCU-PANCY:** Being forced to work in close proximity with the owner's personnel because he has moved in and taken over part or all of the project for his own use.

22. **RIPPLE:** The direct effect of change orders or delays from one contractor to the schedule or sequence of work of another contractor.

23. **ACCELERATION:** Shortening the overall project schedule of one or more subcontractor's schedule.

24. **PROJECT EXPANSION:** The increase of the amount of man-hours required to perform the original contract.

25. **INTERRUPTED BUSINESS:** The stoppage of normal business by one or more of the principals involved in the project.

26. **CONTRACT ORGANIZATION:** The organization of project responsibility delineated in the contract.

27. **PROJECT ORGANIZATION:** The organization of project responsibility and authority.

28. **CREW SIZE:** The number of workers per supervisor. Crew size is often determined by the amount of supervision available on a project or the type of work to be performed.

29. **EXTERNAL SUPERVISION:** The supervisory personnel required at the project site for the safe and productive execution of the contract work.

30. **INTERNAL SUPERVISION:** The supervisory personnel required to coordinate activities between all principals involved in the project: owner, architect, engineer, manufacturer, supplier, inspector, subcontractor, external supervision, support office personnel, and so forth.

31. **NONWORKING SUPER-VISION:** Project site supervisory personnel who do not perform work with "tools." Complete time is spent supervising other workers.

32. **WORKING SUPERVISION:** Project site supervisory personnel who supervise other workers and also work with "tools."

33. **START-UP SUPERVISION:** Supervision necessary during the time of placing the installed equipment in working operation.

34. **PREINSPECTION:** Determination of the correctness of material and equipment prior to installation.

35. **WORKING INSPECTION:** Determination of the correctness of material and equipment installed with conformity to original contract drawings and specifications during the progress of the project.

36. **PUNCH LIST:** A list of all items of work not in conformance with the original contract drawings.

37. **FINAL INSPECTION:** Determination of the correctness of material and equipment installed with conformity to as-built drawings that the owner has approved.

38. **SCHEDULE STABILITY:** The amount of time variation that is reasonably expected in the original project construction schedule.

39. **DESIGN STABILITY:** The state-of-the-art architectural and engineering development of the project to be constructed.

40. **PERFORMANCE SPECIFICATIONS:** Contract specifications written by the owner that specify only the end result of the project acceptable to the owner.

41. **DETAIL DRAWINGS:** How-to drawings required to manufacture and install equipment and material.

42. **AS-BUILT DRAWINGS:** Modified original contract drawings that delineate all deviations from the original drawings made during construction.

43. **OPERATING MANUALS:** Written instructions from manufacturers and engineers on the correct procedures for operating the equipment installed by the contractor.

44. **MAINTENANCE MANUALS:** Written instructions from manufacturers and engineers on the correct procedures for maintenance of the equipment installed by the contractor.

45. **REPAIR MANUALS:** Written instructions by manufacturers and engineers on the correct procedures for repair of the equipment installed by the contractor.

46. **ADDENDUMS:** Additions or deletions made by the owner to the original contract specifications normally before construction begins.

47. **REVISIONS:** Improvements made by the owner to the original contract drawings either before or after construction begins.

48. **APPROVALS:** Owner's acceptance of materials and equipment to be used in the construction of the project.

49. **START-UP:** Placing the equipment installed by the contractor in working operation.

50. **STIPULATED PRICE CHANGES:** A fixed-price change that is provided for in the original contract documents.

51. **UNILATERAL CHANGES:** An authorization in the original contract documents that gives the owner the right to direct the contractor to proceed with a change prior to an agreement on price and time extensions.

52. **TIME-AND-MATERIAL CHANGES:** Owner-authorized changes that are paid on a time-and-material basis.

53. **CONSTRUCTIVE OR UNAUTHORIZED CHANGES:** Changes in work necessary to proceed with the project schedule.

54. **UNIT-PRICE CHANGES:** Changes authorized by the owner based on unit prices provided by the contractor in his bid.

55. **CHANGES IN CODES AND REGULATIONS:** Changes in various regulatory codes and regulations that occur after the awarding of the contract.

56. **CONCEALED CONDITIONS:** Conditions that were not recognized when the contract was awarded but proved to be at variance with contract documents at a later date.

57. **DEFECTIVE PERFORMANCE:** Any fault or error by company personnel that is not in accordance with the project plans and specifications.

58. **ERRORS AND OMISSIONS:** Work that is incomplete, poorly completed, or not completed at all.

59. **DEFECTIVE PLANS AND SPECIFICATIONS:** Term applied to a project completed correctly by a contractor from plans and specifications that he has altered to correct any defective portions of those plans and specifications.

60. **ENGINEERING ERRORS AND OMISSIONS:** Term applied to a project completed incorrectly by a contractor from defective plans and specifications as a result of engineering errors and omissions.

61. **ACCEPTANCE TIME LAG:** The time between when a physical change in the work is required, to when it is authorized and planned for in the project schedule.

62. **REJECTED CHANGE ORDERS:** Owner-requested engineering work and cost estimates of changes in the original work, that is subsequently rejected or ignored.

63. **DEFECTIVE APPROVAL:** The owner's refusal to approve adequate substitutes for specified materials or methods when specified materials are unattainable or specified methods are impossible.

64. **DEFECTIVE REJECTION:** The owner's rejection of work or material, that requires the contractor to rework what has already been installed in accordance with the contract documents.

65. **DEFECTIVE PAYMENT:** Any deviation from the terms of payment of the original contract documents.

66. **DELAYED PAYMENT:** The owner's late payment for correct work performed and invoiced by the contractor.

67. **IMPOSSIBILITY OF PERFORMANCE:** Performance as specified in the contract documents which cannot be completed by any contractor.

68. **STRIKES:** Direct and indirect labor strikes that affect the timely execution of the contract.

69. **ESTOPPELED SCHEDULE DEVIATIONS:** Expressed contract document provisions that anticipate and provide for schedule deviations, limit or preclude the contractor's right of recovery, or provide no reasonable basis to expect the contractor to complete the work in a fixed period of time.

70. **LIQUIDATED DAMAGES:** A specified amount of dollars required to be paid to the owner by the contractor for each day the contractor takes to complete the project in addition to the time allotted in the original project schedule.

71. **UNCONSCIONABLE CLAUSES:** Clauses in the contract documents that do not provide for both party's benefit or protection.

72. **UNCONSCIONABLE ACTIONS:** Actions taken by others that any reasonable person would consider outrageous.

73. **SUSPENSION:** Suspension of any part of the contract work for a period of time.

74. **ABANDONMENT:** Termination of all field work before the contract is completed.

75. **TERMINATION:** A point in time when all work is completed in accordance with the contract documents.

76. **EXTERNAL PROJECT TERMINATION:** A point in time when all project site work is completed in accordance with the contract documents.

77. **INTERNAL PROJECT TERMINATION:** A point in time when all project work required by the contract of the contractor's management and support office personnel is complete.

78. **CONVENIENCE TERMINATION:** Termination of the contract for the sole convenience of the owner.

79. **DEFAULT TERMINATION:** Termination of the contractor's work at the project site by the owner physically taking control of the contractor's work, tools, and materials.

80. **EXTERNAL PROJECT DEFAULT TERMINATION:** The owner's termination of the contractor's project site work.

81. **INTERNAL PROJECT DEFAULT TERMINA-TION:** The owner's termination of required project work being done by the contractor's internal project management and support office personnel, caused by the contractor's failure to proceed with the diligence to ensure completion of the contract within the time specified in the contract documents.

82. **LABOR ESCALATION:** The increase in hourly wage rates relevant to the wage rate anticipated in the project bid.

83. **PREMIUM PAY:** Any payment to workers in addition to the "going" rate or union agreement.

84. **SHOW UP TIME:** Compensation for workers who show up for canceled work.

85. **TRAVEL:** Payment to workers for their travel expenses.

86. **HAZARDOUS PAY:** Premium payment to workers for work performed in hazardous conditions.

87. **OVERTIME:** The time worked "beyond" that of a normal workday in the area where the project is being built.

88. **SHIFT WORK:** When more than one eight-hour working period per day is utilized on a project.

89. **MATERIAL PROCURE-MENT:** All work and costs associated with the purchase of materials.

90. **FBO:** Normally refers to materials that are Furnished By Others.

91. **MATERIAL ESCALA-TION:** The increase in the price of materials between the time of order and the time of payment.

92. MATERIAL STORAGE: All storage of materials, either on the job site or in an off-site warehouse.

93. REMOVAL OF DEBRIS: The removal of debris from the job site, such as equipment packing materials.

94. TOOL RENTAL: The commercial rental rate for all tools used on a project.

95. MACHINERY RENTAL: The commercial rental rate for all machinery used on a project.

96. FREIGHT: The total costs for the transportation of tools and materials from the manufacturer, supplier, or warehouse to the project site by commercial carrier.

97. CARTAGE: The total costs for the transportation of tools and materials from manufacturer, supplier, or warehouse to the project site by other than commercial carrier.

98. INSURANCE: All insurance related to the project and its activities, such as Worker's Compensation, hospitalization, bonding, and special policies.

99. COMMERCIAL INSURANCE: Third party insurance. Pertains to who is the insurer and to whom the premium is paid.

100. SELF-INSURANCE: First or second party insurance. Pertains to who is the insurer and to whom the premium is paid.

101. WARRANTY RISKS AND COSTS: Warranties provided by the contractor and manufacturers.

102. INTEREST: The cost of borrowing money to finance the contractor's labor and material costs.

103. FINANCING: Charges incurred for working capital to benefit work beyond the scope of the contract documents.

104. TAXES: The obligation to federal and state governing authorities relevant to labor and material.

105. CONTRACT AWARD COSTS: The costs incurred by the owner or contractor in bidding and obtaining or awarding the final contract.

106. START-UP COSTS: All costs associated with commencing work on a project.

107. SHUT-DOWN COSTS: All costs associated with stopping a project.

108. EXTENDED DIRECT JOB EXPENSES: Additional job site expenses incurred due to schedule delays.

109. EXTENDED MAIN OFFICE OVERHEAD: Additional main office expenses incurred due to schedule delays.

110. ANTICIPATED PROFITS: The amount of profit originally expected from the base contract and provided for in the contractor's bid.

111. CLAIM RECOVERY AND SETTLEMENT COSTS: All expenses incurred by the claimant while pursuing payment.

If any of a number of these conditions exists on a project, fixed expenses automatically increase, which in turn increases the project break-even point. Once your project break-even point has increased, you must then boost your revenue in order to pass the break-even point before you can again earn a profit. On the other hand, if payment is not billed and received, profits will decrease by the same amount. For a fuller explanation of these important sources of impacted damages, see Chapter 2.

The items listed have come to be known as impacted damages because of their relationship to project scheduling and profit. In fact, it was with the development of PERT and CPM scheduling that many of these costs first became apparent to a group of large contractors doing work for the United States government through the General Services Administration (GSA). The matter of impacted damages has been pursued to such an extent over the past twenty years that the GSA has set up an entire internal legal redress system for claims settlement. It was this very system and the settlements it made with its contractors that provided a body of case law for civil courts to consider when dealing with contractors in the private sector.

SUMMARY

Contractors lose money because of their crippling lack of profit management. In this chapter, you have learned the difference between technical management and profit management and why you need to master both areas to be a successful contractor. The basic tools of profit management were identified, and you learned the importance of knowing the profit equation, how to use break-even, how to schedule and analyze break-even, how to identify losses, and how to identify impacted damages. You have discovered the difference between new time and float time and their effect on "how" and "when" you perform your contract. You have also learned to identify the profit of impacted damages, which includes the profit of new time and the profit of float time.

In short, you have just taken your first step on the road to success. Now that the groundwork has been laid, you can focus your attention on the four elements of profit management: risk management, bid management, money management, and collection management.

Chapter 2 examines the secrets of risk management, identifies the risks you are now accepting in your contracts, and shows you how to control those risks.

Chapter 3 tells how to quantify contract risks and invoice for more than the original contract, with a case example from a real-life claim.

In Chapter 4, after you are comfortable with the types of contracts that yield those big profits, you will find out about bid management and learn how to go about winning those big contracts—the ones you most need and want.

After you discover how to win those contracts, Chapter 5 will demonstrate how to maximize big profit opportunities with money management. And Chapter 6 will show you how to collect those profits with collection management. You will also learn how to use the company break-even schedule to win your next big contract.

Finally, and most importantly, Chapter 7 will combine the information illustrated throughout the previous chapters and explain how to guarantee those big profits time after time with positive action management.

How to Achieve Project Control and Maximize Profit with Risk Management

WHY A CONTRACTOR IS AN INSURANCE COMPANY

Chapter 1 explained "bonding" jobs and taking on the risks of others. Simply put, all risks written into a contract commonly fall on the shoulders of the *contractor*.

Once you understand that a contractor is not only a builder but an insurer as well, you can begin to clarify the contractor's role as a profit manager. Insurance companies charge high premiums to protect themselves from risk. They understand risk. Since a contractor is assuming the risks of others, doesn't it seem logical that a contractor must also learn to protect himself from risk? You must learn to profit from the successful management of this risk. In this respect, a contractor is literally an insurance company. All risks written into the contract become his.

> PROFIT GUIDE: A CONTRACTOR IS AN INSURANCE
> COMPANY

How Risk Management Works

What do you have to know for project control and big profits? The answer is simple: *risk management*. Risk management is the first element of the profit management system. Risk management means knowing what the risks are, knowing how they can be controlled, and taking action to effectively control the risks that fall upon your shoulders.

The first stage of risk management is the identification of all risks. After you have identified your risks, you must then determine precisely which of these risks have been contracted for and which have not.

In order to determine risks that have been contracted for, you must begin by understanding your contract; this means you must be able to read your contract, and, more specifically, take the time to read it. Notice I said *your* contract. No one is more interested in your welfare than you are. And no one will take the time to protect your best interests better than you. A Harvard lawyer would miss the things in a contract you will find. Why? First of all, *you're* reading *your* contract for *your* benefit. Second, after you've read this book, you will have learned exactly what to look out for.

PROFIT GUIDE: KNOW YOUR CONTRACT

A contractor with strong risk-managing skills knows the secrets that allow him to *control* the risks he has assumed in the contract, and he knows the secrets of *collecting* reimbursement for impacted damages caused by the risks he has not assumed in the contract.

How Risk Management Allows You to Realize Large Profits

The preceding chapter explained why contractors lose money. Most contractors are simply technical experts and not profit experts. You learned why a successful contractor must be an expert at both. A contractor must learn the dynamics of the profit equation and understand the concept of break-even payment and how it is used, billed, and collected. Also discussed was the system a contractor must have for keeping track of his losses in order to stop them and guarantee his profits.

The next step will be to reinforce your understanding of the relationship of risk management as a working tool of profit management. Effective risk management will realize big profits that you are entitled to from each project.

Having previously made the distinction between the company break-even point and the project break-even point, you will now proceed to develop a model that will allow you to better understand risk management. This requires a more complete understanding of project break-even, a key concept used to understand and identify risk and a key factor in the profit equation.

RISK AND ITS IMPACT ON THE PROFIT EQUATION

The profit equation and its expansion into the project profit equation is the foundation of risk management. The equations that follow clearly indicate that losses will have an adverse effect on profit because full payment will not be received. Losses are a guaranteed result of not receiving full payment. Losses can also be a result of contracted risks that are realized. Whatever the cause of the losses, whether planned for or ignored, the result is the same—*lost profit.*

Let's review briefly two equations discussed in Chapter 1. The profit equation states that:

$$\boxed{\text{PROFIT} = \text{FULL PAYMENT}}$$

The project profit equation states that

$$
\begin{aligned}
\text{PROFIT} &= \text{FULL PAYMENT} \\[6pt]
\text{Project Profit} &= \text{(Break-even Project Payment)} \\[6pt]
&\quad + \\[6pt]
&\quad \text{(Change Order Payment)} \\[6pt]
&\quad + \\[6pt]
&\quad \text{(Contract Payment)}
\end{aligned}
$$

The project profit equation says that profit is the same as full payment, which is equal to break-even project payment plus change order payment plus contract payment. If you do not receive full payment, you receive dollar losses. However, these dollar losses are unnecessary and are controllable under an efficient risk management plan.

To receive full payment and realize big profits, you must identify and control risk with a strong information and control system, use the correct break-even, and collect all impacted damages from risks not contracted for. In addition, you must also mitigate all impacted damages contracted for and control all those that are self-inflicted.

HOW TO CONTROL RISK WITH CONTRACTS

Many contractors go to great pains bidding and tracking out-of-pocket job costs and expenses relative to their profit. But only a select few know the real job costs. Why? Because most contractors use their original bid as the sole standard to determine whether money was made or lost. Little attention is given to what type of contract they have and to its effect on profits. They ignore the questions: "Who assumed which risks?" and "How can they be controlled?" This is a common example of technical management at work with no regard to profit management.

PROFIT GUIDE: YOU MUST KNOW AND CONTROL RISK

Contracts: A Matter of Knowledge, Not Magic

Many contractors freeze at the thought of signing a contract because they are afraid to take risks. They have no knowledge of risk management. Without having an understanding and control over your risks, you effectively become an "employee" of those who offer "handshake" contracts. Why settle for low-profit-negotiated work?

There is no magic to contracts. All you need is common sense and the time to understand. There are many different types of contracts: time and material, cost plus, not to exceed an estimated price, owner profit participation, partial material supplied by owner, labor only, and fixed price, to name a few. Despite the various different types of contracts, one thing is certain...

PROFIT GUIDE: THERE IS NO MAGIC TO CONTRACTS

How the "Cost Plus" Contract Works

Let us focus our attention on the "Granddaddy" of construction contracts, the "cost plus" contract. Cost plus contracts provide that the owner, who is the sole beneficiary of all improvements made to his property, will assume all risks and pay all costs plus an agreed upon profit for all improvements made to his real property. If an owner awards a contract for a project to be executed on cost plus, he controls the project he wants and pays all costs and expenses plus a profit for the contractor. As long as the contractor satisfactorily completes the project, he is guaranteed his profit.

This is the way many billion-dollar projects are contracted. With a cost plus contract, all the cards are on the table. The contractor is paid all costs and expenses for the one contract **plus** an agreed upon profit. You are probably thinking, "What about the sales expenses of obtaining the project? And what about hiring and search costs? The owner will not pay these!" In short, you are both right and wrong. Depending on the individual owner, these expenses are either paid or declined by the owner.

Risk Shifting

Now you can see why there are so many other types of contracts that add their own forms of restrictions. Each type further restricts the contract until the paper on which the contract is printed weighs more than the project you are trying to build. Surely this is an exaggeration, but it draws attention to the fact that these constraints often do not change the physical improvement to the real property. Instead, they change the conditions under which the physical improvements will be made.

There are as many combinations and permutations of cost plus contracts as ingenuity can devise. All deviations from cost plus contracts are, in many cases, simply devious ways to improve real property at someone else's risk. This "risk shifting" does so at the expense of someone other than the owner...the *contractor*.

Risk and the Fixed-Price Contract

Many risks are "shifted" onto others through *fixed-price contracts*. Under a fixed-price contract an owner awards a contract with constraints, such as the project must be (1) completed in a fixed amount of time and (2) completed at a predetermined "fixed price." This type of contract forces a contractor to assume all the risk to complete the project within the specified time period. To the contractor, the constraints of fixed time and fixed price have now become part of his fixed expense!

Under a fixed-price contract, the contractor must pay whatever money it takes to complete the project over and above the amount of tne contract out of his own pocket. Under a fixed-price contract, the contractor is not guaranteed a profit as he is under a cost plus contract.

When working under a fixed-price contract, the owner's risk (Is the project going to be completed on time and on budget?) shifts onto the shoulders of the contractor. The risk becomes the contractor's, built right into the contract. He is now an insurance company! For example, assume it rains for ten days. The project stops. As soon as the weather clears, the workers have to work overtime to catch up. Who pays for the overtime? According to the fixed-price contract, the contractor must pay for the overtime salaries out of his own pocket as a part of his fixed expenses!

Let's look at another constraint that affects those working under a fixed-price contract. The owner hires an architect/engineer to draw plans and write specifications for the project. Now the architect/engineer is no dummy; he knows that it is impossible to think of everything, so he includes a paragraph in the specifications that reads something like this:

> These plans and specifications are intended to define the scope of the work required but do not limit the work required to produce a complete and working system. It is the responsibility of the contractor to include in his proposal all items not shown but required to produce a complete and working system.

By accepting this clause, the contractor personally assumes the risk of providing all items that are not shown but *required* for a complete working system. Do you know what just happened? The architect/engineer has "passed the buck" onto the contractor! He realizes that he can't think of everything, so he includes this clause in his drawings, forcing the contractor to be the one responsible to "think of everything"! Not only must the contractor think of everything, but by assuming this risk, he must pay for it. *All the items that add risk to the contract become part of the contractor's project fixed expense,* just as the fixed amount of materials needed to do the project are a fixed expense.

THE EXPENSE OF RISK IN CONTRACTS

To continue with contract risk and its relationship to project fixed expense and the project break-even point, let's look at a typical summary of a fixed-price estimate:

Figure 2.1: Typical Fixed-Price Estimate

Labor	$100,000
Overhead 15%	15,000
	$115,000
Profit 10%	11,500
	$126,500
Material plus 10%	23,500
Total Estimated Price	$150,000

As you analyze this typical fixed-price estimate, one obvious question should be, "Where are the fixed expenses for the list of contract risks?" Quite simply, they are not included. In fact, they are rarely ever included. Why? Because any contractor will tell you that if he included his contract risks in his fixed-price estimate, he would never win the contract. Does this mean that these risks are not real? Of course not. When payment is required, the contractor must pay from his own pocket! This is another reason why the owner wants the job "bonded." Once the job is bonded, if any of these risks cause the contractor to go broke, the owner can then turn to the bonding company for payment.

PROFIT GUIDE: RISK DETERMINES PROJECT BREAK-EVEN

The contractor assumes the risks of an insurance company when working under a fixed-price contract. Therefore, it is the contractor's assumed *expense* of this "insurance" that should determine the final project break-even point relevant to project *time*.

Assumed expense of contracted risk (AECR) is the dollars, similar to an insurance premium, required to protect the contractor against those risks he has accepted in the project contract documents. To better understand the assumed expense of contract risks in fixed-price contracts let's take another look at the Project Cash Flow Table from Chapter 1 which is shown in Figure 2.2.

Figure 2.2 shows fixed expenses and cash flow in time periods 1, 2, and 3 at $30,000 for each time period, or a total contract value of $90,000. The contractor is literally "insuring" project completion for three time periods and being paid a $30,000 premium for each time period. If the contractor cannot perform for $30,000 in any time period, he must pay the difference to complete the job in that time period from his own pocket. Therefore, the project break-even point of $30,000 per time period should include all the expense for risks the contractor has assumed in the contract.

Figure 2.2: Project Cash Flow

PROJECT BREAK-EVEN AND CASH FLOW ANALYSIS

Time Period	1	2	3	4	5
Task 1	$10k	—	—	—	—
Task 2	$10k	$20k	—	—	—
Task 3	$10k	$10k	$30k	—	—
Total Cash Flow	$30,000	$30,000	$30,000	$0	$0

However, what happens when the project is extended into time period 4 or into time period 5? In the case of extending jobs into additional time periods, the contractor is also entitled to the "insurance" for the extension of the assumed risks in the additional time periods. (He is also entitled to performance losses in time periods 1, 2, and 3 because he was stopped from reducing the project break-even point.) This is exactly what you discovered in Chapter 1: Float Time and New Time Losses.

Fixed Expense and Its Relationship to Project Break-even

To demonstrate, in another way, the impact of project fixed expense (directly affected by the assumed expense of contract risk) on the break-even point of a project, consider the relationship of project fixed expense to project break-even as illustrated in the mathematical derivation below:

$$\text{Project Break-even; (Percentage)} = \frac{\text{Fixed Expense}}{\text{Fixed Expense} + \text{Margin}} \times 100$$

$$\text{Project Break-even; (Dollars)} = \frac{\text{Fixed Expense}}{\text{Fixed Expense} + \text{Margin}} \times \text{Total Contract \$ Value}$$

$$= \frac{\text{Project Break-even \%}}{100} \times \text{Total Contract \$ Value}$$

$$\text{Project Break-even; (Days)} = \frac{\text{Fixed Expense}}{\text{Fixed Expense} + \text{Margin}} \times \text{Total Contract in Days}$$

$$= \frac{\text{Project Break-even \%}}{100} \times \text{Total Contract in Days}$$

The only two factors used in the calculation of project break-even are *project fixed expense* and *margin*. Clearly, fixed expense which is dependent on the assumed expense of contract risks, determines the project break-even point.

At this point accountants and economists may ask, "What happened to the variable (marginal) cost shown in Chapter One?"

The answer is that there is no *project* variable cost when considering only one project. You must remember here that a contract is one project and we are not manufacturing multiple projects. In other words, there is no marginal cost because we are manufacturing (building) only one item.

One contract is completely different from multiple contracts. This is why the company's break-even point is not the same as the project break-even. This is also one primary reason why the contractor is entitled to compensation for noncontracted external risk items that negatively affect the project break-even point; it is reasonable that these items be calculated and reimbursed relative to the individual project and not the company. The contractor must use the correct break-even point for a true analysis of profit and losses. Unless this is done correctly, project break-even point payment cannot be billed or collected.

The Risks Involved in Using the Wrong Break-even Point

If the company break-even point is used when the project break-even should be used to calculate project profit and loss, project losses will not exceed the amount of the contract. The project and not the company break-even point must be used when calculating impacted damages.

PROFIT GUIDE: YOU MUST USE THE CORRECT BREAK-EVEN

If you use the wrong equation to calculate the dollar value of impacted damages, it will not exceed the original contract amount. The reason for the difficulty caused when the wrong break-even point is used is that the costs of many items from the previously developed list of "sources of impacted damages" (or project risks) are often absorbed in overall company operations and do not properly show up as project expenses.

For example, equipment may have long since been amortized by the company and is no longer carried on the company's books. If this is the case, the contractor may not charge for equipment (if he uses the company break-even point for project break-even calculations) that no longer costs him. The "company books" show zero cost. Even though this is a slight exaggeration, you can see the problem. The "company books" have nothing to do with the "project books."

Another illustration of the serious mistakes that can be made by using the company break-even point instead of the project break-even point is the owner's wish to use company profits of 2 percent to 4 percent in calculating expected profits to which the contractor is entitled on an individual project. These unfair calculations are commonly used when no profit has been realized by the contractor because of noncontracted, externally caused impacted damages. In other words, damages caused by someone other than the contractor, which are not written into the contract, are collectible with profit and have no relationship to industry-average profits.

PROFIT GUIDE: YOU MUST USE THE CORRECT PROFIT

If the wrong break-even is used, no monetary consideration will be given to the risks assumed on a fixed-price contract. This is especially true when the contractor has made money on the original contract. The cost and profit losses of time delays "melt away." This does not mean that the losses were not real; it means only that they have been ignored because of improper analysis and presentation. Remember, the company break-even point does not provide for the risk assumed in each time period of the project. This can be provided only by the use of project break-even analysis.

IMPACTED DAMAGES AND PROJECT BREAK-EVEN

Another way of determining the amount of dollars that have been lost when project break-even is changed is to calculate the cost and profit loss of each applicable item from the list of impacted damages and *add up* the individual losses. This may seem faster and easier than determining your expense of project risk and project break-even, but remember, just billing the owner for your impacted damages isn't enough. You must be able to *collect* reimbursement for your impacted damages. And in order to collect, you must first be able to *identify* your losses, *understand* why you are entitled to reimbursement for these losses, and then be able to *explain* why you are entitled to reimbursement. The specifics of this process will be discussed in greater detail in the following chapters.

The task of identifying and defining the items and their expense that change your project break-even point is a complicated process which must be reduced to its individual parts to be clearly understood. The Expense of Project Risk (EPR) can be separated into (1) the Assumed Expense of Project Risk (AEPR) and (2) the Assumed Expense of Contracted Risk (AECR).

EPR (The Expense of Project Risk) is the amount of dollars, similar to an insurance premium, chargeable to impacted damages. It is the total amount of project impact damage liability divided between the principals involved in the project.

AEPR (The Assumed Expense of Project Risk) is the dollars, similar to an insurance premium, required to protect the owner against those risks of impacted damages he has accepted in the project. In the case of the owner these risks are the ones he is left with, those that have not been accepted by his contractors.

As we have learned earlier in this chapter, *AECR* (The Assumed Expense of Contracted Risk) is the dollars, similar to an insurance premium, required to protect the contractor against those risks of impacted damages he has accepted in the project contract documents. In order to control these risks, you must first identify and keep track of all the variables that have a direct impact on the profit of any single project. This task can be simplified by the use of a model that will help us better understand and keep track of these variables. This model comes in the form of a checklist. Once you have such a checklist (see pages 268 through 271), you can easily use it to identify these variables (or conditions) and quickly develop an appropriate information and control system to track a variable's impact on your profit.

There are many confusing articles that have been written, which attempt to organize these variables into neat little packages. Some articles categorize these variables by "what has caused them," "who has caused them," or even "what the general result of these causes has been." Unfortunately, one item often fits into more than one category, things easily become muddled, and the entire organization of such "packages" becomes utterly confusing.

Such overgeneralized organizing attempts only partially succeed in providing a method of accounting as well as a method of fixing responsibility. The factors that affect the project break-even point are not always easily identified by simply determining "who" or "what" initially caused them. For example, unapproved change orders may result from the neglect of the owner to find sufficient funds for the change or from the architect/engineer failing to sign the approval. However, the effect could well result in several items that create losses (such as out-of-sequence work or loss of beneficial occupancy).

To take this example one step further, an unapproved change order may cause a delay, but such delays may also cause loss of productivity due to a negative effect on attitude and morale. Such a side-effect is difficult to foresee and necessitates a more accurate form of identifying and tracking these items.

Therefore, we shall use the list of items that can affect project break-even as a means of providing a tracking system for each project. It is much easier to first identify the occurrence and then look for the cause, as opposed to identifying the cause, *then* trying to speculate on all the occurrences that may possibly develop. For example, men standing around waiting for a new job assignment is a common occurrence on job sites. It is a problem that requires identification. Once you have identified the problem (men waiting for new assignment), you can then determine the cause (for example, a delayed change order). This is easier than sitting down with a delayed change order in hand and trying to predict all the things that it may cause, which will ultimately affect your project break-even point before you even attempt to figure out what caused the delayed change order (which you may *never* find out).

The occurrences and risks that affect project break-even are listed following for this purpose. Also included are explanations that provide possible effects on profit. When referring to this list, you should keep in mind that a construction project is a dynamic process, and one item will often have multiple effects on profit.

THE CAUSES AND EFFECTS OF 111 SOURCES OF IMPACTED DAMAGES (SIDs): CONTRACT RISK

1. *DELAYED COMPLETION:* The extension of the original contract time schedule, requiring work to be performed in "new time," which is a period not originally shown on the contract schedule or planned for by the contractor. This can be caused by a variety of reasons (such as delayed start, delayed equipment deliveries, and project modifications). An increase in the project break-even and lost profit will result, regardless of the cause of delayed completion.

2. *ENVIRONMENTAL CONDITIONS:* The effects on worker productivity of temperature, humidity, wind, rain, snow and sleet, freezing rain, temperature extremes, dense fog, ground freeze,

drying conditions, temperature inversions, and flooding. Employee productivity is directly affected by weather. Some of these are important throughout the year, while others affect only winter construction, as well as specific times of the day. To find the remarkably great amount of time lost through cancellation of work due to early morning weather conditions, you can refer to Bulletin 1642, Bureau of Labor Statistics, U.S. Department of Labor.

3. *UNFORESEEABLE DELAYS*: All project delays beyond the contractor's control. Unforeseeable delays include acts of another contractor, acts of government, acts of public enemies, strikes, fires, floods, epidemics, quarantine restrictions, freight embargoes, and weather. Although the blame for these delays is not to be placed on the contractor, in all cases the contractor is responsible for notifying the owner for a project time extension.

4. *SITE ACCESS*: Security regulations necessary to obtain clearances for workers or other special conditions required to enter the work area that can cause additional expenses. Quite often, parking requirements for workers require the contractor to bus them to the site. Difficulties also arise with the placement of office and work trailers on the job site. Trailer positions are often decided by the owner's representative with little regard to the sequence of work. Needless job delays are caused by the relocation of trailers in order to clear the area for equipment and workers during the course of a project.

5. *SITE OBSTRUCTIONS*: Anything that physically prohibits workers from proceeding with their work. Ground conditions at the site, lay-down areas, and available electrical power are only a few items, not to mention your own company trailer (as mentioned under site access.) A project scheduled for winter construction can turn into a swimming hole if delayed until spring. A delayed project can cause material to be stored on the site in areas that require rehandling and trucking to move them to the lay-down areas.

6. *OUT-OF-SEQUENCE WORK*: Work that does not follow a logical path to produce maximum productivity. This may be caused unintentionally by one contractor to another. This is due to the fact that what may be a very logical way of doing one contractor's work may cause out-of-sequence work for another. Not only does this play havoc in the field, but it can also seriously impact suppliers and the office work. This chain reaction can even be traced to payment difficulties.

7. *REASSIGNMENT OF MANPOWER:* The changing of the job assignments of the crew or individual workers once they have been hired, trained, and scheduled. Reassignment normally occurs when there has been no orderly schedule planning. As a result, workers stand around while waiting for assignments. Poor planning often involves the scheduling of equipment as well. Expensive equipment sits idle or unscheduled equipment is needed. In addition, material usage is often affected, creating immediate or later shortages that will cause project delays.

8. *MANPOWER UNAVAILABILITY:* The unavailability of qualified and productive workers, which necessitates retaining less productive workers in order to maintain sufficient manpower to meet original schedule. When qualified workers are not available, search costs increase and less productive workers are often paid premiums just to get them to "sign on." This often results in the paying of premiums to all workers for retention purposes. This is often caused by project delays or contract changes.

9. *LEARNING CURVE:* The time required to become familiar with the work, supervision, other workers' habits and abilities, types of tools available, where tools are stored, procedures regarding working, and safety are all factors of the learning curve. The curve starts with low productivity (when a worker first starts a job) and increases as a function of the length of time spent. The more time on the job, the more the worker learns and the more productive is his work.

10. *STACKING OF TRADES:* Multiple crews of different trades working in a confined area, thus reducing the ability of working in an orderly and efficient manner. These situations are extremely difficult to manage for the contractor. This stacking is commonly caused by previous delays that result in a rush to complete the project on time. Changes in individual work items or terms of a contract are also a cause.

11. *INTERRUPTED UTILITIES:* The unplanned interruption of utilities at the project site, which are required for the productive execution of the contract work. These utilities include electricity, heat, light, compressed air, and water. Whether the utilities are furnished by owner or contractor, interruptions are often ignored. Proper sizing of demand and maintenance of utilities are critical to the success of the project and can be a major cause of interruption.

Interruption of utilities when documented accounts for large losses in productivity.

12. *ATTITUDE AND MORALE:* The general perception of workers and supervisors on the project relevant to whether they believe it is a well-run project and one they are proud to be working on. Productivity is drastically affected when attitude and morale are poor. There are many things that can affect attitude and morale, such as change orders or errors and giving the impression that no one knows what to do. Workers need a sense of control over their environment. Items that negatively impact this will cause productivity losses from attitude and morale.

13. *SABOTAGE:* Intentional damage done to job site material and equipment. Construction crime is a serious problem on many projects. This can be caused from labor as well as management disputes. It has been estimated that the costs of sabotage in the United States although decreasing from $19.3 million in 1983 to $8.8 million in 1984* is still a major loss factor to both owner and contractor because of the hidden productivity losses.

14. *EQUIPMENT THEFT AND VANDALISM:* Unauthorized removal or destruction of equipment and tools stored on the project site. It is a category of construction crime that delays the productive execution of the contract. This can be caused from improper project site security precautions and procedures. In the United States, equipment theft is estimated to be the most expensive construction crime, accounting for $274.2 million in 1983 and $361.3 million in 1984.*

15. *UNAVAILABILITY OF ADEQUATE TOOLS AND EQUIPMENT:* Unforeseen tools and equipment that are required, which delay work and affect everyone's schedule on a project. The need for equipment not originally planned for can cause special procurement problems and, if impossible to obtain, will require alternative methods for performing the work. This may produce a loss of productivity, greatly affecting the crew's perception of how the project is being managed.

16. *MATERIAL THEFT AND VANDALISM:* Unauthorized removal or destruction of material stored at the project site. Serious schedule delays are the result, as well as losses in productivity.

*Statistics made available by Associated General Contractors of America.

Additional dollars often are lost in show-up time payments by the contractors when materials are not available. In the United States, material theft and vandalism are estimated to be the second most expensive construction crime, accounting for $141.2 million in 1983 and increasing to $165.5 million in 1984.*

17. *VANDALISM TO STRUCTURES:* Intentional damage done to material and work already performed and installed at the project site. This can be the result of public vandals as well as labor and management disputes. In the United States in 1983, it was estimated at $15.2 million, which increased in 1984 to $20.1 million.*

18. *NEW WORK DAMAGE:* The costs incurred to restore completed work to its original condition because of unintentional damage done by others. When the project schedule fails to consider the sequence of work to be done, one contractor is often required to climb on or to stage off another's work. Consequently, when this occurs, previously installed work is damaged in the process. As a result, this previously installed work must be restored to its original state.

19. *DILUTION OF SUPERVISION:* The decrease of supervision productivity due to a diversion of supervision from the original contract work to other matters. Even the task of hiring additional workers to maintain the same amount of supervision further dilutes supervision. Dilution directly affects worker productivity by increasing the possibility of workers' error and omission on the original contract work.

20. *JOINT OCCUPANCY:* When work area is occupied by another organization performing tasks not stipulated in the original bid documents. Basically, this refers to two conflicting groups in the same place at the same time. Joint occupancy causes losses in productivity and delays.

21. *BENEFICIAL OCCUPANCY:* Being forced to work in close proximity with the owner's personnel because he has moved in and taken over part or all of the project for his own use. Because the owner has taken possession and beneficial use of the project, productivity decreases and serious delays in the final acceptance of the project by the owner and payment of the contractor's retainage may result.

*Statistics made available by Associated General Contractors of America.

22. *RIPPLE:* The direct effect of change orders or delays from one contractor to the schedule or sequence of work of another contractor. This is quite simply likened to a "ripple effect." Ripple invariably increases costs to the second contractor, whether involved with the change or not.

23. *ACCELERATION:* A project is accelerated when the overall project schedule is shortened or when one or more subcontractor's schedule is shortened. Planned acceleration often can give the contractor additional profits. However, such factors as dilution of supervision, the learning curve, and the like must be closely evaluated against the potential gain.

24. *PROJECT EXPANSION:* The increase of the amount of man-hours required to perform the original contract. This increase can come from a multiplicity of causes, such as loss of productivity requiring additional man-hours to complete the original contract work or original contract terms allowing the owner to expand the original contract work as required. Whatever the cause, it is often the basis for the owner's removing a contractor who does not respond productively and taking over the work with his own forces or another contractor. When the scope of the work is expanded beyond the capabilities of a contractor to respond productively, tremendous increases in project fixed costs will be experienced through no fault of the contractor. This can be due to the productive size of his organization or current labor and material conditions.

25. *INTERRUPTED BUSINESS:* The stoppage of normal business by one or more of the principals involved in the project—owner, architect, engineer, supplier, manufacturer, or contractor. This can be a result of physical disaster such as fire or financial disaster such as bankruptcy. No matter what the cause, the result will be contract delays.

26. *CONTRACT ORGANIZATION:* The organization of project responsibility delineated in the contract. It is the method of bidding and the ultimate contract that determine who signs contacts with whom. What is referred to as "the Canadian method of bidding" is one example of bidding and ultimate contract that is intended to determine a single line of project responsibility. This is intended to allow the owner to assign one contractor the responsibility for the entire project. It also is intended to provide the owner the lowest complete fixed-price contract. Here's how it works. First the owner accepts bids from all subcontractors. Then

he awards the subcontracts and instructs the prime contractor to include the various subcontractors and their prices in the total price of the prime contractor. The mania for single line responsibility by the owner can substantially increase project costs with delays. Whenever the owner tries to limit his responsibility, muddled and unclear work scope and communications will result, which is the very thing the owner has tried to avoid. The owner can delegate authority, not responsibility. He is responsible to every contractor on the project. Whenever contracts are devised to legally shield the owner from this responsibility, project delays will result from such items as acceptance time lag and defective approvals.

27. *PROJECT ORGANIZATION:* The organization of project responsibility and authority. The method by which the owner or his respresentative (architect/engineer or construction manager) organizes authority and lines of communication largely determines the success of the project for everyone concerned. An owner who squarely accepts his responsibility for the project and delineates clear lines of authority with smooth working lines of communication between himself and all contractors, suppliers, and manufacturers will build the best quality project for the lowest total dollars. Lines of communication include verbal and visual as well as written communications. Project progress meetings and reports with *all* contractors, suppliers, and manufacturers are fundamental to precluding all impacted damages.

28. *CREW SIZE:* The number of workers per supervisor. Crew size is often determined by the amount of supervision available on a project or the type of work to be performed. All union contracts contain minimum supervision requirements and provide for a safe and orderly flow of work. Once the crew has been formed and a working rhythm has been established, any new changes will seriously affect productivity.

29. *EXTERNAL SUPERVISION:* The supervisory personnel required at the project site for the safe and productive execution of the contract work. Minimum amounts of supervision must be in compliance with regulations of the federal and local governing authorities. In addition, all union contracts contain minimum supervision requirements. Contractors and owners who circumvent these requirements often create serious productivity losses, if not safety problems. More often than not, the minimum requirements

are not sufficient and should be increased by the contractor. In productivity gains alone, it will pay him to do so.

30. *INTERNAL SUPERVISION:* The supervisory personnel required to coordinate activities between all principals involved in the project, including owner, architect, engineer, manufacturer, supplier, inspector, subcontractor, external supervision, and support office personnel. Lack of internal supervision is always immediately apparent; for example, in lack of project schedules, improperly fabricated materials, improperly manufactured equipment, continuous arguments between principals over contract drawings and specifications, to name a few. Lack of internal supervision can be on the part of the contractor or the owner. It is often caused by the owner's lack of construction sophistication. If this is the only construction project, the owner may feel that full-time supervision by the architect or engineer is not required. This does not alleviate the coordination required. It only shifts the burden onto another party.

31. *NONWORKING SUPERVISION:* Project site supervisory personnel who do not perform work with "tools." Their complete time is spent supervising other workers; these are normally foremen and superintendents. Union contracts prescribe minimum amounts of foremen and superintendents that must be used relevant to crew size. The concept that they will perform no work with tools is often a local practice but one that is so ingrained that it has far-reaching effects on productivity when opposed. Any occurrence that increases crew size increases the requirement for nonworking supervision, and increased project break-even will result.

32. *WORKING SUPERVISION:* Project site supervisory personnel who supervise other workers and also work with "tools." This can be accomplished on small or large projects. The determining factor is crew size. A small crew could have a working supervisor. However, compressing the project schedule will increase crew size, making this impossible. Productivity losses are significant when compared with the productivity that could have been expected with working supervision. This often occurs on large projects. Although large, they are made up of many small jobs; when this is ignored, contractors who have planned on small crew sizes to work over a long period of time experience negative profit impact. This is also an item that is often overlooked when calculating the costs of extra work orders.

33. *START-UP SUPERVISION:* Supervision necessary during the time of placing the installed equipment in working operation. This is a critical time for all principals: owner, architect, engineer, manufacturer, and contractor. It is also one of the most unplanned for. Believing that everything is perfect and will work the first time is naive. Construction is complex, and if qualified start-up supervision is not available at the same time in the same place, serious problems causing delays can be expected. These delays will ripple through the entire project schedule, resulting in lost productivity and payment difficulties. It is also an item that is often overlooked when calculating the costs of extra work orders.

34. *PREINSPECTION:* Determination of the correctness of material and equipment prior to installation. This required inspection at the manufacturing plant and/or project site before installation is now first appearing in contract specifications. The time and costs incurred during the performing of inspections or tests, including written and/or verbal reports, is well worth the effort. The availability of inspectors and test equipment is critical to avoid needless delays in work flow and progress. "Prevention is better than a remedy" is a major principle that applies to inspection (as well as to any other problem). A potential problem that is detected and corrected at the manufacturer would cost you 385 percent more to correct in the field. It is critical that this concept and the procedures for project inspection be brought out in the open in the beginning stages of the project. Inspection and testing is normally one of the most poorly defined items in most contract documents. However, it is a concept that is the secret of a happy owner and a working project.

35. *WORKING INSPECTION:* Determination of the correctness of material and equipment installed with conformity to original contract drawings and specifications during the progress of the project. Without the proper timing of inspectors during work progress, projects will be delayed or job "cover-over" occurs without the proper inspection before proceeding. Additional costs are incurred upon the completion of a project and the moving out by a contractor from the job site. Many a contractor is forced to return to a completed site just because an inspector failed to be present at the original completion time for final inspection. Such an instance incurs additional project start-up and shut-down costs.

36. *PUNCH LIST:* A list of all items of work not in conformance with the original contract drawings. This is sometimes
referred to as the owner's "wish list." The items on this list are not
to be taken lightly or ignored. They are the owner's opinion of the
contractor's variation from the original contract specifications. It is
incumbent upon the contractor to obtain this list well before the
scheduled completion of his work. Time is then provided to correct
or finish this work productively. If left to the end of the project, it
will have been a constant point of contention between contractor
and owner. Often it is the cause of tremendous delays in final
payment.

37. *FINAL INSPECTION:* Determination of the correctness of
material and equipment installed with conformity to as-built
drawings that the owner has approved. This inspection occurs after
"start-up" when all equipment is operational. It is imperative that
all principals be present at this inspection. It is incumbent upon
the contractor to make sure that all decisions makers are present.
This is the time when all punch-list items are resolved and final
retainage released for payment.

38. *SCHEDULE STABILITY:* The amount of time variation
that is reasonably expected in the original project construction
schedule. This is often a well-guarded secret. The reasons are
complicated but are based on the individual interests of each
individual principal. For example, the owner's main desire could
be to take occupancy as soon as possible to alleviate manufacturing
bottlenecks, or he may wish to delay the project completion until
after his vacation. The myriad reasons that can affect the original
project construction schedule are not always in the best economic
interests of the principals involved. Completing the project in the
shortest period of time is not always the goal. When this condition
exists, and it often does, job delays will result and the project break-
even point will increase. The result will be impacted damages.

39. *DESIGN STABILITY:* The state-of-the-art architectural
and engineering development of the project to be constructed.
Obviously, projects that have been constructed numerous times
before can be expected to generate a minimum amount of difficulty
with prudent supervision. However, projects that are one of a kind
or new architectural and engineering concepts can be expected to
be difficult projects that require large amounts of design and

supervision. Although obvious, this is often ignored. Each project must be evaluated in terms of design stability to determine the amount of risk involved. Risk should determine the amount of design and supervision required by the owner, contractor, and manufacturer alike. When this is not done, serious project delays will result.

40. *PERFORMANCE SPECIFICATIONS:* Contract specifications that specify only the end result of the project acceptable to the owner. Performance specifications are a result of incomplete architectural and engineering design. Performance specifications intend to shift the responsibility for the project coordination and design from the owner to the contractor and/or manufacturer. Increased costs will result. If the design has not been thought out, you can bet the schedule has not been thought out. The reason for the incomplete architectural and engineering design is another matter. When the reason is to save time or the initial investment of the owner, he is well advised to spend the necessary time and money for detailed design, for nothing will be gained.

41. *DETAIL DRAWINGS:* How-to drawings required to manufacture and install equipment and material. This is a case of if some is good, more is better. Every hour spent on detail drawings will save more than ten hours in the field. This is the fundamental method of communication between owner, manufacturer, and contractor. Project delays are an exponential function of the lack of detail drawings. It is the responsibility of everyone involved to make as many detail drawings as required. The lack of detail drawings is the basis of evaluation of many impacted damage claims.

42. *AS-BUILT DRAWINGS:* Modified original contract drawings delineating all deviations to these drawings made during construction. The obligation to make as-built drawings normally rests between the contractor and engineer. The contractor is normally required to draw all changes on the original contract drawings in red pencil, and the engineer is responsible to make the changes to his original tracing and give the revised prints to the owner. Failure of either the contractor or engineer to perform his responsibility can result in chaos later on. Work has become covered over and drawings made from memory are often not accepted by the owner. Delays in start-up and payment often result.

43. *OPERATING MANUALS:* Written instructions from manufacturers and engineers on the correct procedures for operating the equipment installed by the contractor. Because of the recent fervor in product liability, contractors should think twice about operating manuals. Those involved in the marine industry have learned that in many instances when they perform work, they are considered manufacturers by the courts. This means they have the responsibilities and liabilities of a manufacturer. Complete and correct operating manuals go a long way to cure this problem. They will also expedite inspection and approval. Changes in original contract work require new or changed operating manuals. This item, although often costly, is often overlooked when calculating invoices.

44. *MAINTENANCE MANUALS:* Written instructions from manufacturers and engineers on the correct procedures for maintenance of the equipment installed by the contractor. Maintenance manuals are expected to include all installation techniques that have been used by the contractor that have a direct bearing on how the maintenance must be performed. If the preparation of these manuals is left until the end of the project, serious payment delays can result. Changes in original contract work require new or changed maintenance manuals. This item, although often costly, is often overlooked when calculating invoices.

45. *REPAIR MANUALS:* Written instructions from manufacturers and engineers on the correct procedures for repair of the equipment installed by the contractor. These manuals are used not only by the owner but also by the contractor. They are of great use to the contractor during start-up. Repair information is the most difficult to obtain from manufacturers. If the preparation of these manuals is left until the end of the project, serious payment delays can result. Changes in original contract work require new or changed maintenance manuals. This item, although often costly, is often overlooked when calculating invoices.

46. *ADDENDUMS:* Additions or deletions to the original *contract specifications* made by the owner normally before construction begins. Original contract documents often provide the owner the right to add to or delete from the scope of the contract. The contractor is obligated to furnish the owner with revised pricing and work schedules. Deletions as well as additions can

often cost more than the money saved on the equipment and work deleted. Time revisions affecting how and when work is performed are tremendously costly to the contractor. In addition, deletions do not require that the contractor delete his provision for overhead and profit.

47. *REVISIONS:* Improvements to the original *contract drawings* made by the owner. Revisions can apply before or after construction begins. Original contract documents often provide the owner the right to add to or delete from the scope of the contract. The contractor is obligated to furnish the owner with revised pricing and work schedules. Deletions as well as additions can often cost more than the money saved on the equipment and work deleted. Time revisions affecting how and when work is performed are tremendously costly to the contractor. In addition, deletions do not require that the contractor delete his provision for overhead and profit.

48. *APPROVALS:* Owner's acceptance of materials and equipment to be used in the construction of the project. The requirement that all material and equipment be submitted to and approved by the owner is a prerequisite to completing the project on time and within budget. Whenever approvals are not final, delays will result. This is often seen when owners stamp submittals with a stamp that says something like, "This is approved for general conformity with drawings and specifications only." This legal footwork to duck responsibility does not serve the owner's best interest. It often delays the owner's final acceptance and beneficial occupancy.

49. *START-UP:* Placing the equipment installed by the contractor in working operation. Many unions have rules governing required manpower during start-up. Serious delays can result when start-up procedures are not properly planned for by the owner in the contract specifications and by the contractor with adequate manuals and manpower. They delay beneficial occupancy for the owner and payment for the contractor. Improper start-up procedures will often cause disputes among manufacturers, owners, and contractor—especially when additional work is required to correct errors caused during start-up.

50. *STIPULATED PRICE CHANGES:* A fixed-price change that is provided for in the original contract documents. Normally, such a change occurs as a written amendment to the original contract documents. This amendment is based on information

provided to the owner by the contractor, which sets forth additions to or subtractions from the original contract sum and alterations to the completion time. The amendment normally provides that all change orders must be signed by persons having authority to amend the original contract. The determination of such persons and the obtaining of written notification of this authorization from the owner should be done immediately before or after the contract is accepted. Most certainly this should be done before any field work commences.

51. *UNILATERAL CHANGES:* An authorization in the original contract documents that gives the owner the right to direct the contractor to proceed with a change prior to an agreement on price and time extensions. This authority is often exercised when the owner is dissatisfied with the contractor's proposed price changes. Therefore, to avoid delays (caused by price negotiations) the owner can force the contractor to proceed with the changes before any negotiation takes place. Although all changes require the contractor to pursue prompt payment, the unilateral change order requires special attention for the contractor to receive prompt payment during the progress of and upon completion of the change. The very minimum collected must be an amount that the other party considers to be proper. The balance to which the contractor is entitled must be negotiated, subject to the arbitration or litigation provisions of the contract.

52. *TIME-AND-MATERIAL CHANGES:* Owner-authorized changes that are paid on a time-and-material basis. All time spent on these changes is normally calculated and paid out of the contractor's out-of-pocket cost plus a fixed amount for overhead and profit. Materials are paid for at contractor's cost plus a nominal amount for overhead and profit. When numerous small changes are authorized, the amounts paid for overhead and profit are completely inadequate. In addition, hidden costs such as dilution of supervision can be tremendous, causing a ripple through the entire project. If payment for these changes is not vigorously pursued, a contractor's cash flow can be seriously impaired.

53. *CONSTRUCTIVE OR UNAUTHORIZED CHANGES:* Changes in work necessary to proceed with the project schedule. This is a common occurrence and a primary cause for misunderstandings between the owner and contractor. Even if the owner feels that the changes were justified, he can avoid responsibility by

contesting that he did not previously authorize the changes. Basically, the owner is saying, "I don't have the money to pay for that change!" In addition to changes based on scheduling constraints, the presence of an unreasonable number of errors in the plans and specifications due to architect/engineer errors is another basis for constructive changes. A system of documentation and owner notification is essential. After such a change, if contested by the owner, an expert should be hired for his evaluation of the necessity of the work and of the damages that have been mitigated for the owner.

54. *UNIT-PRICE CHANGES:* Changes authorized by the owner based on unit prices provided by the contractor in his bid. These changes are then incorporated into the contract documents by the owner. Despite how these unit prices are determined by the contractor, one cannot predict and plan for the many conditions that can impact the performance of any change. Furthermore, these unit prices do not make provisions for special tools or equipment that may be necessary. Unit-price requests often appear on projects that have been altered to a "fast track." Fast track is a type of performance specification. This means that bids are requested and contracts are signed before all the engineering and design work has been completed. These projects require an immeasurable amount of bookkeeping and negotiating. Because the architect/engineers are "winging it," they are not really sure what they are doing. There is no schedule stability, and design stability is often not measurable.

55. *CHANGES IN CODES AND REGULATIONS:* Changes in various regulatory codes and regulations that occur after the awarding of the contract can cause serious cost overruns. Building codes, municipal regulation codes, and state and federal safety regulations are a few examples of the types of codes and regulations that seriously affect the contractor when changed. This has become an increasing problem in the construction industry due to the substantial increase in construction activity every year.

56. *CONCEALED CONDITIONS:* Conditions that were not recognized when the contract was awarded but proved to be at variance with contract documents at a later date. Most contract documents provide that the contractor is to visit the project site and familiarize himself with the existing conditions. However, many conditions may be concealed, and unless there is good communication between the field and the office, the costs incurred will be

absorbed by the contractor unknowingly when his supervisor goes ahead with the work. The failure to include complete project schedules with bid documents is a common concealed condition overlooked by many contractors. Unless each contractor can evaluate the impact of work done by other contractors on his own work, serious job delays and conflicts can arise. And what I call the superintendent's disease will govern: "Proceed and complete the project at *any* cost." Field superintendents are the worst offenders, but without correct communications and control, this will be the governing criteria.

57. *DEFECTIVE PERFORMANCE:* Any fault or error by company personnel that is not in accordance with the project plans and specifications. Defective performance includes both office and field work, such as materials ordered incorrectly by the project manager in the office.

58. *ERRORS AND OMISSIONS:* Work that is incomplete, poorly completed, or not completed at all. Errors often occur when working long hours or in an illogical sequence. Crash programs that require rushed work to meet a project schedule are a prime cause of errors and omissions. Errors quickly escalate costs and often require increases in inspection and testing, which negatively affect union relationships. Most union agreements provide that workers will only redo work that *they* have done incorrectly. However, when the contractor under accelerated conditions is responsible for the error, the entire project is negatively affected.

59. *DEFECTIVE PLANS AND SPECIFICATIONS:* A term applied to a project completed correctly by a contractor from plans and specifications that he has altered to correct any defective portions of those plans and specifications. In other words, the equipment and work furnished does not conform to the original plans due to improvements and alterations made by the contractor. Under such a circumstance, all liability becomes that of the contractor's, even though his alterations were necessary to make the project a success. The owner or the architect/engineer is no longer liable once the contractor takes matters into his own hands. The contractor is responsible for his changes should complications arise in the future. Such alterations incur additional costs to the contractor. He is required to provide as-built drawings to the owner upon completion.

60. *ENGINEERING ERRORS AND OMISSIONS:* A term applied to a project completed incorrectly by a contractor from defective plans and specifications as a result of engineering errors and omissions. In other words, the completed project conforms to the original plans, but the result is a defective project due to the engineer's defective plans. Under this circumstance, the engineer is solely liable for his errors. The work must then be done over in accordance with new drawings at the engineer's expense. Many times, however, the work is changed without new drawings. Such a circumstance is a disaster for the contractor, because there is no documentation of the changes, which often increases liability for the contractor.

61. *ACCEPTANCE TIME LAG:* The time between when a physical change in the work is required to when it is authorized and planned for in the project schedule. Assuming that the physical change in the work is necessary for a complete and working project, this lag time can have a ripple effect on every contractor. This will produce serious profit losses for each contractor. Unless the project schedule is actually changed showing the revisions, and each contractor then evaluates the impact this new schedule will have on his preformance, many contractors will experience serious profit losses without ever knowing what has impacted them.

62. *REJECTED CHANGE ORDERS:* Owner-requested engineering work and cost estimates of changes in the original work that is subsequently rejected or ignored. This is a source of high costs for the contractor, diluting supervision and delaying parts of the project that are potentially affected by the request. The contractor is entitled to reimbursement for the work he has done and for all negative impacts from the original contract.

63. *DEFECTIVE APPROVAL:* The owner's refusal to approve adequate substitutes for specified materials or methods when specified materials are unattainable or specified methods are impossible. Outside expert opinions are necessary to document these occurrences properly. Although work may proceed, the owner must be notified immediately of the action the contractor is taking in preparation of his claim.

64. *DEFECTIVE REJECTION:* The owner's rejection of work or material, which requires the contractor to rework what has already been installed in accordance with the contract documents. This situation must be documented before rework is commenced.

Documentation should include notification, outside verification, and photographs.

65. *DEFECTIVE PAYMENT:* Any deviation from the terms of payment of the original contract documents. In order to protect constructive change recovery rights, notification must be made upon failure of payment in accordance with contract documents. If notification is not made, it can be found later that the contractor agreed to the change by quiescence. In other words, by failing to make notification, the contractor "said nothing when he had the chance."

66. *DELAYED PAYMENT:* The owner's late payment for correct work performed and invoiced by the contractor. This is a serious infraction by the owner. It is disregarding his fiduciary duties. When this occurs, it is often legal justification for the contractor to cease work. However, if the contractor continually accepts delayed payment with no protest, then a custom of usage may be established. The court may not consider the contractor's later ceasing work as justified. Delayed payments create negative cash flow and loss in productivity because of the contractor's inability to man and supply the project properly.

67. *IMPOSSIBILITY OF PERFORMANCE:* When performance as specified in the contract documents cannot be completed by any contractor. The job is impossible to perform according to the existing contract. For example, a requirement that the contractor use and furnish materials that are no longer manufactured is grounds for impossibility of performance. There are times when the owner unreasonably insists that it is the contractor's obligation to manufacture the materials as specified. This occurrence should be documented and recovery sought under impossibility of performance.

68. *STRIKES:* Direct and indirect labor strikes that affect the timely execution of the contract. Direct and indirect labor strikes at the project site are immediately apparent. However, indirect labor strikes not at the site may be another matter. A strike affecting the supply of material to a manufacturer of equipment required on a project may be unnoticed by the contractor. Timely notice to the owner will not be made by the contractor, thus creating loss of profit.

69. *ESTOPPELED SCHEDULE DEVIATIONS:* Expressed contract document provisions that anticipate and provide for schedule

deviations, limit or preclude the contractor's right of recovery, or provide no reasonable basis to expect the contractor to complete the work in a fixed period of time.

Often these express contract provisions that preclude the contractor's right of recovery are perceived by the contractor as the final word. In other words, there is no legal way to recover damages caused from delayed completion (particularly if there is no reasonable basis to expect the contractor to complete the work by a fixed period of time). This perception is wrong because it focuses on the result and not the cause. Depending on the cause of delayed completion, contract provisions precluding the contractor's right of recovery may not apply.

For example, if delayed completion exists because of the *interference* of others, the contractor is entitled to recovery; founded on the doctrine of good faith. Such interference can be direct or indirect.

Direct interference would be overt occurrences that delay the timely and productive execution of the contract. This would include such things as site access, interrupted utilities, joint occupancy, inspection, and attitude and morale.

Indirect interference would be covert occurrences that delay the timely and productive executions of the contract. This would include such things as ripple, contract organization, project organization, and design stability.

70. *LIQUIDATED DAMAGES:* A specified amount of dollars required to be paid to the owner by the contractor for each day the contractor takes to complete the project in addition to the time allotted in the original project schedule. This negative incentive for the contractor is intended to define clearly the owner's intention to complete the project on time. This increases the stability of the original project schedule for the owner. However, it does not necessarily increase the stability of the schedule for the contractor. This can be done with a premium being paid to the contractor by the owner for each day ahead of schedule that the work is performed. Then there is little question that it is the owner's and contractor's intention to complete the project on time.

71. *UNCONSCIONABLE CLAUSES:* Clauses in the contract documents that do not provide for the benefit or protection of both parties. These clauses can often be quite outrageous. Many exculpatory contract document clauses and "broad form hold

harmless" clauses are good examples of these types of clauses. Normally, such clauses will not hold up under close scrutiny in arbitration or litigation and should be treated as such by the contractor.

72. *UNCONSCIONABLE ACTIONS*: Actions taken by others that any reasonable person would consider outrageous. An example would be the owner requesting that the contractor perform an impossible task.

73. *SUSPENSION*: Formal documented delay of any part of the contract work for a period of time. This can be based on the convenience of the other party or because contract payment has not been made in accordance with the contract documents. Suspension often results in many charges, such as "move out" and "move in" costs, the learning curve, and so forth.

74. *ABANDONMENT*: Termination of all field work before the contract is completed. Such termination can occur at the owner's request, in which case the owner has normally breached the contract. On the other hand, if the contractor is responsible for the termination of work, the contract breach is his. Both parties require expert legal counsel before taking such drastic action. Contractor-initiated abandonment is a harsh action that should be based only on extreme cases of owner's nonpayment.

75. *TERMINATION*: A point in time when all work is completed in accordance with the contract documents. It is important that the contractor postpone termination of his job site activities until he has received full payment. Termination is the proper time to file lien if full payment has not been received. Otherwise, the contractor will preclude one of his most valuable rights of recovery.

76. *EXTERNAL PROJECT TERMINATION*: A point in time when all project site work is completed in accordance with the contract documents. The completion of project site work does not necessarily mean the contract work is complete. Often, contract documents require manuals and drawings to be prepared by the contractor. Premature external project termination is a serious problem. External project termination should not be taken until written final acceptance is obtained from the owner. It also protects the contractor's lien rights.

77. *INTERNAL PROJECT TERMINATION*: A point in time when all project work required by the contract of the contractor's

management and support office personnel is complete. This includes items such as manuals, as-built drawings, and payment of insurance premiums relating to the project. It also includes the productive time taken to pay costs such as worker's compensation or unemployment compensation incurred by the contractor for the project.

78. *CONVENIENCE TERMINATION:* Termination of the contract for the sole convenience of the owner. In such a case, the contractor should immediately initiate his rights of recovery and prepare his recovery claim. In addition, he should invoice the owner for all anticipated costs he expects to incur in the preparation of the recovery claim. These expenses include consultant's fees, lawyer's fees, interest, and financing.

79. *DEFAULT TERMINATION:* Termination of a contractor's work at the project site by physically taking control of the contractor's work, tools, and materials by the prime contractor because of the contractor's failure to proceed with the diligence as to ensure completion of the contract within the time specified in the contract documents. This is a judgment call made by the prime contractor. The contractor must vigorously pursue full payment from owner and prime contractor of all costs, expenses, and profit.

80. *EXTERNAL PROJECT DEFAULT TERMINATION:* The owner's termination of the contractor's project site work because of the contractor's failure to ensure completion of the contract within the time specified in the contract documents. This is a judgment call made by the owner. The contractor must vigorously pursue full payment of all costs, expenses, and profit.

81. *INTERNAL PROJECT DEFAULT TERMINATION:* The owner's termination of required project work being done by the contractor's internal project management and support office personnel. The termination is due to the contractor's failure to proceed with the diligence to ensure completion of the contract within the time specified in the contract documents. This is a judgment call made by the owner. The owner's execution and liability is not as clear as in the case of external project default termination. Many questions remain to be resolved. For instance, whose time and liability are involved with insurance payments? In any case, the contractor must vigorously pursue full payment of all costs, expenses, and profit.

82. *LABOR ESCALATION:* The increase in hourly wage rates relevant to the wage rate anticipated in the project bid. This escalation may occur if a project has been delayed and extended beyond the original project schedule. The increased base hourly rate will also increase insurance and benefits that are tied to the total dollar amount of wages paid.

83. *PREMIUM PAY:* Any payment to workers in addition to the "going" rate or union agreement. Premium pay may be necessary for many reasons, such as unavailability of manpower, attitude and morale, crew size, and so forth.

84. *SHOW-UP TIME:* Large amounts of money are lost due to union contracts that provide for compensation for workers who show up for canceled work. The contractor must pay his workers for a prescribed minimum number of hours even though no work was performed, regardless of the reasons for cancellation. Job delays of all sorts are a major cause of money being paid in show up time. The amount of money paid becomes a function of how many men are employed on the project.

85. *TRAVEL:* Payment to workers for their travel expenses. Many union contracts provide that if workers are required to report for work at a project beyond certain mileage points, they are to be reimbursed for their travel at set rates. A job delay, causing project schedule extension, automatically requires drastic increases in travel costs over and above those previously anticipated.

86. *HAZARDOUS PAY:* Premium payment to workers for work performed in hazardous conditions. Union contracts normally provide for additional hourly premiums to be paid for work considered to be hazardous. One such example is "high time," a premium paid to union electricians for work performed 40 feet or more above grade on smokestacks. Hazardous work may also require special types of safety equipment and dress which also affect worker productivity.

87. *OVERTIME:* The time worked beyond that of a normal workday in the area where the project is being built. This is normally all hours worked in addition to the first eight. However, this does vary relative to the geographic area of the project, the trades involved, and the shift that is being worked. Overtime normally produces losses in productivity, which almost exponentially increase with the amount of hours worked and the number of

days the overtime is continued. Most contractors' associations have published information that quantify these productivity losses.

88. *SHIFT WORK:* When more than one eight-hour working period per day is utilized on a project. In many geographic areas there can be multiple shifts worked with increased pay and reduced working hours for those shifts other than the day shift. In general, most journeymen stay clear of shift work, because it is normally viewed as a way of beating them out of their overtime. Therefore, it is avoided by contractors but commonly requested by owners or their representatives.

89. *MATERIAL PROCUREMENT:* This refers to all work and costs associated with the purchase of materials. This includes such items as telephone calls, telegrams, research, lab testing of products, and routing.

90. *FBO:* Normally refers to materials that are Furnished By Others to the contractor. These materials must be monitored for timely shipment, completeness, and defects. When no delivery schedules are shown in the contract documents, formal delivery requests are the responsibility of the installing contractor. Method of shipment and liability become important considerations, as well as factory testing for conformance with contract documents. In many cases, these liabilities are not considered until the damage has been done.

91. *MATERIAL ESCALATION:* The increase in the price of materials between the time of order and the time of payment. Escalation can occur because of delays in shipment due to job site obstructions or ripple from contract delays. Another source of material escalation comes in the form of interest penalties charged by suppliers for late payment. Such penalties are often the result of late contract payment to the contractor.

92. *MATERIAL STORAGE:* All storage of materials, either on the job site or in an off-site warehouse. Storage can be a source of enormous costs that are often overlooked when preparing the bid. Special handling and storage are often required when equipment is added to the project not specified in the original contract documents. In such cases, the need for such storage has not been identified until the actual arrival of the equipment at the site. In cases of project extension, special storage sheds are necessary to protect materials from adverse weather. If sheds cannot be con-

structed on the job site, warehouse space must then be rented for this period of time, adding additional expenses.

93. *REMOVAL OF DEBRIS:* The removal of debris from the job site, such as equipment packing materials. This can be a costly expense that is easily overlooked. Many projects make it the contractor's responsibility to ensure that all packing materials, construction byproducts, and demolition byproducts be removed from the project site before final payment is made. This item is also overlooked when estimating change orders.

94. *TOOL RENTAL:* The commercial rental rate for all tools used on a project. Many contractors have a separate rental company just to keep track of and to record all tools used at the going commercial rental rate and to ensure that all tools get back to the shop.

95. *MACHINERY RENTAL:* The commercial rental rate for all machinery used on a project. This includes all service and setup time. The reason for keeping track of these costs is the same as for tools. Commercial rental rates must be used rather than amortizing equipment for the project. Otherwise, all costs will not be accounted for, such as storage and financing.

96. *FREIGHT:* The total costs for the transportation of tools and materials from the manufacturer, supplier, or warehouse to the project site by commercial carrier. This includes transportation, physical handling, and potential loss. It is important to understand that materials shipped "FOB point of origin" become the title and ownership of the contractor as soon as the carrier picks up the material and loads it on the truck at the warehouse of the manufacturer or supplier. This means any damage that is incurred during shipping is the responsibility of the carrier and the contractor. This is a major problem for contractors. As a matter of fact, uncollected shipping damages are estimated to be in the hundreds of millions of dollars nationwide. Whenever possible, purchases should be made "FOB job site," which dictates that title does not transfer to the contractor until the material arrives at the job site. The shipping responsibility is therefore retained by the manufacturer or supplier.

97. *CARTAGE:* The total costs for the transportation of tools and materials from manufacturer, supplier, or warehouse to the project site by other than commercial carrier. This includes transportation, physical handling, and potential loss. The contractor is

normally totally responsible for loss or damage derived from cartage. Cartage is often forced upon a contractor to maintain compressed project schedules. The substantial increase in risk must be calculated either as commercial insurance or self-insured premiums.

98. *INSURANCE:* All insurance related to the project and its activities, such as worker's compensation, hospitalization, bonding, and special policies. Special policies may be necessary when lifting an expensive piece of equipment by crane or helicopter, to protect those items in the care and custody of the contractor and all other items as well. These policies are normally taken on a daily basis. Policies relating to product liability or errors and omissions are other examples. Whether the contractor is self-insured or not, this falls under the title of "risk management." In other words, these policies may be placed with an independent carrier or carried by the contractor himself.

99. *COMMERCIAL INSURANCE:* Third party insurance. Pertains to who is the insurer and to whom the premium is paid. Commercial insurance requires a premium to be paid to a third party (the insurance company) via an insurance agent or broker. Insurance rates can escalate during the progress of the contract. Rate escalation can be caused by the insurance company's inspection of project site conditions. Timely notice must be given to the owner when this occurs.

100. *SELF-INSURANCE:* First or second party insurance pertains to who is the insurer and to whom the premium is paid. In the case of the contractor it is the contractor's assumption of the risk as opposed to transferring it to a commercial carrier by obtaining a policy and paying a premium for the coverage. By assuming the risk himself a contractor is said to be "self-insured." He can create a reserve for losses by accumulating the equivalent of a premium he would otherwise pay to a commercial carrier. It should be noted that a contractor is self-insured on risk where commercial coverage is unobtainable. On large projects such as utility plants, casualty liability insurance coverage is often provided by the owner. The owner self-insures the project and accepts the contractor's casualty liability.

101. *WARRANTY RISKS AND COSTS:* Warranties provided by the contractor and manufacturers. Normally, the contractor

provides "pass-through" warranties provided by the manufacturers. However, the manufacturer's warranty begins when the equipment is shipped. On projects that are delayed, the warranty may expire before placing the equipment or material in service. In addition, in some industries such as the marine sectors, anyone performing work is coming to be considered a manufacturer. This tremendously broadens the liability of the contractor.

102. *INTEREST*: The cost of borrowing money to finance the project. Interest is the actual money paid to financing sources to purchase all materials, equipment, and labor.

103. *FINANCING*: Charges incurred for working capital to benefit work beyond the scope of the contract documents. When the owner or contractor is unable financially to carry on operations, financing is often incurred by one or the other. This is done to protect the investment already made in the project. These costs may be actual interest paid to financing sources or the capital lost opportunity cost of performing the work. All search and organizing costs are also included.

104. *TAXES*: The obligation to federal and state governing authorities relevant to labor and material. There may exist a wide variation in tax liability, depending on the location and type of project being built. For example, when subcontractors calculate their taxes in bids to prime contractors, and the prime contractors add taxes to their inclusive bid, double taxation is incurred. An example of project type is a project that is given preferential tax treatment, such as air pollution control. In this case, the air pollution aspects of the project are tax-exempt. However, if the design changes during the progress of the project, this exempt status can change and unexpected tax liability can be incurred.

105. *CONTRACT AWARD COSTS*: The costs incurred by the owner or contractor in bidding and obtaining or awarding the final contract. These costs must be included in the project break-even point. Under conditions of unexpected project terminations, these are costs that must be recovered.

106. *START-UP COSTS*: All costs associated with commencing work on a project. Some examples of start-up costs are cartage, unloading, tool setup, crew size build-up, the learning curve, scheduling, financing, and supervision. These costs may also be referred to as "move-in" costs when work suspension has occurred.

107. *SHUT-DOWN COSTS*: All costs associated with stopping a project. Some examples of these costs are material and tool loading, cartage, job site cleanup, material and tool storage, and testing. These costs can be incurred when terminating or suspending a project. When associated with suspension, these costs are referred to as "move-off" costs.

108. *EXTENDED DIRECT JOB EXPENSES*: Additional job site expenses incurred due to schedule delays. Some examples of these expenses are office and work trailer rental, telephone, TWX, copy machine, computer, and salary for a secretary.

109. *EXTENDED MAIN OFFICE OVERHEAD*: Additional main office expenses incurred due to schedule delays. These are sometimes applied to change orders. In delay situations, a common formula is the Eichleay formula based on the ruling of the Armed Services Board of Contract Appeals (Decision 5183, December 27, 1960). This ruling recognized that overhead is a function of time as well as of prime cost. It assumes that all field office overhead is recovered as direct job expense. The formula is as follows:

A. $\dfrac{\text{Billings for Delayed Contract}}{\substack{\text{Total Company Billings} \\ \text{During Delay Period}}} \times \substack{\text{Total Company Overhead} \\ \text{During Contract Period}}$

B. $\dfrac{\text{Allocable Overhead}}{\text{Actual Days of Contract}} \times \substack{\text{Daily Overhead Allocable to} \\ \text{Contract Performance}}$

C. Daily Overhead $\times$ Number of Days Delay = Amount Claimable

110. *ANTICIPATED PROFITS*: The amount of profit originally expected from the base contract and provided for in the contractor's bid. Profit loss is often the result of the inability to achieve timely performance by increasing the project break-even point. This includes provision for profits of impacted damages, profits of float time, and profits of new time.

111. *CLAIM RECOVERY AND SETTLEMENT COSTS*: All expenses incurred by the claimant while pursuing payment. This includes legal counsel, accountants, claims consultants, and court costs.

SUMMARY

Effective risk management is knowing your contracted risks, knowing how they can be controlled, and taking action to control effectively the risks that fall onto your shoulders.

In this chapter you have learned that a contractor is an insurance company. You learned about the relationship of the risks in fixed-price contracts to the project break-even point and the importance of using project break-even to calculate project profit and loss. You have discovered what SIDs are and how they negatively impact your profit. All 111 SIDs have illustrated the critical importance of a strong information and control system.

Next, in Chapter 3 you will learn how to document, explain, and monetarily quantify the risks of big-profit, fixed-price contracts. You will also discover the secrets of how to invoice for more than your original contract amount.

CHAPTER 3

What You Have to Know and Do to Prepare Your Invoice for More Than the Original Contract

THE RECOVERY CLAIM:
KEY TO PREPARING YOUR INVOICE

In previous chapters you learned the importance of the profit equation and the management of risk. You saw how project profit is affected by risk and the management of internally and externally caused impacted damages. In other words, you saw how profit is affected by the project break-even payment (a factor of the project profit equation, first stated in Chapter 1 and repeated following).

PROFIT = FULL PAYMENT

Project Profit = (Break-even Project Payment)

+

(Change Order Payment)

+

(Contract Payment)

You learned the importance of identifying and tracking those damages that negatively affect the project break-even payment. Now, in the case study presented in this chapter, you will learn the secrets of how to invoice the costs of those impacted damages caused by others. Such an invoice is the necessary substantiating report. This is called the *recovery claim*.

Although a contractor is well advised to avoid all claims, damages caused by someone other than the contractor (not written into the contract) are collectible with profit and are absolutely necessary to actualize growth strategies. The contractor must depend on himself to mitigate and to prevent all self-inflicted damages, but he can only advise others of the damages they are causing him. Therefore, the contractor is entitled to and must recover the costs of those damages caused by others.

The preparation of a claim depends on your documentation of every event or occurrence throughout the course of the project. This is one of the primary responsibilities of an information and control system. A claim is "built" over time, not thrown together after the fact. In other words, the process leading to the formal preparation of the claim constitutes the claim itself. Properly documented occurrences interfaced with the project schedule and substantiating evidence such as photographs, weather reports, vendor invoices, outside professional service charges, and so forth are essential for the preparation of a recovery claim. These evidenciary elements are gathered and documented over time. Each element must answer the questions of who, what, where, when, and how much.

THE ANATOMY OF THE RECOVERY CLAIM: FOUR MAIN PARTS

In order to prepare your own recovery claim successfully, you must first understand the intricacies of the substantiating report. There are four main parts to a report: credibility, entitlement, quantum and appendix. Let's look at each of these parts and their sections more closely.

The Credibility Part

The *credibility part* should be the first page following the Table of Contents of the recovery claim report. It should clearly state (in one to three pages) who has prepared the report and the qualifications of those who have expressed their opinions. It should also identify all standards or the higher authority that has been used in preparing the report. This section should by no means be slighted or burdened with a clumsy list of Ph.D.'s or professional engineers. Depending on the circumstances, a foreman with ten years of experience is more than qualified to serve as an expert. What is needed is a simple, straightforward, and complete credibility section.

The Entitlement Part

The *entitlement part* will require a great amount of writing. It must detail to the best of your knowledge and in chronological (date) order, exactly what happened, how it happened, and your opinion as to the effect it had on the work. As you prepare the sections of this part, cross-reference each occurrence with your exhibit section so the reader can easily find your documentation of the occurrence you are describing. This will save you days of explanation later. It will also give you an idea of what you can and cannot substantiate with documentation. In addition, it's advisable to have these sections read by disinterested parties to ensure that it has not become a documented venting of your frustrations. Even though this may prove to have some therapeutic results, it will not be well received by those who pay the claim, and thus serves no constructive purpose to receive payment. Try to be objective.

Keep the report focused only on the problems and on the people to the extent of documented actions. This will allow the reader to objectively determine the impact of each occurrence and establish you as the professional you are.

Always open your entitlement with a *summary*. The higher the report goes up the corporate ladder, the less the chances of it's being read closely. Corporate executives will not take the time to read everything, so be sure that you provide summaries that contain everything you want to say. Summaries are a way of saying, "Hey, this is important, read this!" Start with a short summary, then a longer summary, and finally the whole detailed report. You will find it to your advantage to follow the old axiom, "Tell them what you are going to tell them, tell it to them, then tell them what you have just told them."

The more time and effort that you spend on this part, the less trouble you will have negotiating or receiving payment. Properly prepared entitlement sections with substantiating exhibits will overwhelm the opposition. Remember, you are writing this so that if you have to go to court and present this to a judge and jury, they will understand and believe what you are saying. If you follow this advice, 99 times out of 100 your presentation is going to be so strong that payment will be a foregone conclusion. This is for you! In order to survive, your entitlement sections must be complete. It is like the old story of the hound and the hare. The hare always gets away even though the hound is stronger and faster. Why? Because the hare is running for its life, while the hound is running for sport. Don't hold back. You're not running for sport!

The Quantum Part

This is the *financial part* and develops the cost of each occurrence. This part comes almost last. However, it is by no means any less important than the previous two parts. You should realize that proof of entitlement does not mean that you have been monetarily damaged. You can be wronged, but if you have not been damaged you will not receive monetary compensation. This is one important reason for understanding project break-even. Project break-even is fundamental to monetary recovery. By evaluating each item that affects the project break-even, monetary compensation values are calculated.

The financial section should follow the same format used in the entitlement section. It should begin with a financial summary, and each of the following segments should have a written entitlement with appropriate indexed exhibits. If you have prepared your report correctly, the quick reader should be able to look at the invoice, read the entitlement and financial summary, and have a good sense of what is going on.

A major benefit of preparing the report is that you will immediately see where your project information and control system needs to be improved. As you go through the report you will find ways in which you could have made your information and control system more effective. As you will see in Chapter 7, the stronger your project information and control system, the less you will have a need for recovery claim reports. Instead, you will know what to look for and how to stop negative profit impacts as they occur. This should be the goal of every successful contractor.

The Appendix Part

This part consists of endnotes and exhibits. The endnotes are particular references required for clarity and denoted as subscripts in the document.

The *exhibit section* provides visual evidence to the preceding three parts of credibility, entitlement, and quantum. The visual evidence includes confirmed telephone conversations, letters, photographs, previously issued drawings, schedules, reports, and invoices. The exhibits focus only on the problems and on the people to the extent of documented actions. Properly prepared exhibits, substantiating the entitlement and financial sections, will overwhelm all opposition and objections to what really happened.

The exhibit section will immediately show you deficiencies in your information and control system. For instance, when you write "He said..." in the entitlement section and cannot find the written confirmation in your files to place in the exhibit section for substantiation, you will know that an improvement must be made in your system.

This is the part of your system that ensures that thoughts, understandings, directions, and orders are being communicated. The exhibits must not only exist in your files, they must also exist in everyone's files. For example, telephone confirmations must have been sent to the party (or parties) with whom you talked. They must have had the opportunity to respond to your understanding of what was said.

Drawings, schedules, and reports must have accompanying letters of transmittals. Special tools that were needed must have substantiating job site confirmation from the superintendent or foremen. Materials must have substantiating price quotations or invoices from suppliers. Manhours expended on particular jobs must have substantiating reports from the supervising foreman. Think of it this way, if someone told you "He said..." or "We said..." what would you accept as proof? (Many of the forms for this use are provided for you in Chapter 7.)

Since the report is being prepared throughout the course of the project and not thrown together after the fact, a missing confirmation or photograph of a serious situation will show up immediately and can be corrected. The primary reason for this work is to mitigate all internal as well as external damages. And you cannot expect to accomplish this either internally or externally unless everyone knows from the beginning that the damage is real.

HOW TO NEGOTIATE A SUCCESSFUL RECOVERY CLAIM: A CASE EXAMPLE

The following recovery claim is a real-life case of what was done to receive full payment. The recovery claim circumscribes all impacted damages caused by risks not assumed in the original contract documents. In this claim, which was quite successfully negotiated to the contractor's benefit, the original contract value was $150,000, which escalated to $630,353! The claim covers $368,475 that was still owed at the time it was submitted for payment. The amount of this claim is the amount required for project break-even payment, which includes the profit of impacted damages, the profit of new time, and the profit of float time.

You can use this case as a working model to prepare your own claim. The names and places have been changed and are intended to bear no similarity to real places, companies, or people, and exhibits also for this reason have been omitted, and are not required to learn how to prepare a successful recovery claim. Now, let the case speak for itself.

COVER PAGE

ELECTROSTATIC PRECIPITATOR INSTALLATION
BIG CITY ELECTRICAL GENERATING STATION
UNIT #10 BIG PLACE, TEXAS
OWNER—BIG CITY ELECTRIC COMPANY

TWELL DIVISION OF EQUIPMENT CORPORATION
Manufacturer/General Contractor
ELECTRICAL SUBCONTRACT NO. EC-22923/S087

ABLE BODY CONTRACTORS INC.
Electrical Subcontractor
PROPOSAL NO. PP-7029

TABLE OF CONTENTS

(Note: This Table of Contents is separated into Parts I, II, III
and IV only to illustrate the overall structure of the
claim. Therefore, the headers on Parts I, II, III and IV
would not be included on an actual claim.)

DESCRIPTION   *PAGE*

TABLE OF CONTENTS

TABLE OF CONTENTS

*Note: For this sample recovery claim, exhibits have not been included. (See Chapter 7 for the forms that you can use for this purpose.)

PART 1: CREDIBILITY—SECTION 1: AUTHORS

This report has been jointly prepared by Able Body Contractors Inc. (ABC) and Deerfield Consultants & Associates, Inc.

Able Body Contractors: Incorporated 1956, state of Delaware. Report prepared by:

Mr. Roger Thornhill, P.E., 27 years construction experience, 10 years president of Able Body Contractors.

Mr. Birch Kelly, E.E., 25 years construction experience, 15 years general superintendent for Able Body Contractors.

Deerfield Consultants & Associates Inc.: Incorporated 1965, state of Illinois. Report prepared by:

Mr. Robert Lyons, P.E., 31 years construction experience, 15 years manager of claims consulting for Deerfield Consultants & Associates. Inc.

Mr. Murray O'Neil, M.B.A., 19 years construction experience, 8 years staff executive for Deerfield Consultants & Associates, Inc.

Mr. William Jackson, J.D., 23 years construction experience, 6 years manager of the legal department for Deerfield Consultants & Associates, Inc.

PART II. ENTITLEMENT—SECTION 2: OVERVIEW

OVERVIEW

This report sets forth, in detail, the money now due Able Body Contractors (ABC) under Proposal No. PP-7029, dated August 5, 19X1, Twell Division of Equipment Corp. Subcontract No. EC-22923/S087 dated November 8, 19X1 and Letter Agreements dated May 22, May 23, and June 5, 19X2, for the high and low voltage installation work on two Twell electrostatic precipitators installed at the Big City Electrical Generating Station owned by Big City Electrical Co., for undue damages incurred by ABC due to major project problems caused by Twell such as the lack of materials, work areas, equipment, administration, and payment.

This report substantiates the project construction schedule delays, extensions, and unpaid invoices to the amount of $630,353.15 of which a balance of $368,475.95 is now due and payable to ABC.

PART II: ENTITLEMENT—SECTION 3: PROLOGUE

PROLOGUE

This report sets forth the impact of various project delays and project time extensions affecting labor productivity, extra work, contract documents, contract payments, extra work processing, extra work payment, project schedule, equipment shipment, project coordination, work areas, safety, proper equipment sizing, equipment availability and usage, crew size efficiency, beneficial occupancy, site access, reassignment of manpower, learning curve, errors, and omissions.

Attention has been specifically directed to the following items: project schedule duration, work complexities, productivity, and cooperation. Appropriate information sheets, graphs, and exhibits are included in this document.*

*Note: As previously stated, information sheets, graphs, and exhibits are not included or required for this sample claim.

PART II: ENTITLEMENT—SECTION 4: SUMMARY

SUMMARY: HIGH AND LOW VOLTAGE INSTALLATION

ABC's contract for the high and low voltage installation for the two Twell Division of Equipment Corp. (Twell) electrostatic precipitators at the Big City Generating Station for Unit #10 located at Big Place, Texas for Big City Electric Co. (BCEC) was initiated by Twell's request for bid from Able Body Contractors, Inc. (ABC) (Exhibit #1).

Twell, as the manufacturer/general contractor, accepted ABC's electrical subcontract Proposal No. PP-7029 dated August 5, 19X1 (Exhibit #2) and forwarded a letter of acceptance, based on ABC's proposal and a project completion date of April 30, 19X2 (Exhibit #3). Twell's letter of acceptance, dated August 15, 19X1, was received on August 19, 19X1, and ABC immediately commenced work at the Big City Station on August 22, 19X1 (Exhibit #3A).

In accordance with normal practice, ABC notified the owner (BCEC) of its presence and work on its Big City Station electrostatic precipitator project (Exhibit #7).

Twell forwarded its electrical subcontract No. EC-22923/SO87 to ABC on September 30, 19X1, which was received on October 3, 19X1 (Exhibit #4).

On November 8, 19X1, ABC duly signed and executed Twell's contract after first clearly denoting changes and addendums to the formal printed form, in conformance to ABC's subcontract proposal. While Twell received the revised contract, it never returned a signed copy to ABC.

Also on November 8, 19X1, ABC forwarded its authorized invoice for work through October 31, 19X1 (Exhibit #6). Twell did not pay this invoice until February 13, 19X2, leaving a balance to date (Exhibit #53). The problems of improperly delayed and insufficient progress payments were to continue throughout the project and cause debilitating money management problems for ABC.

Commencing at the beginning of the project, ABC diligently worked with the Twell project superintendent, Mr. Donald Morris, and Twell's electrical project administrator, Mr. Robert Thomas, in

PART II: ENTITLEMENT—SECTION 4: SUMMARY

developing an in-depth program to meet the specified April 30, 19X2 project completion date. This program considered the major areas of interface between ABC electricians and other crafts.[a]

Two Weekly Schedules and How They Monitored Progress

In order to actualize and visually display the construction program and to monitor progress effectively on a weekly basis, ABC in concert with Twell prepared and delivered a coordinated "CBM" schedule to Twell on November 22, 19X1 (Exhibit #8).[a]

The "CBM" schedule considered and displayed the following: (1) the various job functions to be performed, (2) the calendar dates during which the job functions were to be performed, (3) the duration of the job functions, (4) the sequence in which the job functions were to be performed, (5) the job functions that must be completed before the next function could be commenced, (6) the calendar dates when materials and equipment were to be on the jobsite, and (7) the electrical manpower required on a weekly basis.

The "CBM" schedule was color-coded for easy reference: blue was used to show the total elapsed time to date of issue, and red to show the current progress on respective job functions. The dashed lines with directional arrows indicated which job functions should be completed first, to proceed in a productive manner and produce optimum results (Exhibit #8).

Examples of Twell's Lack of Coordination and Supervision in Project Administration

Although the "CBM" schedule was developed in concert with Twell for maximum productivity and optimum interface, Twell failed to administer and follow its part of the work program. The following examples demonstrate how the normal degree of care was not exercised by Twell in the project administration of the required physical work and financial payments.

For example, according to the agreed upon program, the precipitator top sections were to be "dressed out" by November 28,

PART II: ENTITLEMENT—SECTION 4: SUMMARY

19X1. This was delayed until January 9, 19X2, then continued for a period twice as long as contemplated, because of material handling equipment shortages and site congestion during the time the work was actually performed (Exhibit #9).[b]

On December 1, 19X1, ABC forwarded its authorized invoice for work through November 30, 19X1 (Exhibit #6). Twell waited two and one-half months until February 16, 19X2 to make partial payment on the approved invoice, leaving a balance to date (Exhibit #53). This resulted in money management inefficiencies such as complicating jobsite payroll procedures.

By December 1, 19X1 the sidewalls and stairs were to be assembled and erected. The sidewalls were not completed until February 14, 19X2, which was two and one-half months late, producing a Twell productivity loss exceeding 300 percent and a ripple effect for ABC (Exhibit #9).

One major factor contributing to this productivity loss was the insufficient physical size of a rubber tire crane furnished by Twell. This was corrected on December 13, 19X1 by the addition of a larger capacity crawler type crane; under ABC's contract Twell was to provide all hoisting equipment such as crane and cherry picker, and all required transportation equipment for ABC's use in performance of the contract.

Three Major Problems Caused by the New Crane

Although the new crawler type crane solved Twell's initial problem of not being able to pick up the precipitator sidewalls (as they had been assembled at the jobsite), the new crane created three additional major problems which went unresolved.[b]

The first major problem that the arrival of the new crane caused was the total "tie-up" of all the material handling equipment (Exhibits #2 and #5). The original rubber tire crane, cherry picker, and trucks were all used to assemble the new crane, thereby excluding ABC from their scheduled productive use. Of course, this impeded ABC's job performance, causing rescheduling, overall jobsite congestion, and consequent labor productivity losses.

PART II: ENTITLEMENT—SECTION 4: SUMMARY

The second major problem caused by the new crane was the loss of credibility; serious questions were raised relevant to Twell's construction ability, which were created by the common knowledge that Twell's original crane was too small. The time loss also caused a tremendous demoralizing effect on the men.

The third major problem caused by the arrival of the new crane, and one which was to have far-reaching effects on the entire project from this time forward, was the lack of ground preparation and maintenance, a situation which was soon to turn the job site into an unbelievable "muck hole" (Photograph Exhibit #11). This condition was created when the new crane, which was a "crawler" type crane substantially larger and of substantially more weight than the original smaller "rubber tire" crane, was used with no ground preparation on the unstable earth of the work areas. Since neither crane mats nor crushed stone (or a combination of both) were used to prepare the work areas, the new crawler crane daily produced an effect similar to that of making pancake mix in a mix master. This mix was three feet deep (Photograph Exhibit #11A).

This situation was intensified and aggravated by the addition of a *second* crawler crane (Photograph Exhibit #11). These work area problems caused significant labor productivity losses and delays, including out-of-sequence work, manpower reassignment, dilution of supervision, concurrent operations, learning curve expense, stacking of trades, and a loss of positive credibility, morale, and attitude.

Delays in Schedule Caused by Late Arrivals of Equipment

The "CBM" program scheduled the control room electrical equipment, being supplied by Twell, to be delivered on December 19, 19X1 (Exhibit #8), in preparation for the assembly of the control house. When assembled the control house was expected to provide a major *dry* work area in which to preassemble equipment in order to proceed in a productive sequence (Exhibits #8 and #9). However, the control house electrical equipment was not delivered and available for installation until two months later than the scheduled time; e.g., the last week of February (Exhibit #9).

PART II: ENTITLEMENT—SECTION 4: SUMMARY

The late arrival of the electrical equipment did delay the erection of the control house framework for two months, but the framework was further delayed for four weeks more after the electrical equipment arrived due to (1) the unavailability of material handling equipment and (2) the addition of linear reactor mounting racks. This addition was unscheduled work made more difficult by ice and snow that had gathered on unprotected mounting surfaces. This put the project further behind schedule. To make matters worse, material handling equipment (such as trucks) were not provided by Twell to ABC in accordance with the electrical subcontract No. EC-22923/SO87 (Exhibits #2 and #5).

Twell's chronic failure to provide material handling equipment for ABC was to continue throughout the project. Indeed the problem was intensified by the ripple effect of site congestion and additional quantities of equipment demanded for later operations which were forced into concurrent time spans caused by the compression of the performance schedule.

Outdoor Work in Winter Causes Morale Problems

After the control house framework was finally erected by Twell, the roof was installed on the control house three and one-half months late on April 5, 19X2 (Exhibit #9). These Twell delays forced ABC to work outdoors during winter months, causing productivity losses and morale problems further contributing to manpower problems. Many of our best workers refused to work under these conditions. When the first reasonable opportunity presented itself, they quit, leaving ABC with the task and expenses involved in hiring and retraining workers. In addition, when ABC pointed out that the control panels and linear reactors required the roof on the control house for protection of the electrical equipment and for its personnel from the inclement weather, Twell refused to erect the roof and forced ABC to "make do" with mere drop cloths (Exhibit #12).

Between December 19, 19X1 and January 6, 19X2, the precipitator top sections were scheduled to be set on top of the precipitator sidewalls so that (1) the internals (plates, wires, and

PART II: ENTITLEMENT—SECTION 4: SUMMARY

weights) could be installed (Exhibits #1, #8, and #9) providing a major sheltered work area, and (2) to enable the weather enclosure to be installed which would also provide a major dry work area (Exhibit #8).

However, the top sections were not completed on schedule, with Twell experiencing a six-week delay and a 200 percent labor productivity loss (Exhibit #9).

Lack of Coordination Between Different Contractors

Twell failed to coordinate the precipitator work with the rest of the project in accordance with Twell's and ABC's contract. Other contractors, working directly for the owner, commenced counterproductive construction activities such as erecting tanks, digging holes, and parking semi-trailers directly in precipitator work areas. This had a devastating effect on both ABC's and Twell's labor productivity throughtout the entire job (Photograph Exhibit #13).

On December 22, 19X1, ABC forwarded its authorized invoice for work through this time (Exhibit #6). Twell waited almost four months until April 28, 19X2 to make partial payment on the approved invoice, leaving a balance to date (Exhibit #53). This continued the serious money management problems for ABC on this project.

Although the scheduled time for Twell to commence setting the compression houses was December 26, 19X1 the work was not started until February. This work was delayed because of the existing congestion in these areas and other schedule delays (Exhibits #8 and #9).

On January 4, 19X2, ABC forwarded its authorized invoice for work through January 4, 19X2 (Exhibit #6). Twell again waited until April 28, 19X2 to make partial payment on the approved invoice, leaving a balance to date (Exhibit #53).

On January 9, 19X2, the installation of internals (by hanging plates) was to commence (Exhibits #1, #8, and #9).[c] This would provide ABC's men with, among other things, a major work area sheltered from the adverse weather conditions. However, this work

PART II: ENTITLEMENT—SECTION 4: SUMMARY

was delayed by Twell until March 23, 19X2 (Exhibit #9). The three-month delay required this major work to be performed under burdensome conditions of limited access and mobility of the material handling equipment because other contractors, working separately and independently for the owner (BCEC), had by then built a tank in this work area (Photograph Exhibit #13).

Productivity Losses Due to Limited Access and Mobility

The problem of limited access and mobility, along with the muck that was generated by the two crawler cranes, caused serious labor productivity losses. For example, instead of being able to place 50 gallon steel barrels containing 30-lb. weights at the place where they were to be used, ABC was forced to place them 40 to 50 feet away and 4 feet below the proper elevation. This required additional men to handle each 30-lb. weight up over the 4 foot elevation and across the additional 40 to 50 feet. This activity took place 90 feet in the air above grade encompassing 5,000 weights (Exhibits #14 and #25).

From January 9, 19X2 through January 20, 19X2, the weather enclosures on the top of the precipitators were scheduled to be completed. This would provide a major work area protected from the adverse weather. The construction of this work area was started on February 15, 19X2; unfortunately, it took Twell eight weeks instead of the expected two weeks to erect the framework (Exhibit #8 and #9).

Why Twell Suffered a 400 Percent Labor Productivity Loss

This six-week delay gave Twell a serious 400 percent labor productivity loss that had several causes and effects on both Twell and ABC:

1. The framework for the weather enclosure was built backwards *twice* by Twell; each time, ABC was required to take down and disassemble the cable tray it had installed. When ABC asked to

PART II: ENTITLEMENT—SECTION 4: SUMMARY

be reimbursed for the additional time that had been spent to reassemble and reinstall the cable tray, the request was refused.

2. ABC was unable to use the material handling equipment to complete the cable tray installation because a separate and independent contractor, working directly for the owner, had dug a hole in one of the precipitator work areas. This required that the framework for both precipitators be built in succession, congesting the only work area left for Twell and ABC. Therefore, if ABC had worked in a logical manner by completing the cable tray on the ground, Twell would have waited to use the work area, which would have given them a serious labor productivity loss by accelerating their schedule. However, it was ABC who waited for Twell and performed its work out of sequence, thus ABC incurred the labor productivity losses.

3. After Twell's second attempt at constructing the weather enclosure framework on the ground, they discovered it did not fit when placed on top of the precipitator, requiring the framework to be rebuilt in the air. This rework in the air on top of the precipitators by Twell caused significant damage to ABC's aluminum conduit that had already been installed on the top portion of the precipitators.

The rework also required that ABC disassemble, remove, and reinstall the aluminum conduit and bracing. When ABC asked to be reimbursed for the additional time it had spent to reassemble and reinstall the aluminum conduit the request was ignored.

Schedule delays, such as those experienced in completing the weather enclosures, created significant work area congestion which was reflected in "tie-ups" of the material handling equipment to ABC's exclusion. This also produced ripple inefficiencies by forcing ABC to move much of its materials in snowstorms and rain, which was the only time left when the limited amount of material handling equipment was not being used by Twell.

After the weather enclosure frameworks were erected, the roof on the South Precipitator Unit was not installed until June of 19X2

PART II: ENTITLEMENT—SECTION 4: SUMMARY

and the roof on the North Unit was not complete by August of 19X2, months after the original contract completion date. These delays required ABC to work outside during the winter months, producing productivity losses and morale problems that contributed to manpower reassignments.

Productivity Losses Due to Delayed Correction of Material

On January 16, 19X2, ABC notified Twell in writing that the emitting beams, as supplied, were not manufactured in accordance with Twell's drawing #1-13419 Section CC and unless corrected now, would require an unreasonable amount of additional corrective work later in the project (Exhibit #15). Unfortunately, this situation was ignored by Twell and did show up later; each wire hanger on the improperly manufactured emitting beams required manual realignment in the field (Exhibits #15 and #25). This work was required during a very difficult time when the internals (plates, wires, and weights) were being installed with composite work crews (made up of boilermakers and electricians). The basic inefficiency experienced from composite crews was multiplied due to the labor productivity loss involving a number of other crews who had to wait on the corrective work. The efficiency losses from limited access were also multiplied by the composite crew size.

During the week of February 6, 19X2, a crane boom failed (dropped and severely damaged by Twell). To solve this problem Twell brought in a second crawler type crane which had to be unloaded and assembled by using the existing equipment, this again rendered any material handling equipment unavailable to ABC.

Five Results of a Job Survey

On February 22, 19X2, a job survey was conducted by Mr. Roger Thomas, Twell construction electrical engineer, Mr. Donald Morris, Twell project superintendent, Mr. Roger Thornhill, president of ABC, and Mr. Thomas May, ABC project manager. The following items were reviewed:

PART II: ENTITLEMENT—SECTION 4: SUMMARY

1. ABC was not provided flagmen in accordance with the provisions in the electrical subcontract (Exhibit #5).

2. ABC was not provided manned trucks and/or trucks in accordance with the electrical subcontract (Exhibit #5).

3. ABC was not provided a manned crane and cherry picker in accordance with the electrical subcontract (Exhibit #5).

4. ABC was performing the following extra work, and had requested authorization for the constructive changes in accordance with the electrical subcontract (Exhibit #5).

   a) Chipping, grinding, and cleaning control house floor and panel mounting channels .... 54 hrs.

   b) Additional mounting rack for linear reactors .... 52 hrs. (15 hrs. N/C)

   c) Straightening compression house on South Unit .... 153 hrs. (70 hrs. N/C)

   d) Unloading and setting additional motor control center sections ..... 33 hrs. (2 hrs. N/C)

   292 hrs. (87 hrs. not charged for)

5. The "CBM" schedule was reviewed along with the physical site conditions, and the following items were agreed upon:

   a) The work areas now available were inadequate because of the ripple effect which was taking place, causing the stacking of job functions and congestion.

   b) Contractors who were working directly for the owner, independent of Twell, were severely reducing the work areas and limiting future access.

   c) The work areas were unsafe and inaccessible because of the "muck."

   d) Required electrical equipment, which was being supplied by Twell, was not being received on time, in accordance with the schedule.

PART II: ENTITLEMENT—SECTION 4: SUMMARY

e) There was not enough material handling equipment such as cherry pickers and trucks.

f) ABC desperately needed the major closed-in work areas in the control room and on top of the precipitators in order to accomplish reasonable labor productivity.

g) ABC invoices were not being paid in a timely and agreed to manner.

During the survey, Mr. Roger Thomas of Twell took photographs for the home office file and concluded that at least 205 hours would be immediately approved for the extra work that had been performed and that the problems concerning site conditions, equipment availability, material shipments, work areas, and payments would be properly corrected.

On February 28, 19X2, ABC forwarded its authorized invoice for work through February 28, 19X2 (Exhibit #6). Twell again delayed paying the progress payment until April 28, 19X2, leaving a balance to date (Exhibit #53).

Four Major Obstacles That Delayed ABC's Schedule

On March 14, 19X2, after several unsuccessful attempts to reach Mr. David White, Twell construction manager, by telephone, ABC forwarded a written report, including a current schedule (Exhibit #16). This report and schedule identified four major encumbrances which were having a detrimental effect on ABC's contract performance, time, and cost.

These impediments of schedule and material delays, lack of material handling equipment, bad site conditions, and lack of payment, forced upon ABC a schedule delay of over ten weeks, a 61 percent labor productivity loss, a 236 percent manpower reassignment, and a 200 percent increase in supervision. ABC requested that Twell advise how it now planned to coordinate, perform, and pay ABC for this project (Exhibit #16).

On March 27 and 28, 19X2, a meeting was held at the jobsite with Mr. Mitchell Sharp, Twell regional construction manager, Mr.

PART II: ENTITLEMENT—SECTION 4: SUMMARY

Benjamin Brown, Twell project manager, Mr. Donald Morris, Twell project superintendent, and Mr. Birch Kelly, ABC general superintendent, to review the February 22, 19X2 survey and the March 14, 19X2 report.

On April 5, 19X2, with apparently no constructive action and after several unsuccessful attempts to reach Mr. David White, Twell construction manager, ABC forwarded by certified mail its written notice, which included a current "CBM" schedule delineating many of the problems ABC was experiencing (Exhibit #17) and a copy of the March 14, 19X2 report and schedule (Exhibit #16).

ABC Suspended Its Jobsite Activities

ABC advised that it would suspend its jobsite construction activities until such time as ABC received reasonable assurances that the matters of schedule delays, increasing productivity losses, and continuing payment difficulties (all of which, as of that date, had resulted in an 85 percent productivity loss, a 283 percent manpower reassignment, and a 200 percent increase in supervision) would be corrected by Twell.

While waiting for Twell's reply, a crane was again damaged on April 13, 19X2. However, this time the crane was not repaired; instead, it was taken out of service and removed from the jobsite. This restricted the use of the material handling equipment during the process of disassembling and loading of the crane, and removed an important piece of equipment needed by ABC. Its removal required ABC to install the balance of the cable tray by first scaffolding the area. This additional work contributed to additional labor productivity losses.

When ABC requested high time premium pay (additional payment for each man-hour worked over 40 feet above grade required by union agreement) in accordance with the electrical subcontract No. EC-22923/SO87 (Exhibits #2 and #5), it was refused (Exhibit #18).

On April 19, 19X2, with eleven days left to the scheduled contract completion date of April 30, 19X2 another jobsite meeting

PART II: ENTITLEMENT—SECTION 4: SUMMARY

was held with Mr. Davis White, Twell construction manager, Mr. Mitchell Sharp, Twell regional construction manager, Mr. Donald Morris, Twell project superintendent, Mr. Roger Thornhill, president of ABC, and Mr. Birch Kelly, ABC general superintendent (Exhibit #19).

Twell Denies Any Monetary Responsibility for Delays

The purpose of this meeting was to resolve the matters surveyed on February 22, 19X2, March 14, 19X2 (Exhibit #16), and April 5, 19X2 (Exhibit #17). Although Twell acknowledged ABC's tremendous losses caused by Twell's inadequate material handling equipment and project management which caused electrical equipment and job delays, along with unmanageable site conditions and congestion, Twell did not assume monetary responsibility. Instead, Twell now argued that it was the owner's project management who was at fault. Therefore, Twell would reimburse ABC whenever and whatever was collected from the owner for a claim that Twell, unknown to ABC until this time, had already initiated.

Twell's New Policy: A Daily Work Schedule

Other areas, such as Twell's conduct in adhearing to reasonable construction schedules, were summarily dismissed by Twell as irrelevant. Moreover, Twell disavowed any intended meaningful participation in the "CBM" schedule and stated that its viability was always meaningless to them, because in its purview *Twell's superintendents would change the job schedule whenever they wanted.* However, from now on, Twell stated they would make out a daily work schedule which was to be strictly adhered to by ABC. Further, if Twell's own boilermakers did not start doing more work, Twell's *new* superintendent would completely shut down the entire project.

In addition, Twell assured ABC that by replacing its project supervision with younger men, the project labor productivity problems and equipment usage problems would be solved.

PART II: ENTITLEMENT—SECTION 4: SUMMARY

In order to ensure that ABC understood Twell's new financial, construction schedule, and management policies, ABC requested that a firm understanding be reduced to writing in order to proceed beyond the scheduled contract completion date of April 30, 19X2. Twell agreed, but because of commitments to another project, Twell's executives would have to conclude these matters formally at a later date.

The time between the April 19, 19X2 jobsite meeting and the next meeting on May 9, 19X2 (at Twell's offices in New York) did not produce any practical solutions for the equipment usage problems (Exhibits #20 and #21) or the lack of sufficient work areas (Exhibits #20, #22, and #23).

On May 1, 19X2, ABC forwarded its authorized invoice for work through April 30,19X2 (Exhibit #6). Partial payment was delayed until July 20, 19X2, leaving a balance to date (Exhibit #53). This redundancy in delayed and incomplete progress payments continued to cause ABC severe money management problems.

The May 9, 19X2 meeting in New York included Mr. David White, Twell construction manager, Mr. John Green, Twell legal administrator, Mr. Roger Thornhill, president of ABC, and Mr. Robert Nice, ABC legal counsel (Exhibit #25).

ABC attended this meeting, believing it to be an earnest attempt to resolve the impediments that were affecting its contract performance, time, and costs. However, it soon became apparent that Twell had no intentions of reaching an agreement on the current project.

Instead of discussing the problems on this project, Twell discussed promises of future and immediate subcontract electrical work on other projects which Twell had under contract such as a $1,600,000 electrical project in Dallas, Texas, and a $150,000 electrical project in Springfield, Florida, and an immediate contract for a $150,000 project in Atlanta, Georgia that had been verbally awarded to ABC some weeks before this meeting.

ABC stressed the urgency and necessity to focus on solving the problems of this project, to make a decision to either correct the serious problems of payment delays, schedule delays, material delays, equipment usage, jobsite conditions, labor productivity

PART II: ENTITLEMENT—SECTION 4: SUMMARY

losses, and contract price escalation, or to engage another electrical contractor. Twell again promised to conclude these matters, but due to problems at another project and its commitments at a new $25 million Miami project, Twell said it would have to get back to ABC in the near future.

On May 11, 19X2 a telephone conference was held with Mr. David White, Twell construction manager, Mr. John Green, Twell legal administrator, and Mr. Roger Thornhill, president of ABC, (Exhibit #26).

ABC's price escalation billing, in accordance with the electrical subcontract No. EC-22923/SO87 (Exhibits #2 and #5), was reviewed (Exhibit #24). ABC's labor productivity losses were not reviewed, since Twell had been too busy to talk with everyone they believed to be involved.

ABC Recommends Twell Hire Another Electrical Contractor

Because of Twell's unresponsiveness to ABC requests, ABC decided it could not continue to work under the arrangements which were being proposed and would not continue to suffer delays. ABC suggested to Twell that another electrical contractor be engaged to take over the project.

Six weeks after ABC's written notice of April 5, 19X2 (Exhibit #17), with no affirmative response from Twell, ABC *discontinued its jobsite construction activities* on May 18, 19X2 and turned over all materials to Twell's superintendent, so that a substitute contractor could continue the project in an expedient manner (Exhibit #27). ABC notified Twell's home office accordingly (Exhibit #28), and this was confirmed by the Twell project superintendent (Exhibit #29).

Payment Reimbursement Plan Accepted

On May 18, 19X2 (the same day ABC discontinued its field activities), ABC received and accepted an offer from Twell for minimum reimbursement for project delay and labor productivity

PART II: ENTITLEMENT—SECTION 4: SUMMARY

losses. ABC agreed to continue work and temporarily defer its full compensation for project delay and labor productivity losses with the understanding as follows:

1. All future contract payments would be promptly paid without delay.

2. ABC would not relinquish any right to recover productivity and delay damages.

3. ABC would assist in presenting Twell's claim to BCEC and would share between Twell and ABC on a 50/50 basis all amounts in excess of the amounts reduced to ABC, along with ABC's expenses in the preparation and presentation of the claim.

4. The immediate objective was to finish the internal precipitator installation because BCEC needed to install the rest of the boiler system to keep its other contractors on schedule.

5. Twell would proceed if necessary, and install the plates out-of-scheduled sequence, and ABC would install the wires and weights later. This would allow Twell to keep BCEC on schedule and allow ABC to establish a small labor force, now the most productive method of finishing the project. It would also save Twell the expense of having two foremen.

6. ABC would keep its present general foreman, (who was guaranteed a 40-hour workweek), even though not required by union agreement.

7. Twell believed once the plates were installed, it would not be necessary for the electrical work to be complete until the entire power plant was completed, probably more than a year away.

8. Because Twell's contract with BCEC required a supervisor to be present on the jobsite whenever a subcontractor was working, Twell would have one of ABC's men designated the Twell supervisor after they were complete. Therefore, Twell would not have to go through the additional expense of paying a supervisor to sit around and watch the electricians.

PART II: ENTITLEMENT—SECTION 4: SUMMARY

9. Twell would repair all deficiencies concerning material handling equipment usage, jobsite conditions, and work area availability (Exhibits #30, #31, #32 and #33).

On May 22, 19X2, a meeting was held at the jobsite with Mr. Ronald Seaton, Twell project superintendent, Mr. Roger Thornhill, president of ABC, and Mr. John Good, ABC general foreman, to review the agreements of May 18, 19X2 concerning the installation of the precipitator internals (plates, wire and weights), material handling equipment availability and usage, and work area availability. The project schedule requirements were discussed and Twell felt that the immediate task of finishing the internal (plates, wire, and weights) precipitator installation was the primary objective to enable the owner (BCEC) to tie in the duct work and complete the boiler system, keeping BCEC's other contractors on schedule.

Mr. Ronald Seaton, Twell project superintendent, said that Twell would ensure that ABC had use of the material handling equipment when needed, but he would have to check with Mr. Mitchell Sharp, Twell regional construction manager, to see what would be done about the "muck."

ABC stressed the importance of this being taken care of as soon as possible to preclude more labor productivity losses. Further, Twell promised to ensure that the roofs would be installed on the weather enclosures immediately.

Lack of Cooperation Continues from Twell

On June 2, 19X2, material handling equipment usage was again refused ABC and, on June 6, 19X2, it was confirmed that Twell was going to do nothing about this problem. It was obviously going to continue to give ABC labor productivity losses (Exhibit #34).

In response to this situation, on June 7, 19X2, ABC forwarded a letter to Mr. David White, Twell construction manager, requesting to know why Twell had apparently changed its mind about ABC

PART II: ENTITLEMENT—SECTION 4: SUMMARY

maintaining a small labor force, and asking if Mr. White was aware of the change in attitude, as several different people were now involved and several different requests for varying amounts of manpower were being received. ABC was not in agreement with these new developments, and went on record that this was an inefficient use of manpower (Exhibit #35).[d] Nonetheless, ABC complied with Twell's new manpower requests to accelerate the construction schedule (Exhibit #55).

On June 12, 19X2, a jobsite conference was held with Mr. Ronald Seaton, Twell project superintendent, and Mr. John Good, ABC general foreman, to discuss the sequence of work on Twell's priority list in relation to normal work procedures. ABC tried to dissuade Twell from proceeding in an obvious unproductive manner; reestablishing the practices that had created needless and ridiculous labor productivity losses for everyone, only to be told that this did not concern Twell and that ABC should proceed the way Twell demanded.

ABC, filled with total frustration and anguish at the absolute lack of cooperation and the vexatious attitude demonstrated by Twell, forwarded its written confirmation of this conference to Twell, requesting any corrections thereto, otherwise ABC would assume the information to be correct. No corrections were returned (Exhibit #36).

Twell Assumes Control of All Electrical Operations

On June 13, 19X2, Mr. David White, Twell construction manager, called Mr. Roger Thornhill, president of ABC, and demanded that he immediately instruct his general foreman to follow all Twell orders concerning sequence of assembly and technique or method in which the electrical work was to be performed and installed.

When ABC agreed, under protest, and pointed out that this approach may create a situation that could cause men to leave, recreating the previous labor productivity problem, ABC was told by Mr. David White, Twell construction manager, "they are my

PART II: ENTITLEMENT—SECTION 4: SUMMARY

dollars and let me spend them the way I want, even if I am wrong!" This was also confirmed in writing on June 15, 19X2 wherein corrections, if any, thereto were requested; otherwise, ABC would assume the information to be correct. No corrections were returned (Exhibit #37).

Later, on June 15, 19X2, Mr. David White, Twell construction manager, telephoned Mr. Roger Thornhill, president of ABC, on a conference call with Mr. Mitchell Sharp, Twell regional construction manager, wherein the following transpired:

1. Twell instructed what the ABC's electricians were going to do at starting time each morning.
2. Twell asked if the general foreman had been told that he was to follow all orders and instructions from Twell during the workday, as Mr. David White had instructed earlier (Exhibit #37).
3. ABC was informed that Twell would "check up" tomorrow at the jobsite to make sure that ABC had actually instructed its general foreman as Twell had demanded.
4. Twell instructed what the electricians were going to do at quitting time each evening.
5. Twell instructed ABC to make all the required arrangements with the union because Twell was sending its own electricians from Memphis.

This telephone conference call was confirmed in writing on June 15, 19X2. Again corrections, if any, were requested, otherwise ABC would assume the information to be correct. No corrections were returned (Exhibit #38).

On June 16, 19X2, two jobsite meetings were held by Mr. Mitchell Sharp, Twell regional construction manager, with Mr. John Good, ABC general foreman.

Mr. Mitchell Sharp, Twell regional construction manager, was "checking up" and wanted to make sure that Mr. John Good, ABC general foreman, had been properly instructed by ABC's home

PART II: ENTITLEMENT—SECTION 4: SUMMARY

office in accordance with instructions from Twell (Exhibits #37, #38, and #39).[e]

Mr. John Good, ABC general foreman, advised Mr. Mitchell Sharp, Twell regional construction manager, that he had been told by the home office to cooperate with Twell on everything.

Mr. Mitchell Sharp, Twell regional construction manager, instructed Mr. John Good that Twell was now going to run this job and that he and Mr. Ronald Seaton, Twell project superintendent, would have the last say on anything pertaining to the electrical part of this job.

These conferences, which certainly accomplished the objective of reducing labor productivity, were confirmed by ABC in writing on June 16, 19X2. Again, corrections thereto were requested, otherwise, ABC would assume the information to be correct. No corrections were returned (Exhibit #39).[e]

On June 16, 19X2, a third jobsite meeting was held. This time it was held by Mr. Ronald Seaton, Twell project superintendent, with Mr. John Good, ABC general foreman, to review the instructions Twell had given ABC regarding starting and quitting time procedures which would be followed and also the assembly techniques to be used in performing the electrical work (Exhibits #37 and #38).

Mr. John Good, ABC general foreman, was told with undue abusive language by Mr. Ronald Seaton, Twell project superintendent, that all ABC personnel were to report to him and follow the same manners as his employees for starting and quitting each day.

Mr. Ronald Seaton, Twell project superintendent, instructed Mr. John Good, ABC general foreman, in the technique the electrical work was now to be performed, and issued a memo to ABC accordingly. In addition, payment would not be made to ABC for work that was not performed in accordance with Twell's new technique and work method instructions (Exhibit #40).

Further, Twell informed Mr. John Good, ABC general foreman, of his demotion to a working foreman, and told him that if he did not perform accordingly, Twell would not pay ABC for the time he worked on this project.

PART II: ENTITLEMENT—SECTION 4: SUMMARY

This meeting was confirmed by ABC, in writing, on June 16, 19X2. As always, corrections thereto were requested, otherwise, ABC would assume the information to be correct. No corrections were returned (Exhibit #39).[e]

On June 16, 19X2, Mr. Roger Thornhill, president of ABC, called Mr. David White, Twell construction manager, to discuss the current attitude and actions. When it became apparent that Twell did not perceive its actions as contrary to reasonable conduct, ABC recommended that Twell exercise its option in accordance with the Letter Agreements of May 22, May 23, and June 5, 19X2 (Exhibits #30, #31, #32, and #33) to engage another electrical contractor. ABC stated it would follow whatever reasonable procedure Twell wished in order to allow for a smooth transition.

On July 19, 19X2 (Exhibit #48), ABC forwarded its letter requesting of Twell the following:

1. To forward overdue payments in accordance with the previous agreements.

2. To advise ABC what Twell's intentions or desires were in accordance with Twell's option to engage the services of another electrical contractor to continue the job since Twell's harassing actions indicated that Twell would prefer someone other than ABC to do the work. This request was made so that ABC could plan and determine its future schedule and, if required, schedule an orderly transition of the work with a minimal loss of time and productivity.

3. To advise Mr. Ronald Seaton, Twell project superintendent, and Mr. Mitchell Sharp, Twell regional construction manager, that their understanding and refusal to sign work orders for work accomplished outside the original scope of work was contrary to the existing contractual provisions.

4. To advise ABC as to when Twell intended to complete preparation of the claim for BCEC as provided in the Letter Agreements (Exhibits #30, #31, #32, and #33) since Twell's failure to commence action in this regard may seriously affect the claim.

PART II: ENTITLEMENT—SECTION 4: SUMMARY

Twell Assesses Unfair Charges to ABC

On June 20, 19X2, Twell notified ABC (by telegram) that ABC's termination has and will cause them excessive delays, expenses, and damages which shall be assessed against ABC's account (contrary to existing agreements) and that Twell will begin a search for the services of another electrical contractor (Exhibit #42). ABC forwarded its clarification of its actions (Exhibit #41).

On June 20, 19X2, a jobsite meeting was held by Mr. Mitchell Sharp, Twell regional construction manager, with Mr. John Good, ABC general foreman, wherein the following transpired:

1. Mr. John Good, ABC general foreman, was reprimanded with undue abusive language for doing his job, by Mr. Mitchell Sharp, Twell regional construction manager.

2. Mr. John Good, ABC general foreman, was informed that if he did not perform to the satisfaction of Mr. Mitchell Sharp, Twell regional construction manager, and Mr. Ronald Seaton, Twell project superintendent, he would be fired by Twell.

3. Mr. Mitchell Sharp, Twell regional construction manager, emphatically stated that he had never authorized ABC to work for Twell.

This meeting was confirmed by ABC, in writing, on June 20, 19X2. Again, corrections, if any, thereto were requested, otherwise, ABC would assume the information to be correct. No corrections were returned (Exhibit #43).

On June 22, 19X2, due to Twell's failure to send its own electricians as it had previously advised (Exhibit #38), ABC forwarded the results of its search for more manpower. The Wisconsin union had offered manpower at specified money rates and Twell was informed of the rates requested (Exhibit #44).

In answer on June 22, 19X2, Twell forwarded its approval to ABC to proceed and expand its labor force, but not at the money rates requested by Wisconsin. Twell unilaterally reduced the individual living expense for the workers to five days, which Twell directed was to cover the individual workers' expenses for seven days (Exhibit #45).

PART II: ENTITLEMENT—SECTION 4: SUMMARY

ABC proceeded as directed. However, the men eventually quit and ABC was faced with more labor productivity loss from learning curve time, morale, errors, and omissions from the reassignment of manpower.

On June 22, 19X2, Twell solicited and reviewed the job site with two local electrical contractors (Exhibits #41 and #42).

On June 26, 19X2, Twell forwarded its letter (Exhibit #46) to ABC, which set forth:

1. No money would be forwarded to ABC since the hours previously agreed to had not yet been worked by ABC. This unauthorized withholding of payments was in contradiction to agreements (Exhibits #30, #31, #32, #33, #47, and #48).

2. In Twell's judgment, ABC was 60 percent complete with the electrical work (Exhibits #46 and #56).

3. ABC had suffered a 99 percent labor productivity loss at the time ABC had been 51 percent complete with its work (Exhibits #5, #46, and #54).

This 99 percent labor productivity loss was a 14 percent increase from ABC's April 5, 19X2 report (Exhibit #17) which determined an 85 percent labor productivity loss, and an additional 24 percent increase from the 61 percent labor productivity loss from Twell's jobsite survey on February 22, 19X2 (Exhibit #16).

ABC continued to suffer labor productivity losses due, in large part, to the vexatious harassments and outrageous, vindictive intimidation of ABC's personnel which demoralized and frustrated the workmen and contributed to a 100 percent turnover in labor force for the month of June, 19X2 (Exhibit #55).

On June 29, 19X2, ABC renewed its request for payments from Twell (Exhibit #47).

On July 31, 19X2, Twell notified ABC (by telegram) that it was exercising the option, provided in the Letter Agreements of May 22, May 23, and June 5, 19X2 (Exhibits #30, #31, #32, and #33) to engage another electrical contractor to complete the work (Exhibit #49).

On August 1, 19X2, ABC received Twell's letter on July 19, 19X2 (Exhibit #50) wherein:

PART II: ENTITLEMENT—SECTION 4: SUMMARY

1. Twell stated that, since ABC has manned the job with an adequate number of men in accordance with the Letter Agreements of May 22, May 23, and June 5, 19X2 (Exhibits #30, #31, #32, and #33), Twell would now pay ABC's invoices. However, as of August 1, 19X2 this had not been done.
2. Twell had authorized payment of subsistence to bring in out-of-area electricians in accordance with the electrical subcontract (Exhibits #2 and #5).

On August 4, 19X2, ABC received Twell's letter of July 31, 19X2, (Exhibit #51) which was answered on August 4, 19X2 (Exhibit #51), wherein ABC confirmed receipt of the July 31, 19X2 letter notifying ABC that Twell had elected, pursuant to the provisions of the Letter Agreements dated May 22, May 23, and June 5, 19X2 between Twell and ABC, to have ABC cease work and, in accordance with Twell's election, ABC was promptly winding up its activities and vacating the premises in an orderly and expeditious manner to effect a smooth transfer of work.

In accordance with Twell's election, ABC considered Twell's decision as a termination for Twell's convenience. Therefore, ABC considered its contractual obligations fulfilled.

However, ABC also pointed out that the Letter Agreements of May 22, May 23, and June 5, 19X2 (Exhibit #30, #31, #32, and #33) specifically provided that while Twell had the option to terminate ABC's performance any time after 9,000 hours had been expended, it also provided that upon exercising this election, ABC shall be entitled to all payments earned through the date of subject cancellation of work; and after the 9,000 hours were completed, 50 percent of the retainage was to be payable while the balance of the retainage was payable upon substantial completion of the work by ABC, or upon Twell's request to terminate the work of ABC, whichever was first to occur.

Furthermore, Twell's statement in its July 31, 19X2 letter (Exhibit #51) that final payment, if any, will be made after all of the work has been performed properly and to specifications, was contrary to the understanding and agreement, as encompassed in the May 22, May 23, and June 5, 19X2 letters (Exhibits #30, #31,

PART II: ENTITLEMENT—SECTION 4: SUMMARY

#32, and #33). While ABC would, as always, attempt to cooperate fully with Twell, make an orderly transition on the job, and assist Twell's substitute contractor in any way it could, ABC must insist that Twell live up to its payment obligations to ABC.

In addition, ABC took exception to Twell's statement that ABC could not perform its contractual obligations since Twell had been advised of the construction problems as far back as January 16, 19X2 (Exhibit #16). Twell's lack of materials, equipment, work areas, and schedule sequences along with the unprofessional manner in which Twell and its owner were performing their obligations under the agreement had caused an undue loss of labor productivity for ABC and extended the time duration for completion of the work. Twell's repeated and continued refusal to promptly pay partial payment and extra work order requests added to the numerous impediments of ABC's timely and efficient performance of its work. While ABC attempted to work out an arrangement with Twell to cover these matters (Exhibit #53), Twell continued to fail to cooperate and continued to withhold payments until ABC notified Twell in April of 19X2 that it would cease its activities unless Twell lived up to its obligations (Exhibit #17). Finally, ABC was forced to discontinue its work.

Twell Attempts to Discredit ABC's Performance

Futhermore, ABC pointed out that Twell was well aware that, since ABC's return to the work following the Twell and ABC Letter Agreements, that Twell had embarked on a systematic program to discredit ABC's performance on the job. ABC believes that this outrageous conduct engaged in by Twell after May 18 illustrated the course that was intended on Twell's part to embarrass and disparage ABC's performance and cloud the issues.

Finally, since the Letter Agreements provided for a sharing on a $50/50$ basis of the proceeds from the claim against BCEC (in excess of the amounts paid by Twell to ABC and amounts previously reduced to ABC along with ABC's expenses in the preparation and presentation of the claim), ABC requested Twell to advise how to

PART II: ENTITLEMENT—SECTION 4: SUMMARY

proceed with this matter. Twell never replied (Exhibits #48, #51, and #52).

Twell's reply was vital to commence preparation of final billing on the entire matter and be properly compensated for the tentative reductions in delay damages and labor productivity losses deferred by ABC at Twell's request.

On September 12, 19X2, ABC forwarded another written request asking Twell how Twell wanted to proceed on the BCEC claim, stating that ABC was ready, willing, and able to work with Twell in presenting a claim (Exhibit #52). ABC also enclosed a statement of account for Twell, showing various payment requests, payments made, and the outstanding balance to August 17, 19X2, for invoices previously submitted, requesting payment (Exhibit #52).

ABC Perfects Its Mechanic's Lien Rights

On September 26, 19X2, after no word from Twell on how it wished to conclude these matters, ABC was forced to perfect its Mechanic's Lien Rights on properties owned by BCEC.

In conclusion, ABC has been damaged and is due funds as shown in the following section.

PART III. QUANTUM—SECTION 5. SUMMARY: FINANCIAL

FINANCIAL SUMMARY

TOPIC

A. SCHEDULE DELAY DAMAGE COSTS
Labor productivity losses until April 30, 19X2,
contract completion

a. Supervision	$16,254.35
b. Out-of-sequence work	$69,702.37
1. Job access continuity	
2. Inefficiency due to unavailable work	
3. Congestion	
4. Lack of material-handling equipment	
c. Manpower reassignments	$35,594.45
1. Learning curve	
2. Errors and omissions	
3. Weather productivity	
4. Work area ground conditions	
5. Morale and attitude	
d. Nonproductive overhead expenses	$57,060.00

B. SCHEDULE EXTENSION COSTS
Project extension April 30, 19X2, to August 4, 19X2

a. Additional labor man-hours	$31,486.36
b. Overhead	47,300.00
c. Supervision	4,616.52
C. UNAPPROVED CHANGE ORDERS (Exhibit #56)	1,942.18
D. UNPAID INVOICES PREVIOUSLY SUBMITTED (Exhibit #56A)	$104,519.72
TOTAL OWING	$368,475.95

Note: All man-hour amounts that have been utilized
in money calculations have been taken from Twell's

PART III: QUANTUM—SECTION 5: SUMMARY: FINANCIAL

Weekly Jobsite Electrical Time Sheets. A summary
is included under Exhibit #54.

The Twell electrical subcontract No. EC-22923/SO87 dated
November 8, 19X1, delineated a scheduled start of September 26,
19X1, and a completion of April 30, 19X2, which provided a firm
lump-sum price (Exhibits #2, #3, and #5).

ABC commenced its work on August 22, 19X1, at the Big City
project and found it impossible to work productively due to
numerous major impediments such as the lack of materials, work
areas, equipment, administration, and payment.

ABC is allowed to recover the money spent for the labor
productivity losses until the April 30, 19X2, contract completion.

These costs have been divided into the following sections:

a. Supervison

b. Out-of-sequence work

c. Manpower reassignments

d. Nonproductive overhead expenses

PART III: QUANTUM—SECTION 5: SUMMARY: FINANCIAL

A. SCHEDULE DELAY DAMAGE COSTS

SUPERVISION

The original scope of work at the Big City project required ABC to have a working supervisor, but due to the problems of out-of-sequence work, site conditions, and manpower reassignments, ABC found it necessary to have a nonworking supervisor, general foreman, and foreman from time to time.

These increased supervision demands have caused ABC substantial dollar penalties, which ABC is allowed to recover.

Although the increased supervision was substantially more than ABC estimated, none of the nonworking supervisor's time, and only 50 percent of the nonworking general foreman's time, along with the nonworking foreman's time, is being reimbursed. This reimbursement is for the period through the contract completion date of April 30, 19X2, Exhibits #2, #3, and #5).

These costs can be determined by multiplying the hours worked by the general foreman or foreman labor rate (Exhibit #2) and then multiplying the average general foreman wage rate by 0.5. This will decrease the general foreman to the nominal amount of 50 percent.

Increased Supervision Costs

$$
\begin{aligned}
\text{General Foreman—1,240 hrs.} \times \$17.37 \times .5 &= \$10,769.40 \\
\text{Foreman—}\quad 236 \text{ hrs.} \times \$16.98 \times 1 &= \underline{\quad 4,007.28} \\
&\quad\ \ \$14,776.68 \\
\text{10\% Margin}\quad &\quad \underline{\quad 1,477.67} \\
\text{TOTAL DUE} \dots\dots\dots\dots\dots\dots\dots\dots &\ \underline{\$16,254.35}
\end{aligned}
$$

PART III: QUANTUM—SECTION 5: SUMMARY: FINANCIAL

OUT-OF-SEQUENCE WORK

Material shipment, equipment, and other problems have been of such a serious nature and so numerous that it was impossible for ABC to follow a logical productive sequence of work at the Big City project. The out-of-sequence work has caused ABC inefficiencies, which have substantially contributed to the increased cost of the project.

These costs have been divided into the following sections:

1. Job access continuity
2. Inefficiency due to unavailable work
3. Congestion
4. Lack of material handling equipment

Job Access Continuity

There are exact and individual time-consuming job functions for each of the processes involved in the installation of electrical work. The labor work estimate is composed of the required man-hours to perform each of the job functions. In the preparation of the labor work estimate, consideration is given to those job functions that are nonrecurring and to those that must continue throughout the life of the project. Job functions involved in moving in and moving out are examples of such. They will be reflected in the labor work estimate only once.

At the Big City Station, ABC has incurred delays from multiple move-in and move-out job functions, causing substantial dollar penalties. ABC is allowed to recover the money spent for excessive moves.

The operation of moving out of an area when work is available or stopped and back in when work becomes available is made up of the following items:

Studying and rechecking plans

Moving to point of usage

PART III: QUANTUM—SECTION 5: SUMMARY: FINANCIAL

Tooling up

Measuring and layout

Cleaning up

Recognized bidding formulas assign values between 4 percent and 30 percent for the sum of these items. For purposes of determining the losses incurred by ABC's excessive moves, use 12 percent.

ABC experienced the following additional moves (move in and move out) in the areas listed (see Exhibit #17).

Compression House	2 extra moves × 12% = 24%	
Control House	4 extra moves × 12% = 48%	
Hopper Area	4 extra moves × 12% = 48%	
Weather Enclosure	2 extra moves × 12% = 24%	
Precipitator Sidewalls	2 extra moves × 12% = 24%	
Top of Precipitators	2 extra moves × 12% = 24%	

The cost of the excessive moves can be calculated by multiplying the additional percentages by the estimated value of the average wage for journeyman labor in each area.

PART III. QUANTUM—SECTION 5. SUMMARY: FINANCIAL

	(EXHIBIT #8) ESTIMATED HOURS	(EXHIBITS #2 and #5) JOURNEYMAN'S WAGES	LABOR $
Compression House	772	× $16.09	= $12,421.48
Control House	924	× $16.09	= 14,867.16
Hopper Area	855	× $16.09	= 13,756.95
Weather Enclosure, Sidewalls, and Tops	2,983	× $16.09	= 47,996.47

Compression House	$12,421.48 × 24%	= 2,981.16
Control House	14,867.16 × 48%	= 7,136.24
Hopper Area	13,756.95 × 48%	= 6,603.34
Weather Enclosure, Sidewalls, and Tops	47,996.47 × 24%	= 11,519.15
Job Access Continuity		$28,239.89

Therefore, for additional cost for job access continuity, ABC is due:

Job Access Continuity	$28,239.89
10% Margin	2,823.99
	$31,063.88

For all possible moves that may not have been caused by Twell deduct	(11,493.63)
	$19,570.25

Inefficiency Due to Unavailable Work

ABC has had to "work around" the other trades, as it were, causing ABC to perform its activities out-of-sequence in an unproductive manner due to the unavailability of work in a productive sequence.

PART III: QUANTUM—SECTION 5: SUMMARY: FINANCIAL

Although ABC's presence was necessary, they were not supplied with sufficient quantities of work to fill the time of crews in work that was in a productive sequence or that could be completed in a productive sequence or area.

Many areas that experienced additional moves (see Job Access Continuity) were also the areas where ABC's crews were confronted with the lack of productive work due to the delays and slow progress of the other trades.

By comparing planned construction (Exhibit #8) to actual construction (Exhibits #9 and #17) in those areas experiencing inefficiencies due to unavailable sequentially productive work, the reader can see graphically how failure to maintain planned volumes of work had caused construction to decelerate, adversely affecting ABC's production.

Unavailability of sequence work and productive work plagued ABC's work crew until February 19X2, after which the problem became congestion. Only the hours worked prior to February 19X2 are subject to a labor correction factor.

Compression House	772 hrs. × $16.09 =	$12,421.48
Control House	924 hrs. × $16.09 =	14,867.16
Hopper Area	855 hrs. × $16.09 =	13,756.95
Weather Enclosure, Sidewalls, and Tops	2,983 hrs. × $16.09 =	47,996.47
		$89,042.06

The labor correction factor for inefficiency due to unavailable work to be preformed in a sequential or productive manner has been suggested between 40 percent and 110 percent. For purposes of determining losses incurred by ABC, use the minimal value of 40 percent.

$$\$89,042.06 \times 40\% = \$35,616.82$$
$$10\% \text{ Margin} \quad \underline{3,561.68}$$
$$\$39,178.50$$

PART III. QUANTUM—SECTION 5. SUMMARY: FINANCIAL

For all possible inefficiencies due to unavailable work
to be performed that may not have been caused by
Twell deduct 37 percent.

$$\begin{array}{r} \times\ .63 \\ \hline \$24{,}682.46 \end{array}$$

Congestion

Work area congestion caused by rescheduling and interruptions in the individual construction schedule job functions have transformed an orderly, sequential work plan (Exhibit #8) into one with many conflicting operations being performed simultaneously (Exhibit #9). Many workmen of all trades were stacked in limited work areas. This situation was further intensified by the encroachment on the work areas of other contractors who were working separately and independently for the owner (Exhibit #13), all of which created a situation in which work could not be performed efficiently. A labor correction factor of 40 percent to 110 percent is accepted for inefficiencies due to stacking of trades or concurrent operations.

For the most part, these inefficiencies have been experienced by ABC in lay down areas #1 and #2 (Exhibit #10), where approximately 75 percent of ABC's time was spent during January, February, and March 19X2, which was the period when the majority of inefficiencies occurred due to congestion.

Inefficiency costs in these areas during this time can be determined by multiplying the number of hours worked in these areas during this time (Exhibit #9) by the average journeyman wage rate to get the labor value. Then the labor value is multiplied by the inefficiency factor conservatively set at 60 percent.

Work Areas #1 and #2

$$\begin{array}{rr}
\text{2851 hrs.} \times \$16.09 = & \$45{,}872.59 \\
\text{Inefficiency factor} & \times\ \ 60\% \\
\hline
& \$27{,}523.20 \\
\text{10\% Margin} & 2{,}752.32 \\
\hline
& \$30{,}275.52
\end{array}$$

PART III. QUANTUM—SECTION 5. SUMMARY: FINANCIAL

For all possible inefficiencies due to congestion that
may not have been caused by Twell deduct approximately 37 percent.

$$\underline{10,886.00}$$
$$\overline{\underline{\$19,389.00}}$$

Lack of Material Handling Equipment

The serious shortage of jobsite material handling equipment,
which was caused by improper sizing and the demands placed on
this equipment from congestion, has caused ABC significant labor
productivity losses.

This equipment, which is normally required on a limited basis
at the proper time, was to be supplied to ABC by Twell (Exhibits #2,
#3, and #5). This equipment was also to be provided by Twell with
flagmen and operators. Because this equipment was normally not
provided at the proper times, and no flagmen or drivers were
provided on much of the equipment, ABC was required to handle
large quantities of material by hand and to provide the necessary
flagmen and drivers when equipment was available.

ABC has experienced inefficiency in material handling for the
materials affecting the control house, top, and internal parts of the
work.

PART III. QUANTUM—SECTION 5. SUMMARY: FINANCIAL

	ESTIMATED HOURS	JOURNEY-MAN'S WAGE	LABOR $ ONE PRE-CIPITATOR
Compression House	772	× $16.09	= $12,421.48
Control House	924	× $16.09	= 14,867.16
Weather Enclosure and Tops	2,983	× $16.09	= 47,996.47
Precipitator Internals	1,314	× $16.09	= 21,142.26
Hopper Area	855	× $16.09	= 13,756.95
			$110,184.32

Inefficiency costs in these areas can be determined by multiplying the number of hours worked in these areas by the average journeyman wage rate by a token efficiency factor of 5 percent.

	$110,184.32
Inefficiency factor	× 5%
	$ 5,509.22
10% Margin	550.92
	$ 5,060.14

PART III. QUANTUM—SECTION 5. SUMMARY: FINANCIAL

MANPOWER REASSIGNMENTS

ABC has experienced detrimental manpower reassignments at the Big City project stemming from the lack of credibility caused by equipment deficiencies, unavailable and/or closed-in work areas, and poor work area ground conditions.

ABC planned for closed-in work areas for its use during the harsh winter months; however, due to the schedule delays, these closed-in work areas were never made available to ABC (Exhibits #9 and #17).

Although ABC's material handling requirements are normal (see Lack of Material Handling Equipment), this equipment was not available to ABC because of work area congestion problems (see Congestion). Therefore, ABC was forced to use the equipment at limited available times (that is, snow and rainstorms) when the other craftsmen were not using this equipment, because they refused to work in these weather conditions. This, along with the difficulties the crawler cranes produced on the unprepared and maintained ground work areas caused a serious morale problem for ABC workers (Exhibit #11).

The morale problem was so drastic that men would literally walk off the job site and past the gate in disgust after falling in three feet of muck, working in the midst of a snow or rainstorm because of equipment shortages, or after receiving childish reprimands from their Twell supervisors (Exhibit #43).

ABC experienced substantial extra money costs from the problems of having 1000 percent more workmen quit than originally estimated. The increased costs suffered by ABC due to manpower reassignments along with the direct causes are divided into the following sections:

1. Learning curve
2. Errors and omissions
3. Weather productivity
4. Work area ground conditions
5. Morale and attitude

PART III. QUANTUM—SECTION 5. SUMMARY: FINANCIAL

Learning Curve

Whenever a new employee is hired, a period of familiarization must be considered until the new employee is oriented to the job, plans, specifications, tool locations, work procedures, and so forth.

At the Big City Station, ABC experienced abnormal conditions that required ABC to go through the learning curve process an extraordinary number of times because of the number of new employees required to replace those who had quit.

The costs for the excessive number of employees to complete the learning curve process can be calculated by taking the average number of union employees ABC estimated, found by dividing the number of estimated man-hours (Exhibits #2, #3, and #5):

$$\frac{7,200 \text{ man-hours (Exhibit \#5)}}{31 \text{ contract (40 hours) weeks (Exhibit \#5)}} = 5.8, \text{ or } 6 \text{ men/week}$$

Then subtract the number of estimated employees from the actual number of employees employed until April 30, 19X2 (Exhibit #55):

(41 actual employees) − 6 = 35 additional union employees

Using two days as a minimum amount of time for the new time to complete the learning curve process, we have:

35 men × 16 hrs. = 560 man-hours

These are the man-hours ABC has suffered from this inefficiency. ABC is due the reimbursement for this time multiplied by the average journeyman wage rate:

$$
\begin{array}{rr}
560 \text{ man-hours} \times \$16.09 = & \$9,010.40 \\
10\% \text{ Margin} & 901.04 \\
\hline
& \$9,911.44 \\
\end{array}
$$

PART III. QUANTUM—SECTION 5. SUMMARY: FINANCIAL

Errors and Omissions

The application of a factor for errors and omissions is justified when job conditions become abnormal. These conditions are working in an illogical manner and continuing on incomplete work left by unhappy employees, all of which increase the normal expectancy of errors.

Although recognized bidding formulas assign values of 10 percent to 12 percent for these items, for purposes of determining the losses incurred by ABC, use only 4 percent.

The costs for errors and omissions can be calculated by taking the average number of union employees ABC estimated, found by dividing the number of estimated contract man-hours (Exhibit #5) by the contract time of 31-40 hour weeks (Exhibit #5):

$$\frac{7200 \text{ man-hours (Exhibit \#5)}}{31 \text{ contract (40 hour) weeks (Exhibit \#5)}} = 5.8, \text{ or } 6 \text{ men/week}$$

Then, subtract the number of estimated employees from the actual number of union employees employed until April 30, 19X2 (Exhibit #55):

41 actual employees − 6 = 35 additional employees
(Exhibit #55)

Using 40 hours as a minimum time period for the new men to be subject to significant errors and omissions and by applying a nominal inefficiency factor for this of 10 percent, you have:

35 men × 40 hours × 10% inefficiency factor = 140 man-hours

These are the man-hours ABC has suffered from this inefficiency. ABC is due the reimbursement for this time multiplied by the average journeyman wage rate as shown:

$$
\begin{aligned}
140 \text{ man-hours} \times \$16.09 &= \$2,252.60 \\
10\% \text{ Margin} &\quad\underline{225.26} \\
&\quad\$2,477.86
\end{aligned}
$$

PART III. QUANTUM—SECTION 5. SUMMARY: FINANCIAL

Weather Productivity

The labor work schedule for the Big City project has been significantly altered by major impediments.

ABC was to be provided major work areas inside the control house, inside the weather enclosures on top of the precipitators, and inside the precipitator shell during the winter months and inclement weather (Exhibit #8). This work was performed outside during harsh winter conditions because these areas were not closed in. This was to have been done by others.

ABC is entitled to recover the lost efficiency that it has experienced while performing outdoor work in winter conditions that should have been performed inside. It is also entitled to recover the lost efficiency that it has experienced while performing outdoor work in inclement weather (such as rain) in time periods other than winter months. The value of the lost efficiency can be determined by multiplying an inefficiency factor by the labor value of activities performed during the period.

The work done during this period is as follows:

WORK AREA	JOB	HOURS
Control Room	Installing cable tray	115
	Installing equipment	294
	Installing conduit	94
	Installing lighting	63
Top of Precipitators	Installing cable tray	172
	Installing equipment and lighting	102
	Installing conduit	509
		1,349

The labor value of the activities will be determined by applying the average hourly journeyman wage rate to the actual hours worked for the activities within the time period. The total labor value of these activities becomes:

PART III. QUANTUM—SECTION 5. SUMMARY: FINANCIAL

1,349 hours × $16.09 = $21,705.41

According to recognized and accepted bidding formulas, the labor correction factor for work performed in winter can be calculated at 30 percent. Accordingly, for work performed in adverse winter conditions, ABC is due:

	$21,705.41
Labor inefficiency factor	× 30%
	$ 6,511.62
10% Margin	651.16
	$ 7,162.78

Work Area Ground Conditions

Bad work area ground conditions due to the lack of ground preparation and maintenance for the type of work being done caused ABC serious work interruptions and inefficiencies (Exhibit #11).

These conditions have created inefficiencies in material handling, work area availability, work area preparation, and restraints on the workmen's physical movements.

These inefficiencies have been experienced by ABC mainly during the months of January and February, through March 19, 19X2. Inefficiency costs can be determined by multiplying the number of hours worked during this time (Exhibit #8) by the average journeyman wage rate to get the labor value. Then the labor value is multiplied by the inefficiency factor, conservatively set at 20 percent.

3,818 hours × $16.09 =	$61,431.62
Inefficiency factor	× 20%
	$12,286.32
10% Margin	1,228.63
	$13,514.95

PART III. QUANTUM—SECTION 5. SUMMARY: FINANCIAL

Morale and Attitude

The morale and attitude of the job labor force affects productivity and, as experienced by ABC on the Big City project, morale and attitude had a detrimental effect on ABC costs.

Whenever an employee is unhappy with his employment and terminates his employment for this reason, a factor for morale and attitude is justified.

ABC has experienced an unusual labor force replacement requirement because of the many factors that have negatively affected the morale and attitude of ABC's labor force.

The costs for the negative morale and attitude can be calculated by taking the average number of union employees ABC estimated and then dividing by the contract time of 31 weeks, which is subtracted from the number of union employees actually employed (see Errors and Omissions).

Now, by taking the number of union employees that have quit (causing morale and attitude losses) on the Big City project and multiplying this number by 8 hours (which is the last day of employment when normally no work is done) you have:

$$35 \text{ men} \times 8 \text{ hours} = 280 \text{ hours}$$

Then multiply by the average journeyman wage rate:

$$280 \text{ hours} \times \$16.09 = \$4,505.20 \text{ (Lost production)}$$

For purposes of determining losses incurred by ABC use a factor of 51 percent.

	$4,505.20
Reduction factor	× 51%
	$2,297.65
10% Margin	229.77
	$2,527.42

PART III. QUANTUM—SECTION 5. SUMMARY: FINANCIAL

NONPRODUCTIVE OVERHEAD EXPENSES

The original scope of work at the Big City project required ABC to allow for normal nonproductive expenses in addition to the 7,200 man-hours to be used at the project site. This was allowed for by ABC in its proposal (Exhibit #2) wherein 9,000 composite man-hours were used for computation purposes, which included 7,200 man-hours to be used at the project site and the dollar value associated with 1,800 hours balance computed at $15.85 per hour for nonproductive expenses.

Therefore, the nonproductive overhead expenses were determined by multiplying the difference of 9,000 composite man-hours (Exhibit #2) and 7,200 man hours to be used at the project site (Exhibit #5).

$$\begin{pmatrix} 9,000 \\ \text{composite} \\ \text{man-hours} \end{pmatrix} - \begin{pmatrix} 7,200 \text{ man-hours} \\ \text{to be used at the} \\ \text{project site} \end{pmatrix} = 1,800 \text{ hours}$$

Then multiply the resultant by $15.85 per hour (Exhibit #2):

1,800 man hours × $15.85 per hour = $28,530 nonproductive overhead expenses

This gives the amount allocated for nonproductive overhead expenses for the eight-month project duration of September 19X1 through April 19X2 (Exhibits #2 and #3).

The amount for nonproductive overhead expenses that was allocated per month can be found by dividing the total amount allocated by the eight-month job duration:

$28,530 ÷ 8 months = $3,566.25 per month nonproductive overhead expenses

PART III: QUANTUM—SECTION 5. SUMMARY: FINANCIAL

However, due to the productivity losses caused by Twell management's insensitivity and unresponsiveness in dealing objectively with the needs and problems of ABC's personnel while on the job site, ABC's nonproductive overhead expense costs were more than four times the amount allowed.

For purposes of determining losses incurred by ABC use the average factor of three times the amount allowed.

ABC is allowed to recover the money spent for the additional nonproductive overhead expenses above the amount allowed.

PROJECT TIME	ALLOCATED NONPRODUCTIVE OVERHEAD	TOTAL DOLLARS
September	$3,566.25 × 3	$10,698.75
October	$3,566.25 × 3	$10,698.75
November	$3,566.25 × 3	$10,698.75
December	$3,566.25 × 3	$10,698.75
January	$3,566.25 × 3	$10,698.75
February	$3,566.25 × 3	$10,698.75
March	$3,566.25 × 3	$10,698.75
April	$3,566.25 × 3	$10,698.75
		$85,590.00

Therefore, the additional cost for nonproductive overhead expenses spent by ABC until the contract completion of April 30, 19X2, is

$$\$85,590.00 - \$28,530.00 = \underline{\$57,060.00}$$

PART III: QUANTUM—SECTION 5. SUMMARY: FINANCIAL

B. SCHEDULE EXTENSION COSTS

The Letter Agreements of May 22, May 23, and June 5, 19X2 (Exhibits #30, #31, #32, and #33), provide for an immediate reimbursement to ABC for the extension of the Big City project past the contract expiration date of April 30, 19X2.

This reimbursement is for items of man-hours in addition to those estimated by ABC for the original contract (Exhibit #5) and for additional overhead and supervision.

ABC temporarily deferred full compensation, causing substantial dollar penalties. ABC is allowed to recover the total money spent for the project extension period from April 30, 19X2, through August 4, 19X2.

These costs have been divided into the following sections:

a. Additional Labor Man-hours

b. Overhead

c. Supervision

ADDITIONAL LABOR MAN-HOURS

ABC is reimbursed for all man-hours spent on the Big City project over and above the 7,200 man-hours ABC expected to be spent in field operations (Exhibits #5, #30, #31, #32, #33, and #54); therefore:

(Exhibit #54)

$$
\begin{array}{lr}
\text{Journeymen} - 2{,}574.5 \times \$16.34 & = \$42{,}067.33 \\
10\% \text{ Margin} & \underline{4{,}206.73} \\
& \$46{,}274.06
\end{array}
$$

Less amounts previously billed by ABC (Invoice EO-2441, Exhibit #53)	(14,787.70)
TOTAL DUE	$31,486.36

PART III: QUANTUM—SECTION 5. SUMMARY: FINANCIAL

OVERHEAD

ABC is reimbursed for overhead spent on the Big City project after the contract completion date of April 30, 19X2 (Exhibits #5, #30, #31, #32, and #33); therefore:

Office Expense (Exhibit #24)

$17,000/month × 3 months (May, June, and July) = $51,000.00

Less amount previously paid ABC (Invoice EO-24 and EO-2448, Exhibit #53)	(8,000.00)
	$43,000.00
10% Margin	4,300.00
TOTAL DUE . . .	$47,300.00

SUPERVISION

ABC is reimbursed for supervision spent on the Big City project after the contract completion date of April 30, 19X2 (Exhibits #5, #30, #31, #32, and #33); therefore:

Superintendent

31 days @ 8 hours/day = 248 hours
248 hours @ $21.78/hour $5,401.44

PART III: QUANTUM—SECTION 5. SUMMARY: FINANCIAL

General Foreman

(including subsistence)	12,322.40
Less amounts previously paid and/or billed (Invoice EO-2410, EO-2411, EO-2412 and EO-2416)	(13,527.00)
	$4,196.84
10% Margin	419.68
TOTAL DUE ...	$4,616.52

PART IV. APPENDIX—SECTION 6. ENDNOTES

ENDNOTES

Note: For this sample recovery claim, exhibits and color coding have not been included.

a. Twell's "Time Grid Master Schedule" (Exhibit #1), determining the time of December 12 through February 6, 19X2 for the installation of "internals" (plates, wires, and weights), and project completion of April 30, 19X2 was used as a basic parameter for the "CBM" schedule and incorporated the interfacing crafts.

b. "Overall 'As Built' Steel Schedule"—the color blue denotes work to be performed by Twell with respect to calendar date, red denotes when the work was actually done, with green arrows added for clarity to follow job function date shifts.

c. On the "Time Grid Master Schedule" in Exhibit #1, the job function of installing the internals is shown commencing on December 7, 19X1. ABC has shown a later date of January 9, 19X2 on the "CBM" schedule, which was the revised thinking of Twell after ABC's proposal.

d. Exhibit #35 consists of ABC's June 7, 19X2 letter to Twell and seven written telephone confirmations dated June 6, 19X2 through June 8, 19X2 enclosed herein. (See Chapter 7 for the form which was used.)

e. Exhibit #39 consists of ABC's June 16, 19X2 written confirmation of three separate conferences. (See Chapter 7 for the form which was used.)

SUMMARY

The secret of invoicing for more than the original contract amount relies on the mastering of the recovery claim.

You now know that claims of damages caused by others are, in fact, collectible with profit. However, you have also learned that contractors are well advised to avoid all claims and litigation for their own benefit if at all possible.

You have learned the importance of a properly prepared recovery claim. You learned the details of the credibility, entitlement, and financial sections to successfully prepare a claim, and you have also seen the identification, substantiation, and monetary quantification of impacted damages from a successful real-life case.

You have seen how this real-life case can be used as a model when preparing your own recovery claim.

You discovered the critical need to identify and control impacted damages with an information and control system and why it is important to avoid claims by controlling the causes.

Now that you have increased your comfort level with fixed-price contracts by knowing how to identify risk (Chapter 2) and how to invoice for losses (Chapter 3), you must move on. Next, in Chapter 4, you will discover the secrets to winning the big-profit contracts with bid management.

CHAPTER 4 ─────────────

Bid Management: How to Win the Projects You Most Need and Want

WHAT YOU SHOULD KNOW ABOUT BID MANAGEMENT

Chapter 2 discussed risk management and its role as the first of the four elements of profit management, as it applies to project control and profits.

Bid management is concerned with winning each project contract and the total profit and growth impact of all contracts won by the construction company. It is important to keep in mind the distinction between a contract (project) and a contracting company. As stated in Chapter 1, the *contracting company* requires not only the management of the contract conditions but also the management of internal and external variables affecting daily business operations. These variables include such areas as pricing, costs, expenses, profits, and market timing.

What do you have to know for company growth and big profits? *Bid management*. Bid management is the second element of the profit management system. Bid management is the determination of strategies to carry out company goals and objectives *and* the development and implementation of tactics to actualize these strategies. In other words, bid management is the managing of your bidding process to best meet the objectives of your company within the prevailing conditions of the marketplace.

As noted in Chapter 1, there are three parts to a business plan: the basic goals and objectives of the organization, the major programs of actions, and the allocation of resources needed to achieve these goals. Once the basic goals and objectives pertaining to company growth and profit are defined, the actual performance of these goals is the responsibility of the bid management plan.

Understanding bid management depends on the knowledge and understanding of several variables: (1) company growth and profit goals, (2) strategies and tactics, (3) internal company strengths and weaknesses, and (4) external market opportunities.

COMPANY GROWTH VERSUS PROFIT: TWO SEPARATE BUT IMPORTANT GOALS

Effective bid management depends on a clear understanding of long- and short-range goals relevant to company growth and profit. You cannot expect to reach your long-range goals overnight; instead, easier-to-obtain short-range goals must be met in order to eventually reach your final destination.

For example, the president of a contracting firm may set a long-range goal to become a market leader in five years. Such a goal obviously requires time to reach, so a short-range goal is set. The short-range company goal may be to obtain a 20 percent compound annual growth in total sales revenue for each year over the next five years. Therefore, in the long run, this firm will become a market leader in five years' time.

On the other hand, many contracting firms may set a long-range goal to realize bigger *profits*. For example, the same contracting firm could set a long-range goal to earn $1 million in net profit after five years. This could be accomplished through a short-range goal of 20 percent compound annual growth in net profit. Thus, at the end of the five-year period, the firm has achieved its long-range goal of a $1 million profit.

The difference between these two examples is essential to understand. The two different goals—to be a market leader or to realize a $1 million profit—are entirely different. The first goal applies to *company sales growth* and the second to *company profits*. Many times these two goals are exclusive from each other, often impossible to achieve at the same time. Whether or not they are mutually exclusive depends on such things as internal company competitive strengths and external market opportunities.

YOUR STRATEGIES AND TACTICS

Once a long-range (or short-range, for that matter) company goal is set, the next step is to determine the proper strategies to achieve the goal and the appropriate tactics to carry out your new strategies. Just as a general must plan his strategy to win the war, and work out his tactics for each battle, so must a contractor do the same with company goals.

Different goals will require different strategies and tactics. For example, the long-range company goal to become a market leader, which necessitated a short-range goal of 20 percent compound annual growth in total sales revenue, may require a strategy to (1) broaden the areas of work being bid on and/or (2) increase market penetration. To carry out either one of these strategies, a tactic that reduces the selling or bid price by 5 percent may be employed.

**PROFIT GUIDE: COMPANY GOALS DETERMINE
STRATEGIES; STRATEGIES
DETERMINE TACTICS**

The previously stated long-range goal of earning $1 million in net profit, which necessitated a short-range goal of 20 percent compound annual growth in net profit, may require a strategy to move into a newly emerging market niche. This strategy may then dictate a tactic of price skimming. This is to say that the company may have to find a new service that no one else is offering, allowing it to charge a premium price.

COMPANY STRENGTHS AND WEAKNESSES

In order to establish a bid management plan, you must also identify your company's strengths and weaknesses. This requires an in-depth survey of the external and, particularly, the internal capabilities and philosophies of your company. Such a study should include management, all employees (past and present), technical management, profit management, and company associations. Company associations with outside vendors and competitors are often overlooked as a viable resource (or strength). You must first identify any potential resources before you can tap them. You must also be aware of your weaknesses so that you can strengthen them.

**PROFIT GUIDE: KNOW YOUR STRENGTHS AND
WEAKNESSES**

Be Realistic About Divulging Company Finances

One of the major weaknesses in many small- to medium-sized companies today is paranoia. Many owners are afraid to open their minds and to look around them. For example, I often start out my consulting survey by asking simple questions about a client's financial position. A "paranoid case" will counter my questions with drawn out stonewalling techniques. For some reason, many contractors feel that their company's financial information is top secret! Can you imagine hiring a business consultant for help and refusing to share with him basic financial information? That's like going to your physician for an annual checkup and refusing to get undressed!

Divulging company information is a sensitive issue, but unless a realistic attitude is taken toward the company's position and its relationship within the business community, real growth will never be realized. Why? How can your company grow if you're always too worried about watching over your shoulder? The man who plays alone will never lose, but he will never win either.

For example, if management plays the role of the paranoid hermit, the possibilities of participating in a joint venture bid are next to impossible. Would you go in on a joint venture deal with some guy who wouldn't share with you information about his financial status? Of course not. This is not to say that you should publish your company balance sheet in the *Wall Street Journal*! Instead, you must find a happy medium. A realistic manner of handling the dissemination of financial material should be based on a need-to-know basis, with a "formal letter agreement" not to disclose any information being furnished.

Create an Information Network

To be successful, a company must build and maintain an information network that works hand in hand with a strong bid management system. Company growth and profits depend on company associations. It is important to keep in mind that the business world is not like taking a test in school where you have to keep your eyes on your own paper. This is real life, so use everything you can, *including* your neighbor. The object of the game is to get the job done and to grow in the process.

As for strengths, exploit them! It's basic. It's simple. You know what your strengths are, so why keep them a secret? Let everyone know about them!

EXTERNAL MARKET PROFIT OPPORTUNITIES

The fourth area you must understand for effective bid management is external market opportunities. Understanding external market opportunities involves a situation analysis that consists of an indepth survey and an understanding of the dynamics of the marketplace. You have to know what is going on out there. You have to know what types of construction are currently in production. And you have to know what the predicted volume is for each of the various types. This is fundamental information essential for planning.

PROFIT GUIDE: KNOW YOUR MARKET OPPORTUNITIES

For example, suppose you were the local hollow-core door manufacturer. Your doors are purchased primarily by contractors who build multiple-family dwellings. These contractors normally order 90 days in advance of when they want their doors delivered. How would you plan your manufacturing schedule? What indicator would you want to look at before buying new equipment or hiring additional help? Obviously, it would be helpful to know the number and dates of building permits presently issued in your trading area for multiple-family dwellings. Sound logical? I think so, but I don't know why I get the answers I do. When I ask contractors what their trading area is, I hear everything from the "United States" to their "home town." Either they really don't know, or they do not understand the importance of knowing.

PROFIT GUIDE: KNOW YOUR TRADING AREA

The importance of being able to answer this question is simple. Every company has a limited amount of resources. These resources are time, money, and human. Therefore, it makes sense to make the best use of your limited resources. This requires a plan. Identifying your trading area will give direction to many things (for example, sales force, advertising, and even where to look for indicators).

"No one knows" is another classic answer I get when I ask questions about trading areas and sales volume. If this is your answer, I suggest you definitely invest in professional marketing assistance. Fast! This is vital information needed to build an effective bid management system. And believe me, it's available!

I remember surveying Tom's company. He was spending five times the industry average on advertising and sales for each bid he won. When I called this to his attention, he said, "It takes a lot to get two or three big orders. You know we specialize in generator repair."

"I know, Tom, but what size generators?"

"Well," he said, "we really are geared for large projects."

"Then why do you send your advertising to all these small companies and only in two states?" I asked.

"Because we have done all our work in those two states for the last two years," Tom said.

"Then do you think your trading area is geographic and only in these two states? And why all the sales calls on small companies?" I asked.

"I guess our business is geographic," Tom replied, "I really never thought much about company size." The more we talked, the more apparent it became to us both that Tom's trading area was electric power plants, which constituted 70 percent of his business. And his trading area was not geographically where he happened to have received his last project. It was where his target market was located.

As we analyzed Tom's trading area, direction to many things began to emerge. We were able to identify a major market segment of electric generating plants. In this segment we were able to zero in on those generating stations that were coal fired and more than 15 years old (these were the ones that needed Tom's company's capabilities). Now we had a target market that we could work on. With this information, Tom could find the facts he needed to increase the cost effectiveness of his sales force and advertising. He could find the right person at the right place to talk with about new work for his company.

For example, once Tom organized a list of qualified electric generating companies, he sent for their annual reports to stockholders and their 10K report (which is an expanded and detailed form of the annual report).

The annual report gave Tom information relative to what the companies' expenditures had been on construction and what their plans were for the next year. The 10K report gave information on company personnel. It shows who is in charge of what, their experience and education, and where their office is located. "This is great," Tom said, "now I know who the right person is to see and I can match the right salesman to the man he has to deal with."

He was beginning to see the light. The next step he took was to plan his sales activities relative to the expected sales potential in his trading area.

PROFIT GUIDE: KNOW YOUR MARKET POSITION

Knowing what the sales volume is for various types of construction in your trading area will enable you to plan your company sales volume. This information will allow you to compare what you think it will be versus what you would like it to be, what new internal company capabilities may need reinforcing, or possibly what new capabilities must be found and added to the company.

One good example of the value of knowing your market position was Mark's company. Like Tom he was spending way above industry averages for advertising and sales relative to each contract he won. "Mark, what do you think the problem is?" I asked. "Your ratio of advertising and sales dollars to the number of contracts you win has dramatically changed this year. Especially when you compare it to the last three years."

"I wish I knew," he answered.

"Well, what percentage of the available work are you winning, Mark?"

"I don't know," he replied. "How can anyone figure that out?"

"Then what you are saying, Mark, is that you don't know if there is any work or not. If there is no work to win, it would explain why your sales ratio is out of whack."

"I know there is some, I bid everything that comes out in the Dodge reports," Tom answered.

"OK," I replied, "that's a start. Now we need to add to that information and estimate what the dollars are that will be spent on the type of work you are doing."

"You're right, there is no sense in chasing work that doesn't exist," Mark said. "I guess my contractor association would be a good place to start and ask about potential sales. Then I could compare that with what was awarded last year to see what the change will be. Am I getting the idea?"

"You sure are, Mark," I answered. "With a clear picture of your trading area and market position, we can start to plan profitable strategies and tactics to win the contracts you need and want."

TOOLS FOR OBTAINING GROWTH AND PROFITS

Once you have gathered information on internal company strengths and weaknesses and external market opportunities, you can begin to plan your strategies and tactics to meet your company goals effectively.

In Chapter 1 you saw the winning of a bid through an understanding of the dynamics of break-even. This was illustrated in the case example "How to Outbid Your Competition with Break-even Analysis." Contractors A's competitor, Johnny Jones, was able to win bids by his use of break-even. However, the factors not looked at in that case were (1) How did Johnny Jones decide that he wanted a particular job? (2) How high could he bid? (3) How low could he bid? and (4) How many bids should he win?

To answer these questions you must understand the dynamics of demand curve pricing, variable costs, fixed expenses, profit, and market timing as the tools for obtaining company growth and profit through bid management.

HOW TO MEASURE PRICE MOTIVATION WITH THE DEMAND CURVE

Unfortunately, pricing is still an art and not a science. The primary reason for this is that cost and revenue data presently available to executives are generally insufficient for exact calculations. Even though this situation is continually improving with new technology, it appears that pricing will continue to be more of an art than a science for some time to come. With this in mind, and because pricing is fundamental to winning contracts, it is essential for us to know what motivates price and to understand the factors that affect the pricing decision.

What motivates price? The demand curve is the basis for what motivates price. Figure 4.1 illustrates a typical demand curve. The factors that affect the pricing decision—cost, expense, and market timing—are discussed in their respective sections following.

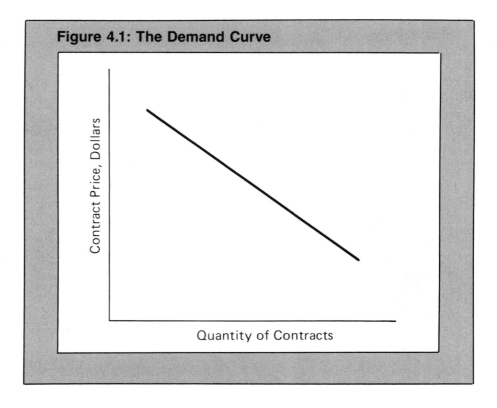

Figure 4.1: The Demand Curve

Contract Price, Dollars

Quantity of Contracts

The demand curve visually demonstrates that you will sell more of your product or service the lower you set your price. It also illustrates that the higher you set your price, the less you will sell. This is a basic fact. Unfortunately, it is not entirely simple. The secret is to know what the demand curve looks like for the projects available to bid. Figures 4.2 and 4.3 show why it is important to know what the demand curve looks like.

The vertical and horizontal demand curves are two extreme conditions for a demand curve. Normally, our demand curve will lie somewhere in between these limits, looking similar to the one shown in Figure 4.1. The vertical demand curve visually illustrates that no matter what price you charge for your product or service, the demand for your product or service is going to stay the same. Under such a circumstance, you can charge anything you wish without losing sales.

A real-life example of vertical demand would be the circumstances that surrounded the OPEC cartel in 1973 and 1979. Because of this cartel the price of oil jumped from \$12 (U.S.) a barrel to \$32 (U.S.) a barrel almost overnight. The member nations of OPEC realized that the United States' demand curve for OPEC oil was vertical. They correctly concluded that they could raise the price of oil with no danger of the U.S. and/or other major oil-using countries finding a substitute that would reduce the demand for OPEC oil. They also realized that U.S. citizens weren't about to stop driving their cars. Thus, the demand curve was vertical, and they could charge anything they wanted without an immediate drop in demand.

Because of the vertical demand curve for oil, OPEC moved the price of oil right on up until the major oil-using countries were able to make economies that shifted the demand curve (for example, reduced speed limits, manufactured gas-efficient cars, substituted forms of energy). This change in the demand curve is probably the only thing that stopped OPEC's price increases.

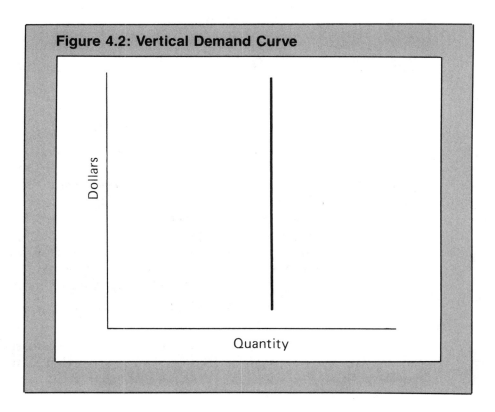

Figure 4.2: Vertical Demand Curve

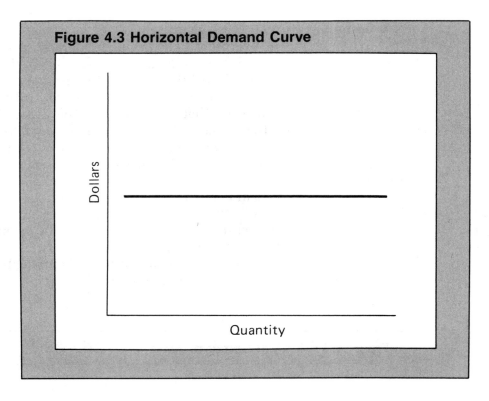

Figure 4.3 Horizontal Demand Curve

The horizontal demand curve in Figure 4.3 could be illustrated by the demand for a commodity such as salt. At the given
market price for salt, you can sell all the salt you want. However,
since all salt is the same and in good supply, if you were to charge
more than the market price, you will sell nothing. Your market will
be lost to your competition. Why pay more for the same thing if you
can find it cheaper? Figures 4.2 and 4.3 illustrate the two possible
extremes that can exist in the marketplace. Your demand curve is
probably somewhere in between and may look more like Figure 4.1.

PROFIT GUIDE: PRICING IS BASED ON THE DEMAND CURVE

The important thing to remember is that pricing is based on
the demand curve. As you will soon see, pricing should not be
based on "cost plus," which is nothing more than what you *think*

you need for overhead and what you would *like* for profit. Also realize that each type of construction has a different demand curve.

Demand curves can change *frequently.* Therefore, it is important to continually update your demand curve. In order to update your demand curve, you must keep track of what your competition is bidding. As noted, this is more of an art than a science, but fitting a demand curve to the types of bids that are consistent with your strategies and tactics will give you a good method of monitoring the external marketplace.

With a good idea of the demand curve for the type of projects your strategies and tactics determine, you can correctly evaluate both the volume and the price of the work. Volume will depend on your internal company capabilities, the availability of bids, as well as the price you charge.

In other words, what work do you want? Can you physically do all the work you want to do? Will there be that amount of work available? You must first know the answers to these questions to determine what price to charge.

THE PROFIT DYNAMICS OF COSTS

Costs are only those dollars spent for materials and services that can be traced directly to the building of the project; this includes labor, material, telephone calls, gasoline for the trucks, and so forth. These costs are often referred to as *variable costs* because their size varies with the total amount of work to be done.

Variable costs are not the same as *fixed expenses,* which are expenses such as office rent, shop tools, and so forth that must be paid whether you perform work or not. Fixed expenses are not "variable"; they do not fluctuate with the total amount of work to be done.

In Figure 1.8 (in Chapter 1) you saw the effect of reformatting a bid to show variable costs and fixed expenses. By reformatting Contractor A's bid to show the real cost of performing the project, a decision with regard to the selling price could then be made. Without this information, your decision will never be an intelligent one. If knowing variable costs is essential for an individual project, then how well will this information work with all projects? What additional information can be obtained from this for decision making?

How Changes in the External Market Affect Profit:
The Most "Bang for Your Buck"

Overall, there are three factors that affect profit: costs, expenses, and sales. You can increase profits by controlling your costs and expenses, or you can increase your profits by increasing sales volume. Before making a decision as to which is more important, you must first consider the potential effects of external market forces. This is particularly important because, by and large, this is beyond your control. Therefore, it becomes a "given" but represents great opportunity. In other words, you must know the rules of the game before making major decisions regarding strategy and tactics.

**PROFIT GUIDE: THE EXTERNAL MARKET AFFECTS
PROFITS**

Let us now look at how changes of total sales volume in the external market (relative to costs) affect profits. It is true that the degree to which you control costs will determine profit. However, it is not only necessary to control, it is vital to identify which type of work will produce the maximum return for the effort put forth. After you know how the external market affects profits (relative to costs), you will, in Chapters 5 and 7, learn the secrets of controlling costs and the effect of cost on profits and growth.

Figure 4.4 illustrates a Segmented Contribution Report for two types of work, formatted to show variable costs and fixed expenses.

Suppose your external market opportunities dictate that you can win more work. You can either take more work like type #1 or more like #2, but not both. Which work should you take? Another way of asking the same question is if you could win 10 percent more work by spending $500 in advertising, which type of work would you advertise?

Both types of work earn a $10,000 profit. So what's the difference? The difference is great. Let's demonstrate why there's a difference via two methods. Figure 4.5 shows a quick and easy method of demonstrating why you should choose one over the other.[1]

It makes good business sense to spend your advertising dollars where they will do the most good. If you spend $500 in advertising on work like type #2, then you will not only be increasing your sales by 10 percent, you will increase your profit by 70 percent. This is determined simply by using the Operating Leverage, which

[1]Ray H. Garrison, *Managerial Accounting*, fourth ed. (Dallas: Business Publications, Inc., 1985), p.203.

Figure 4.4: Segmented Contribution Report for Two Types of Work

	Total Company	Type 1	Type 2
Sales	$200,000	$100,000	$100,000
Less Variable Costs	90,000	60,000	30,000
Contribution Margin	110,000	40,000	70,000
Less Fixed Expenses	90,000	30,000	60,000
Net Profit	$ 20,000	$ 10,000	$ 10,000

NOTE: Both #1 and #2 types of work give the company $10,000 in profit for a total company profit of $20,000.

Figure 4.5: Profit Effects of a 10 Percent Increase in Sales

	Increase in Sales		Operating Leverage		Increase in Profit
Type #1	10%	×	4	=	40%
Type #2	10%	×	7	=	70%

$$\text{Operating Leverage} = \frac{\text{Contribution Margin}}{\text{Profit}}$$

is found when Contribution Margin is divided by your profit. By using this same method with type #1, you increase your profit by only 40 percent.

PROFIT GUIDE: YOU MUST KNOW WHICH CONTRACT TO WIN

Now, for the second method, let's figure out how many more dollars in profit you can expect to earn by doing only 10 percent more work like type #2. Will this allow you to pay for your $500 investment in advertising? Look at Figure 4.6.

Figure 4.6: Profit Effects of a 10 Percent Increase in Sales

	Total Company	Type 1	Type 2
Sales	$220,000	$110,000	$110,000
Less Variable Costs	99,000	66,000	33,000
Contribution Margin	121,000	44,000	77,000
Less Fixed Expenses	90,000	30,000	60,000
Net Profit	$ 31,000	$ 14,000	$ 17,000

Now you can see in dollars and cents just how much difference there is in taking 10 percent more work like type #2 instead of more work like type #1. There is a big difference between making a $17,000 profit or a $14,000 one. Remember in Chapter 1 we talked about "the squeaking wheel" and how you must be able to know which wheel to grease first? Well, the same is true for the type of work that you should be bidding relative to cost.

HOW TO ANALYZE EXPENSES: TWO METHODS TO CHOOSE FROM

Expense can be analyzed as a changing percentage of total sales revenue or as a total dollar amount. The results of the two, however, can be quite different.

The first method effectively implies that you are never going to pay off your fixed expenses, and the other implies that fixed expenses will be paid at a predetermined time. Quite simply, if something is a percentage, it will always exist. On the other hand, if something has a determined total value, it can be paid off. Both statements are true, but they cannot be true at the same time.

PROFIT GUIDE: EXPENSE AS A PERCENTAGE MAXIMIZES GROWTH

If you analyze expense as a changing percentage of sales, your primary interest is growth or increased sales. The reason for this is that you are reducing your selling price by "spreading out" your fixed expenses over the entire year *before* they are paid off. In other words, you have used the lowest possible percentage for fixed expense in calculating your bid and there will be no profit; it will take all year to reach break-even. You have reduced your selling price, which increases the amount of contracts you will win (demand has increased).

PROFIT GUIDE: EXPENSE AS A CONSTANT DOLLAR VALUE MAXIMIZES PROFIT

If you calculate expense as a constant dollar value, your primary interest can be maximum profit. This is especially true if you are using the shortest period of time that you can to pay off fixed expenses before the end of the fiscal year. In this case, to calculate your bid, you use the highest percentage for fixed expense that the market will bear relative to the demand curve for a particular type of work.

PROFIT GUIDE: FIXED EXPENSES ARE NOT FIXED

When you analyze fixed expense as a changing percentage of total sales revenue, you can plan for maximum sales growth. The only thing fixed about a fixed expense is the word "fixed." This is probably the least understood aspect of business economics. Terminology seems to be the underlying reason for this confusion. It is certainly true that the absolute dollar amount is fixed, but calling things "fixed" when they are not fixed relative to time can be tremendously misleading. In the following illustration a more appropriate title would be "total expenses" as opposed to "fixed expenses."

How Fixed Expenses Vary with Sales

The graphs in Figures 4.7 and 4.8 illustrate how fixed expense varies as a percentage of total sales revenue. As the total dollar value of total sales revenue rises, the percentage of total sales revenue (which is fixed expense) decreases. In other words, as sales goes up, the percentage you must allocate in your bid for fixed expense goes down. This is a powerful tool and an important secret for competitive bidding for company growth.

If fixed expense decreases with increasing sales, then you can determine the percentage you should allocate for fixed expenses for a given or projected amount of sales. For example, referring to Figure 4.7, assume you project $1 million in sales. You then move down from the $1 million sales mark in Figure 4.7 to Figure 4.8 and find that your overhead percentage is 6.6 percent. For $2 million in sales, your overhead percentage is 5 percent.

This example determines the applicable percentage of overhead for various sales volumes that can be applied to your bid for zero profit and the lowest selling price relevant to fixed expenses. This focuses attention on the question, "What is your company goal?"

Next, let's consider the second case in which fixed expense is a constant dollar value with focus on maximum profit. With this you are, in effect, holding expenses constant and determining at what sales volume and at what time of the fiscal year all fixed expenses will be paid. It is at this point that you begin to make a profit. Sound familiar? It should. You're back to break-even analysis, which you have already seen in Chapter 1.

Once you determine *when* your fixed expenses are paid, you can then determine the amount of profit that you will realize.

PROFIT GUIDE: FIXED EXPENSES DETERMINE PROFITS

Anything that increases the amount that you are contributing toward paying off your fixed expenses (called the contribution margin) will then lower your break-even point (relative to time), thereby increasing the company's profits. There are several alternatives open that will increase your profits by lowering the break-even point. These are to reduce costs and expenses, to increase selling price, to increase the amount of sales, or to combine a number of these items.

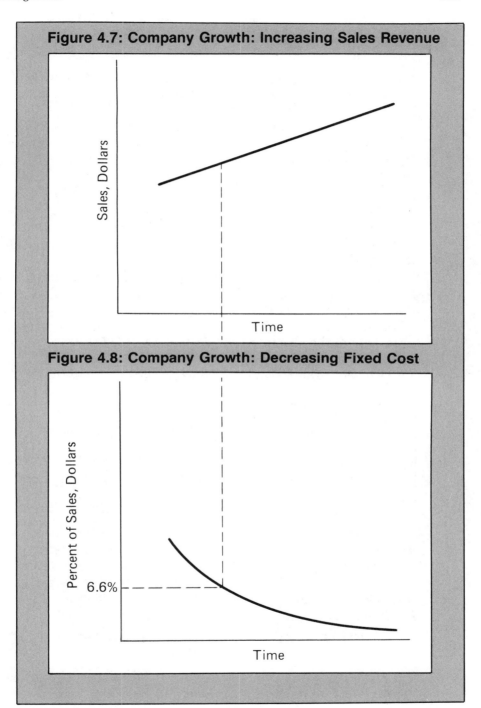

Figure 4.7: Company Growth: Increasing Sales Revenue

Figure 4.8: Company Growth: Decreasing Fixed Cost

HOW TO EARN BIGGER PROFITS AND BID LESS:
THE DYNAMICS OF PROFIT

In order to earn big profits, you can reduce the percentage of profit calculated in each bid. How is this possible? Study for a moment the graphs in Figures 4.9 and 4.10.

How can you earn bigger profits while charging less? Assume you want to make $1 million in profit by the end of the year. Referring to Figure 4.10, the graph for $1 million in profit, you see that as your sales volume goes up, the percentage that is allocated for profit decreases.

This dictates that you can reduce your selling price and *still make big profits.* However, this is possible only if you think of profit as an absolute total dollar amount: allowing sales volume to change, holding profit (in total dollars) constant.

The demand curve illustrates that you can increase sales by lowering your price. Figure 4.10 demonstrates that you can in fact lower your price by lowering the percentage you use for your profit calculation in your bid. Therefore, you can increase sales to the point where the absolute total dollar amount of your target profit is obtained.

Consider the following two examples.

Example 1	Example 2
Sales = $20,000,000	Sales = $40,000,000
Profit @ 5% = $ 1,000,000	Profit @ 2.5% = $ 1,000,000

Clearly, the total profit of $1 million has been made, but in example #1 the profit used was 5 percent of sales, and in example #2 it was cut in half to 2.5 percent of sales. Therefore, you should ask the questions: (1) Does the external market have the opportunity to increase sales? and (2) Do you have the internal company resources to increase your normal workload?

**PROFIT GUIDE: REDUCING YOUR SELLING PRICE WILL
INCREASE PROFITS**

This is an important concept, crucial to a strong bid management plan. The dynamics of fixed expenses and profits show that

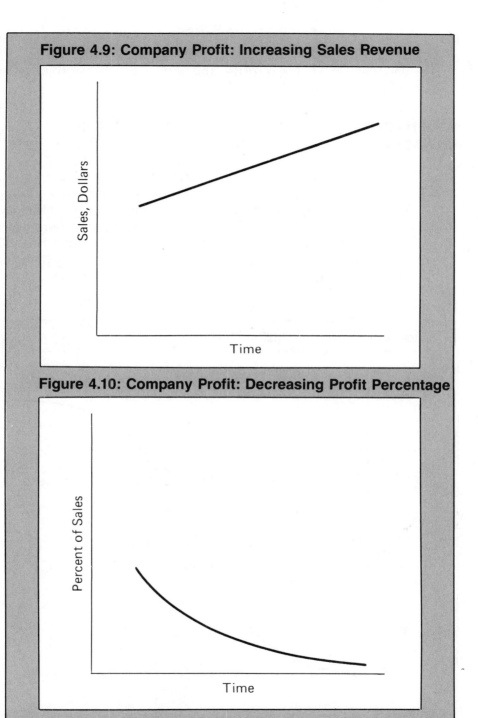

Figure 4.9: Company Profit: Increasing Sales Revenue

Figure 4.10: Company Profit: Decreasing Profit Percentage

you can make big profits *and* still pay all fixed expenses by reducing your selling price.

WHY MARKET TIMING IS CRITICAL TO EFFECTIVE BID MANAGEMENT

Bid management depends on an acute sense of market timing. Knowing *when* to start developing internal company expertise in a newly emerging type of construction project can "save the day" and transform a mediocre bid manager into a company hero overnight. Big profits are made when there is little or no competition. Timing is the key. The adoption curve, shown in Figure 4.11, demonstrates the importance of timing.

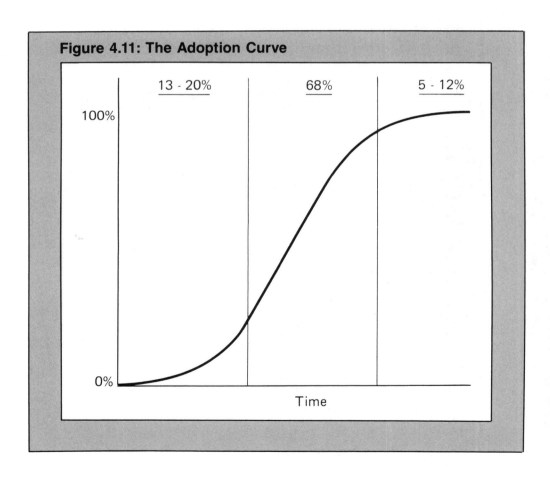

Figure 4.11: The Adoption Curve

This curve illustrates how consumers come to adopt a new product over a period of time. When a new product hits the market, at first only the innovators and early adopters will buy the product. Eventually, as word of mouth spreads and advertising sets in, more and more people will buy the product, assuming there is a demand for the product. If you look at the way various types of construction come into demand when it follows free market forces, you can expect to see the same type of curve. The adoption curve can be an effective tool to analyze where various types of construction are in demand to see how they fit into your strategies and tactics.

This seems reasonable if you consider how projects are financed and built. One example is tax shelters. As tax shelters became more and more popular with consumers, office building construction followed the same curve because the financing was being provided by the purchasers of tax shelters.

The number of construction companies who become interested in particular types of work also follow this curve. When new types of work first appear for bid, there are very few bidders. Then as the work is around for awhile, more companies start competing and submitting bids. In established types of construction (types that are repetitive year after year such as warehouses and docks), companies assign personnel to learn how to do the work and to learn how to bid the work. This means that the salary of these personnel is tied to how much work they win and how well they do it. However, in the case of a newly emerging type of work, no personnel has yet been assigned to learn about it. Until someone is assigned to a particular newly emerging work, it will go unnoticed and unbid.

How Work Can Disappear Overnight

Government regulations can create some pretty distorted curves. There is a danger with these curves. The danger lies not in being too early but rather in staying around too late and investing too much. When free market forces are at work, you can expect to see the type of curve shown in Figure 4.11. Now compare this type of curve with what can happen in Figure 4.12.

The "step" curve shown in Figure 4.12 demonstrates how there can suddenly be a tremendous amount of work and then absolutely no work overnight. Although this may be a slight exaggeration, the potential is there. It points out the tragedy that can occur when

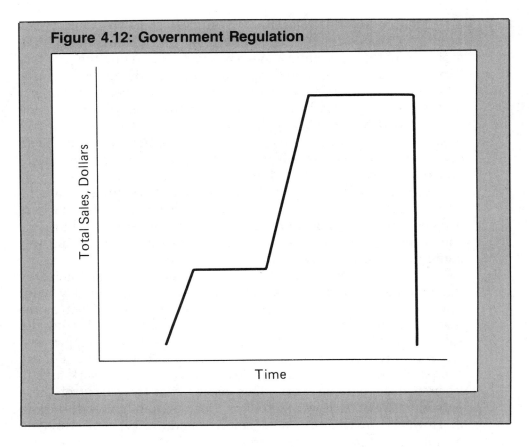

Figure 4.12: Government Regulation

funds are allocated to company fixed expense without bid management. This curve is not far from what happened to the incinerator
construction market in the early 1970s when the Environmental
Protection Agency (EPA) decided to crack down on air pollution,
setting incinerator plants as one of their primary targets. As a
result, the market for new incinerator plants came to an abrupt
standstill.

The rewards for good construction market timing are great (as
with any business). It more than pays for your effort. Take, for
example, the stock market analyst who is searching for a new "hot"
stock. How does one go about finding such a stock? Let's take a look
into an analyst's "bag of tricks" to find out.

PROFIT GUIDE: TECHNICAL AND FUNDAMENTAL
ANALYSIS IS MARKET TIMING

The analyst has two tools at his disposal: technical and fundamental analysis. Technical analysis is the tracking of stock price and volume. Technical analysis assumes that all known information will be reflected in the price of a stock and in the number of buyers and sellers of the stock. If you think about it, this is similar to a contractor who tracks jobs that are coming out for bid. The Dodge Report is an excellent resource for determining what is available for bidding. If, all of a sudden, incinerator plants, water treatment plants, jails, or what have you begin to pop up, this would be valuable information that you would want to know. Just like the technical stock analyst who really does not know or care what is happening elsewhere in the world, in this case you care only about what is happening in the marketplace *now. Construction technical analysis* for bid management is the evaluation of the type and quantity of contracts currently being awarded in the marketplace.

The fundamentalist, on the other hand, is interested in the "big picture." He watches what is happening in the world at large. From everything he sees, hears, and reads, he then deduces the up-and-coming stocks. For the contractor, this means knowing what is going on in the world at large. If politicians are crying about the crime rate and jail overcrowding, then you better learn how to build jails. *Construction fundamental analysis* for bid management is the evaluation of social needs and the anticipated type and quantity of contracts that will be awarded in the marketplace. Market timing depends on *both* a strong technical and fundamentalist approach.

SUMMARY

Effective bid management is the determination of all strategies to carry out company goals and objectives and the development and implementation of tactics to actualize these strategies.

You have learned the importance of setting clear and concise goals. You have identified the difference between the goals of growth and the goals of profit, understanding that growth and profit can be mutually exclusive. You learned that once goals are determined, strategies and tactics can then be devised and implemented to realize your growth and/or profit goals.

You discovered that strategies and tactics are based on company strengths and weaknesses as well as external market opportunities. You have also discovered the dynamics of the tools of bid management: pricing, costs, expenses, profit, and market timing and how they are used to win big profit contracts.

Perhaps most important, you have learned how to choose the type of contract you want, identifying a strong need for an efficient information and control system.

Now that you are comfortable with the large profit contracts (which enable company growth and profit) and have learned how to win those contracts, you will discover how to keep the company growing with money management in Chapter 5.

How You Can Obtain Project Control, Company Growth, and Big Profits with Money Management

HOW YOUR COMPANY CAN FUNCTION AS A "PROFIT MACHINE"

Chapter 2 discussed risk management as it applies to project control and profit. Chapter 4 discussed bid management as it applies to company growth and profit. This chapter discusses an element of profit management common to both project control and company growth: money!

Money management is the management of all assets and liabilities for maximum owner benefit. *Assets* are all things of value (tangible things or intangible rights) owned by the company. Assets constitute the resources of a company.

Liabilities are all things of value (tangible things or services) owned by the company. Liabilities constitute the debts of a company.

Money management includes short-term assets and liabilities as well as long-term assets and liabilities. *Short-term* or *current assets* are all company resources that are expected to be realized in cash within one year. *Long-term assets* or *long-term investments and funds* are all company resources that are set aside in special funds or investments.

Short-term or current liabilities are all company debts that are expected to be paid with current assets. Thus, current liabilities are expected to be paid within one year. Long-term liabilities are long-term debts of a company. They are expected to be paid in a period of time in excess of one year.

To begin to understand money management it is important to realize that assets and liabilities are money. At least once in their life they actually become money, and during their life they are money invested. For example, when an asset such as equipment is purchased, it is paid for with money. When sold, the equipment is converted back to money.

PROFIT GUIDE: ASSETS AND LIABILITIES ARE MONEY

Effective money management determines whether *you* are running the company or whether the *company* is running you. Without money management, the company will not survive. Instead, it will be a ship without a rudder...a machine out of control.

Without a money management plan, all effort will be put into "the problem of the day," running around "stamping out fires." Managing profit exceptions will be impossible with no time for preplanned profit. There will be no attention to serious losses. All growth and profit will be left in the hands of fate. In short, without money management there will be management by *reaction* and not management by *planned action*.

PROFIT GUIDE: PLANNED ACTION IS PREPLANNED PROFIT

In order to realize preplanned profit, you must regard profit as the *first item of expense*. Those in business always find themselves working for whatever their first item of expense happens to be; albeit profit, labor, rent, or whatever. Therefore, it makes sense that if you are working to make a preplanned profit, then your first item of expense should be profit. Preplanned profit is obtained with effective money management, positive cash flow, optimum sources of financing, and realistic budgets.

PROFIT GUIDE: PROFIT MUST BE YOUR FIRST ITEM OF EXPENSE

Effective money management is the ability to maximize the use of all money received for the owner's benefits of growth and profit. This requires being able to determine *when* and *how much* money will be required for current and future operations; *what* the correct available sources of money are; and, of paramount importance, *how* the money will be used to realize growth and profit expectations.

Money is the resource that enables all company operations to produce benefits for the owner. This is the same as saying money is the resource that enables all company operations to produce benefits for the *common stockholders*.

PROFIT GUIDE: COMMON STOCKHOLDERS ARE OWNERS

A simple way to conceptualize a company is to consider a company as a machine whose function is to produce a *constant* profit output. This machine (the company) is equipped with various gauges and dials that the manager uses to monitor and adjust the machine for *varying* sales inputs. The optimum result of these adjustments (planning) is a *constant* profit output. Keeping with this analogy then, what kind of "fuel" does your profit machine run on? *Money.* Effective money management ensures that your machine (company) keeps running by continually controlling the real company financial constraints, thereby providing the money it needs as "fuel."

THE IMPACT OF TIME ON MONEY: HOW TO MAKE SURE YOU DO NOT RUN OUT OF MONEY

When money is *received* and *when* money is *used* is critical to the health and well-being of the company. Therefore, the fundamental focus of money management is time. This forces the company to base its plans on the impact of time. The course line to preplanned profitability cannot be followed without knowing when to "refuel" your engine along the way. In other words, money must be available at the proper time to pay for various operations.

PROFIT GUIDE: YOU MUST CONSIDER TIME

Obviously, the *amount* of money needed for company operations and plans is important, but without knowing *when* the money will be required, action cannot be taken to ensure that you will have the needed money. *When* the money will be needed is a primary question that must be answered.

PROFIT GUIDE: FIRST, KNOW WHEN THE MONEY IS REQUIRED

After having answered the question "when?", you must consider "how much?" The amount of money needed at your predetermined "refueling time" is the second question.

PROFIT GUIDE: NEXT, KNOW HOW MUCH MONEY IS REQUIRED

In order to answer these questions, certain information must be compiled and used. This information consists of project schedules, realistic budgets, and cash flow projections. There is an additional benefit gained from gathering this information: You receive an automatic increase in project accountability which produces company profitability.

Project schedules are the first step in determining the answers to these questions. For example, in order to have money for payroll, you must know when labor is to be paid and how much money is required. Therefore, a *project labor schedule* must first be made to determine when and how much labor is to be used. In order to determine when and how much materials are needed, a *project material schedule* must also be made. In addition, a *project equipment schedule* must then be made to determine when and how much equipment is required. The project schedules of labor, material, and equipment are basic to money management as well as to project and company accountability. This information helps us answer when and how much money, as well as providing project accountability, which automatically increase company profitability.

PROFIT GUIDE: NO PROJECT SCHEDULES MEANS NO CASH AND NO PROFIT

PROFIT VERSUS CASH FLOW

Avoid the "Bookie" Accounting System

Understanding the difference between profit and cash is critical in order to determine the correct available source of money and how it should be best used for growth and profit. Unfortunately, too many contractors tell me, "Don't pay attention to my financial statements. The reports are really not correct. They show a profit, yet there is no money in the bank." Or, even worse, they say, "The loss on the Profit and Loss Statement really doesn't mean anything. There is plenty of money in the bank. So I guess we have already corrected the loss." The assumption seems to be that balance sheets or income statements are the causes of trouble.

These comments remind me of the story about the bookie. It is astonishing how many companies are operated with what I call "bookie accounting." A bookie takes "off track" bets and normally has two pants pockets that automatically track his profit.

At the conclusion of every race, with both pockets bulging, he takes money out of one pocket and puts it into the other. If you ask him what he is doing, he will tell you that one pocket is "his money" and the other is "their money."

In other words, his profit is always the cash in "his" pocket. This may work fine for him, but it won't work for you. Contracting is eminently more complex and requires a great deal more planning because a construction company has many more places to put money other than two pants pockets. A company's profit is rarely the same as that company's available cash.

PROFIT GUIDE: CASH IS NOT PROFIT

Some examples of the places in which money is used (which directly affect the cash in your bank account) are (1) unprofitable operations, (2) retirement of capital stock or payment of dividends, (3) a decrease in any liability account (current or noncurrent), and (4) an increase in any asset account (current or noncurrent). These are examples of items that will reduce the money in your bank account. As you increase company assets (such as buying more equipment, paying debt, or even losing money on a project) the money in your bank account will decrease.

On the other hand, if you have (1) profitable operations, (2) sales of capital stock, (3) an increase in any liability account (current or noncurrent), or (4) a decrease in any asset account (current or noncurrent), the money in the bank account will increase.

Clearly, there are many items besides profit that have a direct effect on the amount of money in the bank. Cash is only the "fuel" with which to accomplish growth and profit, and it is not equal to them.

PROFIT GUIDE: CASH IS FUEL

The following section concerning the tools of money management will enable you to discover the profit management secrets of money management: when and how much money is required, the correct available source of money, and how to use money to maximize stockholders' benefits. These secrets are illustrated with real-life case examples.

FOUR KEY TOOLS OF MONEY MANAGEMENT

A contractor cannot set out to build a major construction project with only a pair of pliers and a screwdriver in hand. He needs the proper tools to do the job correctly. By the same token, if you want to build that major construction project and *still earn a profit,* then you need the proper money management tools.

PROFIT GUIDE: YOU MUST KNOW AND USE THE CORRECT TOOLS

Just as a mechanic needs the proper tools to fix your carburetor, the money manager needs the proper tools to achieve profitable results. The four key money management tools are balance sheets, income statements, budgets, and cash flow projections.

KEY TOOL #1: THE BALANCE SHEET

The *balance sheet* documents the financial health of the company at a specific point in time. It tells us *where* the company is financially. The very heading at the top of the balance sheet is an exact date which lets us know that this is the financial condition of this company on this specific date. Simply put, the balance sheet is a "snapshot" of a company's financial position for a particular moment.

The balance sheet spells out three items: the amount of all company assets, liabilities, and owner's equity. The secret to understanding a balance sheet is that it *"balances"* what the company has in assets against what the company owes in liabilities plus what it owes to the stockholders. Simply put, assets = liabilities + owner's equity. Figure 5.1 illustrates this balance with boxes. The left box represents the company's assets, while the two smaller boxes on the right represent liabilities and owner's equity, respectively. Notice they are "balanced" on a fulcrum. This is exactly what the *balance* sheet tells us. It tells us that assets = liabilities + owner's equity.

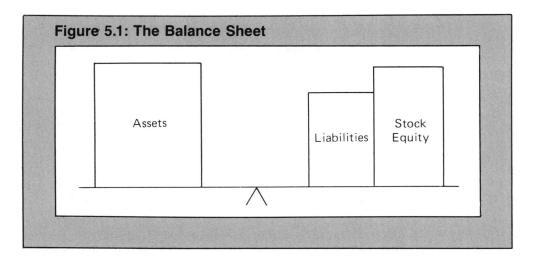

Figure 5.1: The Balance Sheet

The Art of "Crunching" Numbers

Use the numbers from your own balance sheet and draw your own "balanced" illustration. Be sure to proportion the size of the boxes to represent the amounts on your balance sheet. This is the first step in understanding the secrets locked in your balance sheet. You have started to "crunch numbers."

Very simply, "crunching numbers" is the practice of reducing numbers into an intelligible format. It is done by taking a complex value and then separating the component parts of that value into simpler, easy-to-use parts.

Now you can compare the balance illustrated in Figure 5.1 to the typical numerical balance sheet in Figure 5.2 and understand how to read a balance sheet.

PROFIT GUIDE: YOU MUST "CRUNCH NUMBERS"

The balance sheet provides the money manager with vital information so that he can "crunch numbers" for objective decision making. The easiest method of "crunching numbers" required for analytical objectivity is *ratio and trend analysis*.

Ratio Analysis

Ratio analysis is the process of comparing the proportional relationships between two quantities at a specific point in time. Ratio

Figure 5.2: Typical Balance Sheet

THE XYZ CONSTRUCTION COMPANY
BALANCE SHEET
AT DECEMBER 31, 19XX

Current Assets: Current Liabilities:

Cash .... $ 1,000,000   Accounts Payable ... $ 2,000,000
Accounts   Income Tax Payable .   500,000
  Receivable . 4,000,000 Total Current
Total Current   Liabilities .... $ 2,500,000
  Assets ..... $ 5,000,000

Fixed Assets: Long-Term Liabilities:

Land .... $ 2,000,000   Note .... $ 2,000,000
Equipment ... 3,000,000   Bonds Payable   500,000
Total Fixed   Total Long-Term
  Assets ..... $ 5,000,000   Liability .... $ 1,500,000
Total Assets .. $10,000,000 Total Liabilities ..... $ 4,000,000

                                Stockholders' Equity:

                                  Common Stock ..... $ 1,500,000
                                  Retained Earnings ... 4,500,000
                                  Total Equity .... $ 6,000,000
                                  Total Liabilities
                                    and Equity $10,000,000

analysis of financial reports is necessary when judging whether the financial structure of your company should be altered or re-designed to improve overall performance. For example, suppose you need to know the company's current financial ability to pay off current debts. You would start by dividing current assets by current liabilities. Figure 5.3 shows how effective this ratio is in providing the information in an easy-to-understand format. Figure 5.3 illus-

---

Figure 5.3: Company's Ability to Pay Current Debt

$$\frac{\text{CA/CL}}{\text{Ratio}} = \frac{\text{Current Assets}}{\text{Current Liabilities}} = \frac{\$5,000,000}{\$2,500,000} = \frac{\$2}{\$1}$$

---

trates how current assets divided by current liabilities (CA/CL) is one indicator of the company's ability to pay current debt.

Figure 5.3 graphically illustrates that the company has $2 in current assets for every $1 it owes in current liabilities.

The CA/CL ratio is a solvency test that is normally the first item your banker or bonding company evaluates when you apply for a loan or bond. Obviously, they want to be sure you can pay them back. Testing whether you have more assets than liabilities is a basic prerequisite.

PROFIT GUIDE: RATIOS CRUNCH NUMBERS

Many ratios are interrelated. When ratios appear to be out of line, be careful! Go back and determine the cause before taking action from a ratio that appears to be out of line. Always determine *why* a ratio is out of line. For example, cost of goods sold and gross margin are definitely interrelated. As the cost of goods sold increases, gross margin decreases, and vice versa. At times, cost of goods sold may appear to be too high and gross margin may appear to be too low when viewed as a ratio. However, the reason may simply be caused by comparatively low bidding practices. On the other hand, the costs of goods may be too high because of wasteful buying practices.

PROFIT GUIDE: YOU MUST KNOW WHY A RATIO IS OUT OF LINE

Trend Analysis

Balance sheet ratios are also used to identify trends. *Trend analysis* is simply projecting a ratio out over a period (or periods) of time.

Returning to the previous example, if the CA/CL ratio is charted over periods of time, you obtain valuable information. The solid line illustrates what has happened to date and the dotted line projects into the future what can be expected to happen if the current trend continues. Figure 5.4 shows a typical CA/CL chart.

The CA/CL chart shows a company that is accumulating assets and reducing liabilities. Quite often a client will show me a trend chart similar to the CA/CL ratio in Figure 5.4 and ask whether it is a "good" trend or a "bad" trend. As discussed, when studying ratios, a trend chart alone will not give you the entire answer. It is merely a tool that must be combined with other tests and calculations before you can draw a solid conclusion.

PROFIT GUIDE: KNOW WHY A TREND IS OUT OF LINE

For example, the trend chart in Figure 5.4 could indicate that management may be insensitive and unresponsive to operating the company for maximum stockholders' benefit. However, unless return on investment (ROI) calculations also confirm this suspicion (see Case III, p. 214 and ROI), it is not a valid conclusion.

In summary, you must have as much information as possible before you can make a good decision. To do this, the information

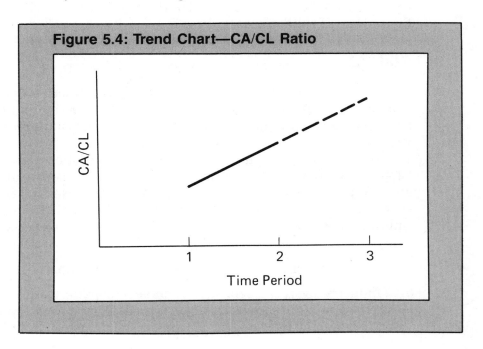

Figure 5.4: Trend Chart—CA/CL Ratio

you gather must be in an easy-to-understand format. If you find yourself asking someone else "Is this right?" then you have a strong indication that either (1) you do not have enough information to answer the question or (2) your information is in the wrong format. Once you have the information in an intelligible format (assuming you have the knowledge to solve the problem), the answer will pop to the surface like a cork in a tub of water.

PROFIT GUIDE: FINANCIAL TRENDS ARE INDICATORS OF THINGS TO COME

Trend analysis of company conditions and operations is crucial to making major business decisions. This just makes good common sense. However, I often wonder whether trend analysis is some well-guarded secret because very few contractors use it in their decision-making process.

KEY TOOL #2: THE INCOME STATEMENT

The *income statement* documents where you have been financially. As in the case of the balance sheet heading, the heading of the annual income statement states "For the Year Ended 19XX" (refer to Figure 5.5). In other words, this is what has happened over the entire year. Simply put, the income statement is *history!*

PROFIT GUIDE: INCOME STATEMENTS ARE HISTORY

Income statements are particularly useful when historically analyzing company operations on a percentage basis. Figure 5.5 illustrates a typical income statement with dollar and percentage variations.

As soon as percentages and percentage variations are calculated, the income statement comes to life. Once these calculations are completed, you can then—and only then—use the income statement to pinpoint areas that should have been controlled. You can now compare your calculations with industry averages as well as with your own experience of past years.

PROFIT GUIDE: USE YOUR OWN PAST EXPERIENCE

Industry averages typically include the performance of the least efficient and the most efficient firms. They do not represent "par." Therefore, your operations should be adjusted to be better

Figure 5.5: Comparative Income Statement

XYZ COMPANY
INCOME STATEMENT
FOR THE YEAR ENDED DECEMBER 31, 19X1

	19X0	19X1	Increase (Decrease) Item by Item 19X0–19X1	Increase (Decrease) Item by Item 19X0–19X1
Sales	$1,394,195	$1,775,818	$381,623	27.4%
Variable Cost:				
Material	476,434	574,855	98,421	20.7%
Direct Labor	461,237	574,948	113,711	24.7%
Payroll Taxes, etc.	107,971	148,390	40,419	37.4%
Other Direct Job Costs	86,198	131,605	45,407	52.7%
Total Variable Costs	$1,131,840	$1,429,798	$297,958	26.3%
Gross Margin	$ 262,355	$ 346,020	$ 83,665	31.9%
Fixed Expenses:				
Administrative Travel and Entertainment .	$ 5,439	$ 6,560	$ 1,121	20.6%
Advertising	2,292	2,369	77	3.4%
Auto and Truck . .	12,597	18,361	5,764	45.8%
Bad Debts	3,781	3,185	(596)	(15.8)%
Charitable Contributions . .	635	783	148	23.3%
Depreciation and Amortization . .	10,231	12,866	2,635	25.8%
Dues and Subscription . . .	1,662	2,083	421	25.3%
Freight and Express	265	341	76	28.7%
Heat, Light, and Water	3,079	2,958	(121)	(3.9)%
Insurance	9,655	12,098	2,443	25.3%
Interest	5,880	11,899	6,019	102.4%

Figure 5.5: Comparative Income Statement (continued)

	19X0	19X1	Increase (Decrease) Item by Item 19X0–19X1	Increase (Decrease) Item by Item 19X0–19X1
Legal and Accounting	$ 4,311	$ 5,489	$ 1,178	27.3%
Employee Benefits	4,643	6,459	3,082	91.3%
Pension and Profit Sharing ..	7,732	11,217	3,485	45.1%
Office Supplies ..	5,440	6,555	1,115	20.5%
Rent	7,233	8,056	823	11.4%
Repairs and Maintenance ..	2,435	3,881	1,446	59.4%
Plans, Bid Bonds	1,627	2,773	1,146	70.4%
Salaries and Wages	114,389	129,096	14,707	12.9%
Small Tools and Shop	2,899	4,215	1,316	45.4%
Taxes and Licenses	5,380	5,282	(98)	(1.8)%
Taxes, Payroll ...	6,684	10,255	3,571	53.4%
Telephone	4,249	4,902	653	15.4%
All Other	4,207	5,355	1,148	27.3%
Total Fixed Expenses	$ 226,745	$ 277,038	$ 50,293	22.2%
Operating Profit ..	$ 35,610	$ 68,982	$ 33,372	93.7%
Income Taxes ...	$ 10,805	$ 27,491	$ 16,686	154.4%
Net Profit After Taxes	$ 24,805	$ 41,491	$ 16,686	67.3%

( ) Decreases are subtracted.

than industry averages. A two-year comparison is demonstrated for you in Figure 5.5.

As you have previously seen with the balance sheet, ratio and trend analysis is used to obtain valuable decision-making information. It provides you with vital information, allowing you to "crunch numbers" for analytical and objective decision making. Figures 5.6 and 5.7 are typical trend charts for the percentage cost of labor and the percentage cost of material for three time periods. They provide information for operational decisions.

The information presented in Figures 5.6 and 5.7 (see page 188) show that you must take positive action to control labor and material costs in order to reverse this negative trend.

PROFIT GUIDE: GOOD DECISIONS REQUIRE TREND ANALYSIS

KEY TOOL #3: THE BUDGET

The discussion thus far of the tools of money management has centered on balance sheets (which document financial position at one point in time) and the income statement (which documents what has happened over a past period of time). This information is history! In fact, by the time a balance sheet is tabulated and presented to management, it has already become history! Like all history, the balance sheet and the income statement tell you where you've been but cannot direct you where to go. To manage your business effectively on a day-to-day basis, it is imperative that you use information that will direct you where to go!

PROFIT GUIDE: YOU MUST KNOW WHEN AND WHERE TO TAKE ACTION

Budgets are the foundation of financial accountability and preplanned profit. Most managers can easily tell me what they want to accomplish and when they want it accomplished. However, unless they have some way of communicating their thoughts and plans to others, they will never accomplish their goals.

Budgets provide a vehicle for communicating these plans throughout the company in an orderly way. A budget states what goals have been set and how they are to be realized. Budgets provide accountability with definite goals and objectives to evaluate performance. They identify bottlenecks in cash flow. Of most importance, they coordinate all the activities of the company, freeing the manager to concentrate on only those items that are over budget. Over-budget items are the "exceptions" to the plan (preplanned profit).

PROFIT GUIDE: BUDGETS PROVIDE PROFITABILITY WITH ACCOUNTABILITY

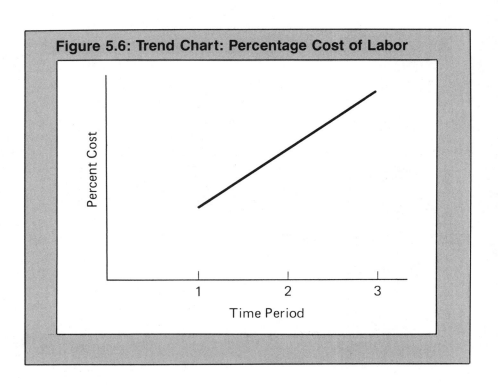

Figure 5.6: Trend Chart: Percentage Cost of Labor

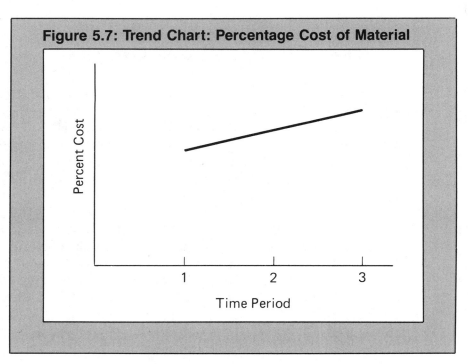

Figure 5.7: Trend Chart: Percentage Cost of Material

In other words, budgets allow you to identify immediately the trouble and the extent of the problem when it occurs, enabling you to take corrective action. This is called *management-of-exceptions*. Management-of-exceptions is a system whereby management knows and acts upon negative variations to preplanned profit.

An *action* "management-of-exceptions" system requires, in addition, the tracking of all SIDs. This system reduces this information into an easy-to-understand format called a Daily Operating Control Sheet, or DOC Sheet (see Chapter 7, about the Information and Control System).

PROFIT GUIDE: BUDGET VARIATIONS CREATE ACTION

Once a budget and DOC sheet are completed, you can readily identify any negative variations of your budgeted amounts, which can then be remedied with positive management action. Once you have mastered and budgeted each item of cost and expense by generating a DOC sheet, you will have activated your own "management-of-exceptions" system that guarantees big profits. But before you can set up your system, you must first take a closer look at basic budgets.

How to Budget Profit, Cost, and Expense Items

In order to identify these "exceptions" properly, each item of cost and expense must be budgeted. Figure 5.8 (see pages 190 and 191) illustrates the positive and negative variations of a typical basic budget for a period of one year. Unfortunately, the budgeted items in Figure 5.8 are about the only items most contractors bother to track.

Keep in mind that in Chapter 7 (Information and Control System) you will learn how to build on the budget from Figure 5.8, adding SIDs and preparing your own DOC sheet.

Also take note that *profit* is the first item of expense listed in Figure 5.8.

KEY TOOL #4: THE CASH FLOW PROJECTION

In addition to the company budget, the *cash flow projection* is another important money management tool. The cash flow projection is a preplanned projection that determines when and how much money will be needed on a day-to-day basis for a project.

Figure 5.8: Cost and Expense Budget

XYZ CONSTRUCTION COMPANY
BUDGET
FOR THE YEAR ENDED DECEMBER 31, 19X1

	Budget	Actual	Over Budget (Under Budget) Item by Item	Over Budget (Under Budget) Item by Item
Costs:				
Material	$476,434	$574,855	$98,421	20.7%
Direct Labor . .	461,237	397,948	(63,289)	(13.7)%
Payroll Taxes, etc.	107,971	102,707	(5,264)	(4.9)%
Other Direct Job Costs	86,198	86,198	0	0%
Expenses:				
Profit	$ 24,805	$ 41,491	$ 16,686	67.3%
Administration Travel and Entertainment .	5,439	6,560	1,121	20.6%
Advertising	2,292	2,369	77	3.4%
Auto and Truck . .	12,597	18,361	5,764	45.8%
Bad Debts	3,781	3,185	(596)	(15.8)%
Charitable Contributions .	635	635	0	0%
Dues and Subscription . .	1,662	2,083	421	25.3%
Freight and Express	265	341	76	28.7%

Figure 5.8: Cost and Expense Budget *(continued)*

XYZ CONSTRUCTION COMPANY
BUDGET
FOR THE YEAR ENDED DECEMBER 31, 19X1

	Budget	Actual	Over Budget (Under Budget) Item by Item	Over Budget (Under Budget) Item by Item
Heat, Light, and Water	$ 3,079	$ 2,958	$ (121)	(3.9)%
Insurance	9,655	8,373	(1,282)	(13.3)%
Interest	5,880	11,899	6,019	102.4%
Legal and Accounting	4,311	5,489	1,178	27.3%
Employee Benefits	4,643	4,643	0	0%
Pension and Profit Sharing	7,732	7,732	0	0%
Office Supplies	5,440	6,555	1,115	20.5%
Rent	7,233	7,233	0	0%
Repairs and Maintenance	2,435	3,881	1,446	59.4%
Plans, Bid Bonds	1,627	2,773	1,146	70.4%
Salaries and Wages	114,389	129,096	14,707	12.9%
Small Tools and Shop	2,899	2,012	(887)	(30.6)%
Taxes and Licenses	5,380	5,282	(98)	(1.8)%
Taxes, Payroll	6,684	10,255	3,571	53.4%
Telephone	4,249	4,902	653	15.4%
All Other	4,207	4,313	106	2.5%

PROFIT GUIDE: NO CASH FLOW PROJECTIONS MEANS FINANCIAL TROUBLE

As previously discussed, you need to plan in advance when and how much money you will need to ensure that you will have the money you need when you need it. Without a cash flow projection, you will discover you need money only as the actual need arises, which is too late. You'll be a day late and a dollar short.

Cash flow projections require that project schedules of labor, material, and equipment be organized in a working format. Figure 5.9 illustrates the format of the *project cash flow projection*.

Once project cash flow projections are made, they can be easily incorporated into an "overall" *company cash flow projection*. Figure 5.9 shows that *when* and *how much* cash is going to be needed throughout the entire project is no longer a mystery. Now, if necessary, you can even go to the bank well before you actually need the money, just as long as you have it available and accounted for when the anticipated need arises. Of equal importance, the cash flow projection tells us when and how you can pay back the bank. For example (in Figure 5.9), month 2 shows a $2,000 "short fall" that can be paid back in month 3.

PROFIT GUIDE: YOU MUST KNOW YOUR FUTURE FINANCIAL NEEDS

Many advantages are gained by planning when and how much money is going to be required *in advance*. By preplanning your projected cash flow, you have the time to ask "What if...?" questions to find the best source of financing available to you. You have the time to "cut the best deal," to determine the best type of work (as you learned in Chapter 4, Figure 4.4), and how to maximize common stockholders' benefits, as you will see in the case examples that follow.

THE IMPORTANCE OF POSITIVE CASH FLOW: WHEN AND HOW MUCH MONEY

The importance of time versus cash has already been discussed. *When* money is received and *when* money is used are crucial to the health and well-being of the company. Now you can build on this understanding using the tools of money management to exploit new avenues that will provide positive cash flow for maximum stock-

Figure 5.9: Project Cash Flow Projection

THE XYZ CONSTRUCTION COMPANY
PROJECT #1
CASH FLOW PROJECTION

	Months			Total 3 Months
	1	2	3	
Cash Balance:				
Beginning	$10,000	$ 2,000	($ 2,000)	$10,000
Contract Partial Payments	30,000	26,000	30,000	88,000
Total Cash Available	$40,000	$28,000	$28,000	$98,000
Disbursements:				
Materials	$10,000	$ 9,000	$3,000	$22,000
Labor	18,000	17,000	8,000	43,000
Equipment	3,000	1,000	1,000	5,000
Other	7,000	3,000	1,000	11,000
Total Disbursements .	$38,000	$30,000	$13,000	$81,000
Excess (deficiency) of Cash Available	$2,000	($2,000)	$15,000	$17,000

holder benefit. In other words, you want to have enough money when it's needed for company growth and profit.

Positive cash flow means that the company is generating money in excess of all of its costs and expenses. In order to accomplish an excess cash flow, *each project* must generate cash in excess of its own costs and expenses at all times.

PROFIT GUIDE: POSITIVE CASH FLOW IS EXCESS CASH

Construction is one of the few industries that provides opportunities for ensuring positive cash flow. Industries that produce products to be sold on a fixed-price basis require the manufacturer to "finance" the entire production himself.

A construction company is analogous to a "job shop" manufacturer who manufactures items to specifications from individual outside orders. Although called a manufacturer, the "job shop" manufacturer is actually a contractor. For the most part, each order is quite different from the previous, requiring the type of machinery and labor that only he can provide.

The primary difference between a construction contractor and a "job shop" manufacturer is that the manufacturer works indoors under his own roof while the contractor, for the most part, works outdoors in the field.

Another important distinction is that the "job shop" manufacturer is normally not paid until the product is shipped, received, and accepted by the purchaser. Not being paid until production is completed means that the "job shop" has a negative cash flow and often suffers from a lack of enough cash to pay all costs and expenses incurred during the execution of a contract.

PROFIT GUIDE: NEGATIVE CASH FLOW MEANS FINANCIAL TROUBLE

Quite simply, if you are not paid until the job is complete, then you will have a negative cash flow. You will either have to borrow the funds required to complete the project from external sources or finance the project yourself. Either way, you will have a negative cash flow.

CASE I: MAKING PARTIAL PAYMENTS WORK FOR YOU

I consulted for a contractor who spent most of the time during our initial conference answering telephone calls from his suppliers and subcontractors, assuring them that his "check was in the mail." (For purposes of this example, I'll call him Charles.)

"The problem with construction is that no one pays their bills," Charles told me. "I've been in this game all my life," he went on to say, "and if I knew some other way to 'make a buck' I'd do it tomorrow."

The more Charles talked about his company, the more intriguing the mystery became. Every project he was working on was projected to make a profit. In fact, his company had turned a seven-figure profit each year for the past six years. However, his credit rating was zero because he was always late paying his suppliers and subcontractors.

"I spend more time with my banker than at the job site," Charles told me. "I know I could get more work if I had more money. In fact, I could actually cut my material costs if I could only pay off my suppliers on time."

Charles was convinced that his problem was a lack of money due to the fact that no one paid his bills. He was right. His problem *was* a lack of money. He was clearly operating with a negative cash flow. However, as you will see, he was also wrong because his negative cash flow problem was not caused by others not paying their bills on time. They weren't paying their bills because Charles wasn't billing them!

Upon close inspection of Charles's contracts, I discovered his cash flow was based on project "partial" payments spread out over the progress of the project. Interestingly, as is so often the case, his partial payment schedule was completed *before* the actual project schedule had even been finalized. Furthermore, each application carried a 15 percent retainage provision that the owner deducted and kept until final acceptance.

To many contractors these contract conditions appear innocuous. They are accepted as more or less "standard fare" for the industry. Depending on how well they are managed, these conditions can either help or hurt you a great deal.

PROFIT GUIDE: CONTRACT PARTIAL PAYMENTS CAN WORK FOR YOU

The underlying theory of partial payment is that payment is made for work as it is completed. However, the idea is not that contractors should become bankers as well as builders by waiting for payments that come after *all* work is complete (although I will admit this sometimes appears to be the wish of some owners). Like anyone else, owners are not going to pay you until they have been invoiced. I assure you, they certainly are not going to follow you around making sure you have enough money to carry on operations (remember: they have your performance "bond"). The key to partial payments is to keep up on your invoices.

When Charles and I reviewed the partial payment applications that he sent to the owner, his problem became obvious. We found that his payment schedules were never readjusted relevant to cash flow according to the finalized project schedule.

PROFIT GUIDE: YOU MUST INVOICE TO BE PAID

Figure 5.10 shows the schedule Charles used when estimating versus the schedule to which the work was performed and invoiced.

Let's evaluate a single item in Figure 5.10 to better demonstrate what had been happening to Charles. For example, structural steel had been initially planned to arrive at designated times during the project, distributing a $600,000 payment during the progress of the project. Remember, each payment includes overhead and profit allocations. Clearly, Charles had originally planned for the distribution of cash, including overhead and profit shown in the Original Schedule of Work for structural steel.

What actually happened was that billing on structural steel was not started until the latter part of the project, as shown in the Actual Schedule of Work, thereby shifting the major dollar amount of his incoming cash flow. This shift seriously delayed the overhead and profit payment included in the structural steel billing.

PROFIT GUIDE: YOU MUST COLLECT OVERHEAD AND PROFIT ON TIME

In addition, the original schedule would have allowed for the structural steel erection to be approved and accepted during the progress of the project, releasing the 15 percent retainage. However, the actual schedule made this impossible.

Front-end Loading

The original schedule provided the opportunity to "front-end load" the project. Front-end loading means that Charles would have had the majority of his overhead and profit out of the project and in his pocket by the time he was halfway done with the project. This would have been accomplished by providing those materials with the largest dollar amounts early in the project that would carry and provide the largest total dollar amounts for overhead and profit.

As it turned out for Charles, the actual schedule did just the reverse. Overhead and profit were locked in until the very end of

Figure 5.10: Original Schedule vs. Actual Schedule of Work

ORIGINAL SCHEDULE OF WORK

Time Period	1	2	3	Total Estimated Amount
Site Work	100K	100K	. . . .	$200,000
Parking Lot	. . . . .10K	40K		50,000
Foundation	80K	. . . .		80,000
Structural Steel . . .	200K	200K	200K	600,000
Total Payments . . .	$390K	$340K	$200K	$930,000

ACTUAL SCHEDULE OF WORK

Time Period	1	2	3	Total Actual Amount
Site Work	100K	100K	. . . .	$200,000
Parking Lot	. . . .	40K	10K . . .	50,000
Foundation	80K	. . . .		80,000
Structural Steel . . .	. . . .	25K	575K	600,000
Total Payments . . .	$180K	$165K	$585K	$930,000

the project. Structural steel (which carried the largest dollar amounts for overhead), profit, and retainage were not scheduled to be paid until the end of the project.

In addition, suppliers and subcontractors were forced to change their schedules, thereby negatively impacting their cash flow as well as his. Needless to say, this placed Charles in a precarious position with his suppliers and subcontractors. He became exposed to their claims against him for impacted damages.

Does this sound familiar? It should. This is exactly what was discussed in Chapter 1. You learned how new time and float time (which are caused by schedule changes) affect your job planning. You now can see how they can strike at the very heart of your company. They can transform a healthy, positive cash flow into a debilitating, negative cash flow condition, robbing you of the "fuel" you need to follow your preplanned profit course line.

Once Charles realized what had been happening to his company, he was able to take the appropriate action. Cash flow projections were made for each project, including the original schedule he bid and the schedule as it was revised. This comparison clarified Charles's negative cash flow problem.

PROFIT GUIDE: SCHEDULES ARE CONTRACTS

Having clarified his problem, Charles could now correctly invoice the owner. Remember, you are entitled to the payments when you were originally promised; this includes overhead and profit. The revised schedule and cash flow projection became the "fuel gauge" for Charles to ensure that he could provide the "fuel" he needed to realize growth and big profits.

PROFIT GUIDE: REVISED SCHEDULES REQUIRE REVISED PARTIAL PAYMENTS

The cash flow projection also provided Charles with the benefit of increased accountability leading to profitability. In order to generate his revised cash flow projections, he first needed to make new labor, material, and equipment schedules for each project. These became the foundation for his budget and partial payments. The budgets tracked exceptions (variations) and provided performance information and definite goals and objectives to evaluate both his performance and the owner's performance for his managers.

CASE II: POSITIVE CASH FLOW AND REAL COSTS

This case considers the importance of identifying and billing all costs. This is fundamental for generating a positive cash flow. Obviously, there can never be a positive cash flow if real costs are not first identified, then billed and collected. However, oftentimes things are not as simple as they appear.

Knowing all of your real costs means that all costs must be identified and correctly calculated. Billing all costs means that correct costs be used for internal as well as external company purposes. Internally correct costs are used for original contract cost estimating. Externally correct costs are used to calculate all extra work added to the original contract. As you will see in the following case from another contractor I had the opportunity to consult for, it was vital that he be able to identify and bill all of his costs.

When we first met, Richard told me that he was in the middle of a $450,000 "short fall." He had just projected out all costs to finish the work he had in house. After subtracting what was left to collect on all the projects (from what it would cost to finish the work), he found that he was left with minus $450,000. "I can't figure out how this could have happened," he explained. "Take a look at these numbers. I hope you can find what I'm missing."

Figure 5.11 shows Richard's calculations.

Figure 5.11: Original Contract Values

	Total Contract Value	Total Material	Total Labor	Other
Project #1	$ 2,898,750	$ 811,650	$1,217,475	$ 869,625
Project #2	2,648,033	741,450	1,112,174	794,409
Project #3	3,536,363	990,182	1,485,272	1,060,908
Project #4	3,059,933	979,179	1,315,771	764,983
Project #5	5,725,711	2,061,255	2,633,827	1,030,629
	$17,868,790	$5,583,717	$7,764,519	$4,520,554

Figure 5.12: Contract Amount Still Owing: *Cash Inflow*

	Balance Owed on Contract	Total "Material" Extra Work and Still Owing	Total "Labor" Extra Work and Still Owing	Total Amount Owing
Project #1	$ 135,000	$ 23,190	$ 34,785	$ 192,975
Project #2	377,675	31,776	47,665	457,116
Project #3	389,000	38,901	58,349	486,250
Project #4	279,977	55,079	82,618	417,674
Project #5	487,678	103,062	154,595	745,335
	$1,669,330	$252,008	$378,012	$2,299,350

Figure 5.13: Work Still to Be Completed: *Cash Outflow*

	Material	Labor	Other	Total
Project #1	$ 70,576	$ 110,389	$ 52,010	$ 232,975
Project #2	181,938	272,909	102,269	557,116
Project #3	257,656	314,915	38,679	611,250
Project #4	189,154	250,741	87,779	527,674
Project #5	· 321,788	362,868	135,679	820,335
	$1,021,112	$1,311,822	$416,416	$2,749,350

Figure 5.14: Summary of Contract Amount Owing and Work Left to Be Completed

Cash Flow Projection	=	Total Cash Inflow	–	Total Cash Outflow
Cash Flow Projection	=	$2,299,350	–	$2,749,350
Cash Flow Projection	=	($450,000)		

Richard was right. He was experiencing a $450,000 negative cash flow that could have, if not corrected, resulted in a serious "short fall."

As I studied Richard's numbers, I became curious about the total amount of extra work he had been billing ($252,008 for extra work material + $378,012 for extra work labor = $630,020 total in extra work). To me, $630,020 in extra work seemed awfully small in comparison with the total contract values. In fact, it was only 3.5 percent of the total contract values of $17,868,790. Extra work normally averages between 10 percent to 20 percent of the total contract. Extra work is normally the result of human error and changing conditions. I have only seen lower percentages (that were supported) when the same projects were being built over and over again.

Upon surveying Richard's system of managing the extras, the mystery began to unfold. Here's how his system worked. Changes were authorized in writing by the owner before extra field work commenced. After field work was completed, inspection was made and acceptance was obtained from the owner (again in writing). At this time the owner was invoiced for labor, material, supervision, and tools plus an added 15 percent for overhead and 10 percent for profit.

To help you follow what I've just described, Figure 5.15 illustrates a typical invoice for Richard's extra work.

Figure 5.15: Typical Invoice for Extra Work

Labor	.... ($16.00/hour × 8 hours)	$128.00
Supervision	.... ($22.00/hour × 2 hours)	44.00
Material	....	235.00
Tool Rental	....	50.00
		$457.00
Overhead 15%	....	68.55
		$525.55
Profit 10%	....	52.55
Total Amount	....	$578.10

Determining an Accurate Man-hour Cost

The system may sound good, but it sure doesn't look good. Bells and whistles went off as soon as I thumbed through Richard's invoices. The low percentage of extras that first caught my attention (and which we shall return to later in this case) was now replaced with an even more fundamental question. *Did Richard know his man-hour cost?* Invoices with amounts ending in zero invariably spell trouble, especially when they are for labor costs. The chances of calculating labor and having the amount come out to even dollars are a million to one. Of course, there is always the possibility that after making careful calculations, the billing department simply rounded off the numbers.

Unfortunately, this was not the case for Richard. This is a major flaw I find with many contractors. To clearly understand what the problem was and its debilitating effect, let's take a closer look at Figure 5.16 to see how Richard's billing department was arriving at the $16.00 an hour labor amount.

Where is the mistake? Well, let's analyze the two that certainly hurt Richard. Keep in mind that Richard's is not a special case. His mistakes are the most common: the proper allocation for insurances.

Figure 5.16: Billing Cost Rate per Man-hour Worked

Cost of Insurance

6.7%	FICA
1.5%	Federal Unemployment
3.7%	State Unemployment
11.9%	

Labor Man-hour Billing Rate

Base Man-hour Rate $12.00
+ 11.9% Insurance 1.43

Contributions to Fixed Funds

Health and Welfare . $1.98
Vacation 15
Pension 40
Apprentice . . . . .04 $ 2.57

*Total Billing Cost
per Man-hour Worked* . . $16.00

Why You Must Allocate Funds for Insurance

There are two general types of insurance that you need to be concerned with in the United States because of their drastic variations. These are *state unemployment* and *casualty insurance*. State unemployment insurance rates are based on experience. Newly formed companies in the United States are initially billed by the states at low experience rates. As time goes on and as the company gains experience, the state adjusts its rates accordingly. Many states adjust rates based on two criteria: (1) the state's cost experience with all employers and (2) the state's cost experience with an individual employer.

In other words, if a company has high employee turnover rate, producing an increasing number of employees collecting unemployment insurance benefits, then that company's insurance rate is adjusted upward by the state. Depending on the state in which you are performing a project, the minimum and maximum limits of unemployment insurance vary drastically. In Richard's case, the variation was 3.7 percent to 7 percent. That's quite a variation!

PROFIT GUIDE: KNOW YOUR INSURANCE RATE

To see what this meant to Richard, minimum and maximum insurance rates have been converted into dollar amounts and shown in Figure 5.17.

By presenting the information in this format, you can see that Richard had a potential dollar savings in state unemployment insurance of $268,703 (which is the difference between the 3.7 and 7 percentage rate). With this kind of total dollar variation, it is obvious that the state's percentage rate should be monitored closely.

PROFIT GUIDE: USE THE CORRECT INSURANCE RATE

Unfortunately, Richard's estimating department was using the lowest percentage rate (3.7 percent) for state unemployment insurance and his accounting department was paying the highest percentage rate. To make matters worse, his billing department was

Figure 5.17: Dollar Comparison of Minimum and Maximum State Unemployment Insurance Rates for Richard

		State Unemployment Insurance Rates for Total Labor		
		3.7%	7%	Variation
Total Contract Labor	$7,764,519	—	—	—
Extra Work Labor	378,012	—	—	—
Total Labor	$8,142,531	$301,274	$569,977	($268,703)

also using the lowest percentage rate (3.7 percent) when billing the owner for extra work. Figure 5.18 illustrates what this was costing Richard both in internal and external company calculations.

Figure 5.18 shows that $256,229 was being lost internally by the estimating department because it was using the wrong rate for state unemployment insurance. In addition, $12,475 was being lost externally by the billing department because it was using the wrong rate to invoice the extras.

As a matter of fact, because the state starts a new company with the lower insurance rate, it actually would have paid Richard to start a new company just to perform the extras. Richard would have saved $12,475 in state unemployment by starting an entirely new company just to perform his own authorized extra work!

Here's another insurance secret of which Richard was unaware. Every contractor carries every type of casualty insurance (listed in Figure 5.19, see p. 208) because he is exposed to all of these risks. Are these risks self-insured or commercially insured?

In other words, are you paying someone else to take the risk, or are you paying yourself to take the risk? If you fail to carry these

---

Figure 5.18: State Unemployment Insurance Rates

INTERNAL COST

		State Unemployment Insurance Rates		
		3.7%	7%	Variation
Original Contract Labor	$7,764,519	$287,287	$543,516	($256,229)

EXTERNAL COST

Extra Work Labor	$ 378,012	$ 13,986	$ 26,461	($ 12,475)

policies with a broker or fail to compute them into your labor rate as self-insurance, you are merely "sticking your head in the sand," which leaves some pretty sensitive parts exposed. This is why insurance brokers refer to contractors who forego buying insurance as "going naked."

The reasons for listing insurance in the format shown in Figure 5.19 is (1) to provide a method for determining "real cost," and (2) to provide a model format to establish an internal company audit system of insurance premiums. Internal company audit systems are a big money saver because you naturally make sure that you are going to pay the lowest premiums. Remember: nobody is more interested in your welfare than you are! I have yet to review insurance premiums paid from insurance company audits that favor the contractor. Is this the fault of the insurance company? Of course not. It is soley the fault of the contractor who does not have his own internal company audit system that can verify the insurance company audit in advance of making final premium payments.

Verify Insurance Rates with an Internal Audit

Always verify your insurance rates in advance with an internal company audit system. This is a vital concept. Workers Compensation premiums alone can vary over 400 percent depending on what insurance classification the worker is categorized under. Consider the "project manager" who is actually the company salesman. Technically, he can be classified under either Workers Compensation Insurance code number 5606 or number 8742. The rate difference between these two code classifications is a substantial 469 percent. Assuming you did not have a complete job description for this salesman, which code rate would you base the insurance premium on if you were an insurance company auditor?

PROFIT GUIDE: VERIFY YOUR INSURANCE RATES IN
ADVANCE

The responsibility of determining insurance code classifications rests solely with you! This is not the responsibility of the insurance company. Insurance companies must be consulted for correct classifications; however, the responsibility for correct classification and payment is yours.

How to Calculate and Bill All Insurance Costs

What were Richard's rates? Figure 5.19 shows what turned up after extensive digging. Take note of two things. First, the insurance coverage has been separated into commercial and company coverage. As previously stated, commercial insurance is provided by paying a premium to a third-party insurance company and company self-insurance is provided by paying a premium to the company itself. Second, all insurance rates have been reduced to an estimated percentage of man-hour labor costs (as shown in Column 4). This is necessary to further solve the mystery of Richard's disappearing $450,000 by finding his real man-hour cost.

There are additional benefits from using the format illustrated in Figure 5.19. The Total Yearly Fixed Cost of Insurance, tabulated in Column 1, provides powerful information for negotiating insurance rates and for calculating your company break-even point as well.

Even though premiums for comprehensive general and contractual liability (as shown in Column 1) are normally advance premiums that will be returned if unused, they do substantially reduce positive cash flow and profit. This is *your* money that gets tied up with the insurance company. Once you establish your own internal company audit system, you can free up this money to put to a more profitable use.

Now that you know Richard's insurance costs (shown in column 4 in Figure 5.19) his real man-hour cost can be recalculated with the 28 percent insurance rate that should have been used for external and internal company transactions. Figure 5.20 (see p. 211) is the revised billing cost rate per man-hour worked.

When you compare Richard's *real* man-hour costs of $19.76 with the $16.00 amount that he was using to estimate his work and bill extras; you discover that his real cost was actually 23.5 percent greater.

$$\% \text{ increase} = \frac{\$19.76 - \$16.00}{\$16.00} \times 100$$
$$\% \text{ increase} = 23.5\%$$

Figure 5.19: Insurance Coverage

Policy and Description	Minimum Fixed Cost per Year	Estimated Annual Premium Cost (note 5)	Estimate Premium Cost per Total Insurance Risk per All Jobs	Percentage Per Dollar of Payroll
COMMERCIALLY INSURED				
I. Comprehensive General and Contractual Liability (note 4)				
A. Premises Operations	$19,000	$0.02/$1	$160,000	2.00%
B. Excess Liability	35,000	3.38/$100	608,800	7.61%
1. Completed Operations				
2. Contractual Liability				
II. Commercial Comprehensive (Umbrella Liabilities Increases Total Coverage in item 1)	10,000	0	10,000	0.13%
III. Worker's Compensation (Required by Each State)	0	0.16/$1	1,280,000	16.00%
IV. Const. Equipment Loss (Insures for Theft, Fire and Mysterious Disappearance)	6,000	0	6,000	0.08%
V. Office Equipment (Theft and Fire)	7,000	0	7,000	0.09%
VI. Nonowned Vehicles (Insures Against Loss and Damages)	9,500	0	9,500	0.12%
VII. Owned Vehicles (Insures Against Loss and Damages)	15,000	0	15,000	0.19%

Figure 5.19: Insurance Coverage *(continued)*

Policy and Description	Minimum Fixed Cost per Year	Estimated Annual Premium Cost (note 5)	Estimate Premium Cost per Total Insurance Risk per All Jobs	Percentage Per Dollar of Payroll
COMPANY INSURED				
1. XCU Coverage (Explosion, Collapse, and Underground Damage to Utilities, Building Foundations, etc.)	$ 1,500	$0.10/$100	$ 18,000	0.23%
2. Custody and Control (Claims for Damage to Equipment Furnished by Others but Handled or Installed by Contractor)	1,200	0.15/$100	27,000	0.34%
3. Builders' Risk (note 4)	0	0.50/$100	90,000	1.13%
a. Loss of Material and Equipment Installed on the Project				
b. Loss of Material and Equipment Furnished by the Contractor That Have Not Been Installed, Resulting from Acts of God, Fire, Theft, Accidents, etc.				
4. Liability (Slander, Defamation of Character, False Arrest, Invasion of Privacy, etc.)	6,000	0	6,000	0.08%
Totals	$110,200	0	$2,223,800	28.00%

Figure 5.19: Insurance Coverage *(continued)*

Notes:

1. Percentage cost of $1 of payroll for fixed cost or minimum dollar amount policies are based on $8,000,000 in annual labor costs.

   For example:

   Construction Equipment Loss

   $6,000 Premium   ÷ $8,000,000 Labor Dollars = 0.0008%/$1 Labor
   % per $1 of Payroll = 0.0008/$1 Labor × 100   = 0.08%

2. Percentage cost of $1 of payroll for estimated premium cost per total annual receipts of $18,000,000.

   For example:

   XCU Coverage
   $18,000,000 Sales × 0.10/$100 Receipts   = $18,000 Premium
   $18,000 Premium   ÷ $8,000,000 Labor Dollars = $0.00225/$1 Labor
   % per $1 of Payroll = 0.00225/$1 Labor × 100   = 0.225%

3. Percentage cost of $1 of payroll for estimated premium cost per total insurance risk per all jobs is based on $18,000,000 annual total sales.

4. Advance premiums that will be returned if not used. To be subtracted from total minimum fixed cost per year to find true fixed cost.

5. Estimated annual premiums are based on $100 per receipts or $1 per labor payroll as shown in Column 2.

To evaluate what this 23.5 percent increase meant to Richard in terms of dollars lost, let's examine Figure 5.21.

We started by looking for a $450,000 loss and instead we discover a *loss of almost $2 million!* This is actually a total loss of almost $2.5 million because Richard forgot to include overhead and profit.

PROFIT GUIDE: DO NOT FORGET OVERHEAD AND PROFIT

The dollar impact of the 23.5 percent increase in terms of total real cost is shown in Figure 5.22. Remember: it is imperative that you find the *total* dollar impact of this increase. Therefore, you must also add overhead and profit allocations.

Therefore, the total dollar impact on Richard as a result of this 23.5 percent increase in real cost resulted in an actual loss of almost $2.5 million (as shown in Figure 5.22).

Figure 5.20: Revised Billing Cost Rate per Man-hour Worked

Revised Man-hour Costs

28.00%	Insurance (from Figure 5.19)
6.7	FICA
1.5	Federal Unemployment
7.0	State Unemployment
43.2 %	

Revised Labor Man-hour Billing Rate

Base Rate $12.00
+ 43.2% 5.19

Fixed Fund
  Contributions

Health and Welfare	$1.98	
Vacation	.15	
Pension	.40	
Apprentice	.04	$ 2.57

Total Revised Billing
  Cost per Man-hour Worked $19.76

Figure 5.21: Dollars Lost: 23.5 Percent Increase in Labor Cost

				23.5% Increase
INTERNAL COST				
Original Contract Labor	$7,764,519	× (0.235)	=	$1,824,662
EXTERNAL COST				
Extra Work Labor	$ 378,012	× (0.235)	=	$ 88,833
Dollars Lost.				$1,913,495

Figure 5.22: Total Dollars Lost: 23.5 Percent Increase in Labor Cost Plus Overhead and Profit Allocations

	23.5% *Increase*
INTERNAL COST	
Original Contract Labor. . . . . $7,764,519 × (0.235) =	$1,824,662
EXTERNAL COST	
Extra Work Labor. . . . . $ 378,012 × (0.235) =	88,833
Total Cost	$1,913,495
Overhead 15%.	287,024
	$2,200,519
Profit 10%	220,052
Total Dollars Lost	$2,420,571

Now that you see how crucial it was for Richard to know his real man-hour cost, let's take a look at the other aspect of Richard's operation that was affecting his positive cash flow problem.

The Impact of Extra Work

You'll remember that Richard's invoices for extras amounted to only 3.5 percent of his total contract value. Remember also that extras normally run between 10 percent to 20 percent of the total contract value due to human error and changing conditions. Let us now calculate how much money is involved if Richard's extras were 10 percent instead of his billing of 3.5 percent, as shown in Figure 5.23.

We were trying to find the reason for Richard's $450,000 "short fall," and we have just found another loss of $1,156,859!

How could he have been losing this kind of money? Simple. Richard was not considering his SID costs. He was billing the owner only for the time the craftsmen spent to perform the extra work, when in reality that extra work was really costing Richard a great deal more.

In previous chapters you learned that schedule changes negatively impact profits. *Float time* and *new time* have a multiplying

Figure 5.23: Extras Billed Versus Extras Anticipated

3.5% Extras Billed	*10% Extras Anticipated*
$17,868,790	$17,868,790
× 3.5%	× 10%
$ 630,020	$ 1,786,879

Difference of
  Extras Billed
  and Extras
  Anticipated . . . . $1,786,879 − $630,020

Total Difference $1,156,859

effect on "when" and "how" work is performed (refer to Figure 1.11). The Sources of Impacted Damages (SIDs) are also caused by extra work. Schedule changes caused by extra work are too often ignored because extra work is often perceived as windfall profits by owner and contractor alike. Nothing could be further from the truth!

PROFIT GUIDE: EXTRA WORK CAN MEAN NO PROFIT

Extra work can injure project profitability tremendously. Schedule changes and ripple effects (already discussed in other chapters) must be included in extra work cost estimates. Not knowing all real costs and not billing for *all* the costs of extra work is a serious common problem.

PROFIT GUIDE: ALL COSTS OF EXTRA WORK MUST BE BILLED

This case has demonstrated how a lack of understanding of all real costs will create serious cash flow problems and profit losses that ultimately diminish owner (stockholders') benefits. And you have seen how correct internal and external company uses of real costs can actually solve these cash flow problems. Next you will learn how to choose the correct source of financing.

USING INTEREST LEVERAGE AND THE CORRECT SOURCE OF MONEY

We have already discussed the importance of profit and cash. Now let's build on our understanding of the tools of money management to exploit further ways to increase stockholders' benefits by using the correct source of financing. Money management increases benefits by providing maximum interest leverage. *Interest leverage* is the securing of funds at a lower rate than invested while producing the highest net return to the owner or common stockholders.

PROFIT GUIDE: BEFORE DECIDING, ASK "WHAT IF...?"

Money management allows you to look at the "bottom line" and know what is happening when it is happening. Most important, money management shows you what can be done internally to increase profit. It allows you to separate each factor that determines preplanned profit and ask *"What if* I do this, then what happens to profit?" The ability to ask "What if...?" *before* suffering a potential loss, rather than asking "What happened?" *after* a loss is critical to successful profit management. Apparently, the "What if...?" question must be another one of those well-guarded secrets, because very few contractors use it.

CASE III: "WHAT IF...?" AND INTEREST LEVERAGE

When consulting with the president of a construction company (whom I'll call "Tom"), I learned that he had just managed to finance a large project that expanded his sales by 80 percent. Tom was one happy gentleman.

He proudly explained that he had initially analyzed two sources of financing: current liabilities and long-term bank financing. "I've always liked current liabilities," he said. "There is no interest charge." Tom preferred to work out long payment terms with his suppliers and "subs," explaining that "It's great when they'll agree to finance me with literally no interest charges just to win the contract." However, Tom explained that his new project was a "special case" because it was labor intensive and wouldn't involve any subs.

Tom negotiated with banks for several months to get the funds he needed to expand sales. The negotiations were quite successful. The bank offered a long-term loan at the current prime interest rate, but Tom managed to do even better. Once he obtained the terms of the bank loan, he turned around and sold preferred stock to his employees (which paid dividends less than what he would have paid the bank on the long-term debt).

Sound reasonable? The bank would certainly ask a higher rate of interest than what they paid their depositors. And the employees (also bank depositors) would be happy with a greater amount of interest than what the bank paid them. Tom realized this and astutely took advantage of the difference between what the employees could obtain as depositors and what the bank wanted to charge him for the long-term loan.

In summary, Tom was happy. The preferred stock cost him less interest than what the bank would have charged. His employees were happy. They were getting more than what they would have been paid by the bank as depositors. And it appeared as though everyone (except maybe the bank) was happy with this arrangement. But were Tom's stockholders happy? Did Tom choose the correct source of financing? Let's see.

The sources of financing Tom considered for the $200,000 he needed were

1. Current liabilities
2. Long-term debt from bank financing at 16 percent interest
3. Preferred stock issued at 14 percent dividend payment

As Tom previously explained, current liabilities were not right for him, leaving him with the following two alternatives:

1. Long-term debt from bank financing at 16 percent interest
2. Preferred stock issued at 14 percent dividend payment

Assume the company will earn the $60,000 expected from this investment. If so, then what is of maximum benefit to the stockholders who own 50,000 shares of common stock?

In order to answer this question, let us begin by calculating the operating results for the two alternative sources of finance available to Tom (shown in Figure 5.24).

According to Figure 5.24, Tom made the wrong decision. He failed to consider *all* of the factors that affect common stockholders'

Figure 5.24: Preferred Stock Versus Bank Long-term Debt

	Preferred Stock	Bank Long-term Debt
Earnings Before Interest and Taxes (EBIT)	$60,000	$60,000
Bank Interest Expense (16% × $200,000)	0	32,000
Net Income Before Taxes	$60,000	$28,000
Deduct Income Tax (40%)	24,000	11,200
Income	$36,000	$16,800
Preferred Stockholders' Dividends (14% × $200,000)	28,000	0
Net Income for Common Stockholders	$ 8,000	$16,800 (a)
Total Common Stock Equity (50,000 Shares × $1/sh)	$50,000	$50,000 (b)
Return on Common Stockholders' Equity (a/b)	16%	33.6%

benefits. By examining Figure 5.24, you can see that Tom forgot about taxes! Net income for the common stockholders [Item (a)] became 110 percent less than what it could have been because the preferred dividends are *not* tax deductible. However, the interest on a long-term loan *is* tax deductible. Things don't always work out as they first appear. Tom assumed incorrectly that by getting the *lowest* interest rate, he was also getting the maximum bottom-line benefit. The effect of taxes decreased net income for common stockholders from $16,800 to $8,000. By fighting only for the lowest interest rate, Tom succeeded in robbing his stockholders of an $8,800 profit!

The Twofold Concept of Interest Leverage

The concept behind interest leverage is twofold: (1) to secure funds at a fixed rate of interest and invest them at a rate of return greater than the fixed rate paid for them (which produces positive leverage for the stockholders) and (2) to maximize interest leverage for the highest possible return on common stockholders' equity by identifying all sources of financing and choosing the correct source.

In other words, interest leverage has two parts: to produce positive leverage for the stockholders and to maximize that leverage for the highest possible return on common stockholders' equity.

Part one—to produce positive leverage—concerns itself with "how to use money," which will be expanded on in the next case with Return on Investment (ROI) analysis. Tom knew how to take advantage of positive leverage. As shown in Figure 5.24, both financing alternatives generated a positive return for the common stockholders.

PROFIT GUIDE: CHOOSE THE CORRECT SOURCE OF FINANCE

Tom knew how to increase profit with interest leverage. He realized that he was responsible for how he used the company's assets once they were obtained. However, Tom did not understand how to pick the correct finance source (which is part two of the concept of interest leverage). Tom's weak analysis cost his stockholders a 110 percent profit.

Had Tom chosen the long-term bank loan instead, he would have realized a 33.6 percent return on the $50,000 invested by the common stockholders. By selling preferred stock as his source of financing, he realized only a 16% return on his investment for the common stockholders.

In summary, the correct source of financing is determined by the bottom line. The full effect of each available source of financing must be analyzed by first evaluating the impact of all factors on the bottom line and then the highest net return to the common stockholders.

PROFIT GUIDE: KNOW YOUR NET RETURN

Why You Must Consider All the Factors

As this case has illustrated, taxes are a factor that cannot be ignored. This case proved that taxes were tantamount to making the best decision. Depending on the source of financing being considered, other factors must also be analyzed.

PROFIT GUIDE: CONSIDER ALL FACTORS

It is imperative that you consider all factors. For example, if bonds are an available source, the total cost must be analyzed. This includes the internal and external cost. Internally, the manpower cost of preparing a bond issue can be burdensome, as well as the external legal fees involved.

HOW TO USE MONEY TO ACHIEVE MAXIMUM RETURN ON INVESTMENT

We have discussed and demonstrated the importance of time and cash as well as the importance of profit and cash. Now let's build on this knowledge with the money management tools to exploit the methods of using your money to increase your stockholders' benefits. A company exists solely for the benefit of the common stockholders. It is not a retirement home or gambling casino for the manager.

Money management increases the stockholders' benefits by providing maximum Return on Investment (ROI) with minimum risk to the common stockholder. As we learned from the previous case of interest leverage, the ability to ask "What if...?" *before* suffering a loss instead of asking "What happened?" *after* a loss is critical to successful profit management.

CASE IV: "WHAT IF...?" AND ROI

Contractors, like many businessmen, seem to fall in love with "things." For some reason they convince themselves that a fancy office with expensive drapes, carpeting, and computers—or the 80-ton crane sitting out in the yard—somehow guarantees success. In the area of fancy offices, contractors seem to rival only bank presidents. Seeing who can have the neatest "things" seems to be part of the glory of being a contractor.

Unfortunately, this propensity has become the demise for many contractors. Remember not so long ago when you could not beg, borrow, or steal a job? You can bet that the boys with those big "yards" were the first to fall.

This is precisely what happened to a client (whom I'll call "Cliff") I consulted for. I remember walking into Cliff's equipment yard, seeing almost everything with a "For Sale" sign posted on it. Unfortunately, when you need to sell your equipment, there won't be any buyers because, most likely, construction is down across the board. Now, I'll be the first to admit that a contractor needs equipment, but how much equipment does one really need?

Cliff was convinced that he needed every piece of equipment sitting in that yard to stay in business. I asked him, "If you need all that equipment so badly, why are you selling it?" Cliff looked at me and in a matter-of-fact tone answered, "I have to...the payments are putting me out of business."

A true paradox. Cliff "needs" all this equipment to stay in business, but the equipment is putting him *out* of business. How did he get into this mess? And, more important, how could he have *avoided* this mess?

PROFIT GUIDE: YOU MUST KNOW AND USE ROI

How to Maintain and Control ROI

One sure method of avoiding such a situation is to know and use the secret of Return on Investment (ROI). In fact, one of the major attractions of even being in construction is the large potential ROI itself. The secret is knowing how to maintain and control that large ROI with minimum risk to the common stockholder.

PROFIT GUIDE: KNOW AND CONTROL ROI

First you must gain a working understanding of the general ROI formula shown in Figure 5.25.

Net income, as well as owner's equity, consists of many separate items. As illustrated in Case III, net income from the correct source of financing is only a part of the company's total net income. In the case of owner's equity, the equipment used to perform contracts is not only a "component" of owner's equity, but often a very significant portion.

Figure 5.25: General ROI Formula

$$ROI = \frac{Total\ Net\ Income}{Total\ Owner's\ Equity}$$

The ability to use ROI effectively to unlock the secrets of the bottom line depends on the ability to ask specific "What if...?" questions. This determines how your profit is made. To do this you must make a further clarification of the ROI formula (illustrated in Figure 5.26).

By separating the ROI formula into its individual component parts of average profit and turnover, you know how profit is made and you are able to evaluate critical items that directly affect your profit. These critical items are (1) the performance of cost and expense control by focusing on average profit, (2) the performance of owner's equity invested in operating assets by focusing on turnover, and (3) the performance of sales by focusing on both average profit and turnover.

Three "What If..." Examples to Consider

The following three examples demonstrate specifically "What if...": (1) sales are increased? (2) cost and expenses are reduced? and (3) assets such as equipment are reduced?

To complete our understanding of the dynamics of ROI, the following examples are compared with Cliff's "good year" financial performance before sales dropped off (shown in Figure 5.27).

Example 1: "What if" sales volume is increased? In Figure 5.27 you saw that Cliff was accomplishing sales of $5,000,000 a year at a 10 percent profit. Now consider a 2 percent sales increase to $5,100,000 in sales with the same 10 percent profit return.

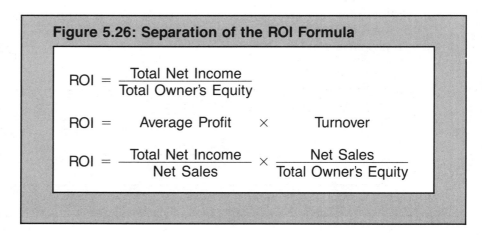

Figure 5.26: Separation of the ROI Formula

$$ROI = \frac{\text{Total Net Income}}{\text{Total Owner's Equity}}$$

$$ROI = \text{Average Profit} \times \text{Turnover}$$

$$ROI = \frac{\text{Total Net Income}}{\text{Net Sales}} \times \frac{\text{Net Sales}}{\text{Total Owner's Equity}}$$

Figure 5.27: Cliff's "Good Year" Financial Performance

```
Sales............................. $5,000,000 (a)
Less: Cost and Expenses..........   4,500,000
Less: Taxes .....................        0
Net Income ...................... $   500,000 (b)
Owner's Equity (Invested in
    Operating Assets of Equipment) . . . $1,000,000 (c)
Profit (b/a) ........................      10%
ROI (b/c) ........................        50%
```

Note: Taxes are shown as zero to simplify calculations.

Figure 5.28: Example 1: Increased Sales Volume

$$ROI = \frac{\text{Total Net Income}}{\text{Total Owner's Equity}}$$

$$ROI = \text{Average Profit} \quad \times \quad \text{Turnover}$$

$$ROI = \frac{\text{Total Net Income}}{\text{Net Sales}} \times \frac{\text{Net Sales}}{\text{Total Owner's Equity}}$$

$$ROI = \frac{\$\ 510,000}{\$5,100,000} \times \frac{\$5,100,000}{\$1,000,000}$$

$$ROI = \quad 10\% \quad \times \quad 5.1$$

$$ROI = \quad 51\%$$

Turnover has increased from 5 to 5.1 and ROI has increased from 50 percent (in Figure 5.27) to 51 percent, which is a total increase of 1 percent in stockholders' (owner's) benefits.

In addition, Example 1 also illustrates that a 10 percent average profit was being made 5.1 times a year. In other words, the turnover (or use of owner's equity) was 5.1 times a year. Furthermore, an average profit of 10 percent was realized on each turnover.

Example 2: "What if" you reduce costs and expenses by 2 percent? This will increase operating income by $90,000 (which is $500,000 net operating income + 2 percent of the $4,500,000 original cost and expenses).

Turnover has stayed the same and average profit has increased 1.8 percent, with an increase in ROI from 50 percent to 59 percent. This is a total 9 percent increase in stockholders' benefits.

Example 3: "What if" you reduce the original $1,000,000 total owner's equity invested in operating assets by 2 percent to $980,000?

Figure 5.29: Example 2: Reduced Costs and Expenses

$$ROI = \frac{\text{Total Net Income}}{\text{Total Owner's Equity}}$$

$$ROI = \quad \text{Average Profit} \quad \times \quad \text{Turnover}$$

$$ROI = \frac{\text{Total Net Income}}{\text{Net Sales}} \times \frac{\text{Net Sales}}{\text{Total Owner's Equity}}$$

$$ROI = \frac{\$\ 590,000}{\$5,000,000} \times \frac{\$5,000,000}{\$1,000,000}$$

$$ROI = \quad 11.8\% \quad \times \quad 5$$

$$ROI = \quad 59\%$$

Figure 5.30: Example 3: Reduced Operating Assets of Equipment

$$\text{ROI} = \frac{\text{Total Net Income}}{\text{Total Owner's Equity}}$$

$$\text{ROI} = \text{Average Profit} \times \text{Turnover}$$

$$\text{ROI} = \frac{\text{Total Net Income}}{\text{Net Sales}} \times \frac{\text{Net Sales}}{\text{Total Owner's Equity}}$$

$$\text{ROI} = \frac{\$\ 500,000}{\$5,000,000} \times \frac{\$5,000,000}{\$\ 980,000}$$

$$\text{ROI} = 10\% \times 5.1$$

$$\text{ROI} = 51\%$$

Turnover has increased from 5 to 5.1 and ROI has increased from 50 percent (in Figure 5.27) to 51 percent, resulting in a total 1 percent increase in stockholders' benefits.

Don't miss the fact that in Example 3 there is a $20,000 reduction in total owner's equity. This means that $20,000 have been "set free" to be returned to the stockholders. Very soon you will see that this fact is the key to evaluating Cliff's performance. But first, let's summarize the powerful profit secrets the examples have given us so far.

When you compare the effect of a 2 percent sales increase (in Example 1) with what happens with a 2 percent reduction in cost and expense (in Example 2), you are comparing a 51 percent ROI (in Example 1) with a ROI increased to 59 percent (in Example 2).

In other words, cost and expense generates the greatest increase in ROI. Fortunately for us, cost and expense are items over which we have maximum control. A 2 percent cost and expense reduction has generated a 9 percent ROI increase relevant to the original 50 percent ROI (in Figure 5.27).

In addition, when you compare increasing sales and reducing cost and expense results with reducing owner's equity, you also realize an increase in ROI plus a reduction in stockholders' investment. Both a cost and expense reduction and a reduction in owner's equity invested in operating assets fall under your direct control. One increases average profit and the other increases turnover. Together, both give you profitability increases and stockholders' benefits.

PROFIT GUIDE: CONTROL MEANS PROFITS

Now we are prepared to evaluate the major aspect of Cliff's problem. How much equipment should Cliff own?

To answer this question, let's compare Cliff's performance with the performance of another manager (whom I'll call "Mark"). The operating results of Cliff's "good year" and Mark's performance are compared in Figure 5.31.

Cliff has a bottom line of $500,000, while Mark has only $250,000. This bottom-line mania is precisely the thing that has led to Cliff's problems.

In order to discover which manager's performance is in the best interest of his common stockholders relevant to his use of

---

Figure 5.31: Financial Performance of Cliff Versus Mark

	Cliff	*Mark*
Sales	$5,000,000	$3,000,000 (a)
Net Income	500,000	250,000 (b)
Owner's Equity (Invested in Operating Assets of Equipment)	1,000,000	500,000 (c)
ROI (b/c)	50%	50%

equipment, we must further simplify the ROI formula. In Figure 5.32, the ROI formula has been simplified to ROI of *equipment*.

As you will recall from Figure 5.24 (interest leverage) only the profit from the interest leverage transaction was used to determine common stockholders' benefit derived from interest leverage. Now let's use only the profit and owner's equity in equipment to determine stockholders' benefits.

The bottom line is important, but you must not lose sight of the most important question: Whose benefit is the manager really working for? Let's assume he is working *only* for the good of the common stockholders.

Stockholders can do many things with money not tied up in assets. In Cliff's case, this amounts to a significant $500,000 more than Mark. The other consideration is, how sure are we that sales will stay at the $5,000,000 level? What will be done with the equipment if sales drop? In other words, what is the risk to the common stockholders?

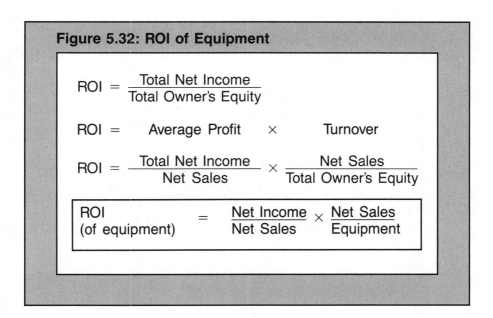

Figure 5.32: ROI of Equipment

$$ROI = \frac{\text{Total Net Income}}{\text{Total Owner's Equity}}$$

$$ROI = \text{Average Profit} \times \text{Turnover}$$

$$ROI = \frac{\text{Total Net Income}}{\text{Net Sales}} \times \frac{\text{Net Sales}}{\text{Total Owner's Equity}}$$

$$\begin{array}{l}ROI \\ \text{(of equipment)}\end{array} = \frac{\text{Net Income}}{\text{Net Sales}} \times \frac{\text{Net Sales}}{\text{Equipment}}$$

How to Evaluate the Risk to Company Owners

To evaluate which manager is the best under these conditions, let's evaluate Cliff and Mark using the ROI illustrated in Figure 5.33.

Figure 5.33: ROI Evaluation of Cliff Versus Mark

$$\text{ROI} = \frac{\text{Total Net Income}}{\text{Total Owner's Equity}}$$

$$\text{ROI} = \text{Average Profit} \times \text{Turnover}$$

$$\text{ROI} = \frac{\text{Total Net Income}}{\text{Net Sales}} \times \frac{\text{Net Sales}}{\text{Total Owner's Equity}}$$

$$\text{ROI (of equipment)} = \frac{\text{Net Income}}{\text{Sales}} \times \frac{\text{Sales}}{\text{Equipment}}$$

Cliff

$$\text{ROI} = \frac{\$\ 500,000}{\$5,000,000} \times \frac{\$5,000,000}{\$1,000,000}$$

$$\text{ROI} = 10\% \times 5$$

$$\text{ROI} = 50\%$$

Mark

$$\text{ROI} = \frac{\$\ 250,000}{\$3,000,000} \times \frac{\$3,000,000}{\$\ 500,000}$$

$$\text{ROI} = 8.3\% \times 6$$

$$\text{ROI} = 50\%$$

Mark has sacrificed 1.7 percent (10 percent − 8.3 percent) of average profit to reduce his assets by 50 percent. Sure, Cliff has a bigger bottom line, but what is the total benefit to his stockholders? The question boils down to an evaluation of risk. How long will sales continue at the present level or increase to a new level? Let us assume that Cliff's and Mark's sales will continue for only one year. Which one will produce the greatest benefit for the common stockholders? Under this condition, total stockholder benefit is shown in Figure 5.34.

Which manager is doing the best job for his stockholders? If you determine that sales will stay at the present level for only one year, then the risk to Mark's common stockholders is half the risk of Cliff's. In addition, the total amount of money in Mark's common stockholders' pockets is one and a half times *greater* than Cliff's.

The graph and table in Figures 5.35 and 5.36 demonstrate Cliff's and Mark's performances for your decision.

The Stockholders' Benefits Graph clarifies Cliff's and Mark's performances as managers. If the expected business cycle is less than two years (as you learned can happen in Chapter 4), then Mark is certainly the best manager.

In Cliff's case, his business cycle was less than two years. Once he learned the dynamics of ROI, he jumped on the road to being a success.

Figure 5.34: Common Stockholders' Benefits

	Cliff's Stockholders	Mark's Stockholders
Profit	$500,000	$250,000
Plus: Cash from Asset Reduction	0	500,000
Total Stockholder Benefit	$500,000	$750,000

Figure 5.35: Stockholders' Benefit Graph

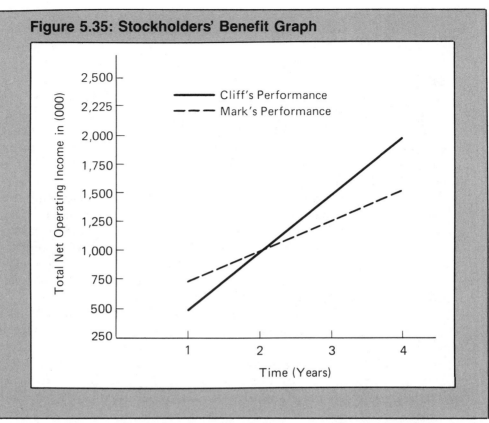

Figure 5.36: Yearly Table: Total Stockholders' Benefits

Cliff's Performance

Year 1	Year 2	Year 3	Year 4
$500,000 Profit	$500,000 (Yr.1)	$1,000,000 (Yr.2)	$1,500,000 (Yr.1–3)
	500,000 (Yr.2)	500,000 (Yr.3)	500,000 (Yr.4)
	$1,000,000	$1,500,000	$2,000,000

Mark's Performance

Year 1	Year 2	Year 3	Year 4
$250,000 Profit	$ 750,000 (Yr.1)	$1,000,000 (Yr.2)	$1,250,000 (Yr.1–3)
$500,000 Savings	250,000 (Yr.2)	250,000 (Yr.3)	250,000 (Yr.4)
$750,000	$1,000,000	$1,250,000	$1,500,000

Note: Time value of money is not considered on the amount of dollars Mark's common stockholders could have earned on their initial $500,000 in savings (shown in Figure 5.34).

SUMMARY

Effective money management is the ability to maximize all money received for growth and profit for the benefit of the stockholders (owners). The importance of money has been considered by realizing that money is the "fuel" that keeps the company running.

To ensure that the company as a "profit machine" continues to have the fuel to operate, critical questions concerning money must be answered. How much money is needed? When will money be needed? Where will the money come from? And how will the money be used?

You have discovered the tools of balance sheets, income statements, budgets, and cash flow projections and how they are used to answer these vital questions. Variation, ratio, and trend analysis provide the necessary information in an easy-to-understand format to answer the critical questions concerning money. You have also discovered, by the effective use of these tools, how positive cash flow, interest leverage, and ROI benefits are realized for the benefit of the common stockholders.

Finally, applications and insights into how these tools can be effectively used to maximize common stockholders' benefits at minimum risk have been demonstrated in case studies of positive cash flow, interest leverage, and ROI.

Again, as in the preceding chapters, you have seen the need for a strong information and control system and the need for "action management of exceptions" for preplanned profit.

Now that you know the secrets of why contractors loss money (Chapter 1), how to identify risk (Chapter 2), how to monetarily quantify risk (Chapter 3), and how to win contracts and maximize their profit (Chapters 4 and 5), you can learn how to collect.

The next chapter, on collection management, will uncover the secrets of how to collect your profits and how to win the next big contract from the one you are now working on.

CHAPTER 6

How to Collect All Your Profits Using the Collection Management System

HOW THE COLLECTION MANAGEMENT SYSTEM WORKS

The preceding chapters discussed the first three elements of profit management: risk management, bid management, and money management. You have also learned how to prepare your invoice. With this understanding, you are now ready to collect your profits. Despite all that you've learned thus far, you are not successful until you hear the ring of the cash register.

What do you need to know to collect big profits? *Collection management.* Collection management is the fourth and final element of the profit management system. Collection management will determine your method of collection, the conditions of collection, and the optimum method of payment for you and your client.

The collection management system requires goals and objectives compatible with the project schedule or business plan. Remember: the project schedule is simply the schedule of events to complete a single project, while the business plan is the overall organizational strategy consisting of the basic goals and objectives of the organization, the major programs of actions, and the allocation of resources needed to achieve these goals. In order to make the necessary decisions that will determine the method of collection, the conditions of collection, and the optimum method of payment, it is imperative that your goals and objectives be clearly defined.

For example, if your intentions are to perform one contract and then retire to Florida, your goals and objectives are going to be drastically different from what they would be if you are building a company to eventually become a market leader. If your case is the latter, your long-range plans could be to offer a full service of installation, product, and engineering.

Your goals and objectives can vary significantly even if you are "Florida bound." You may want all your money immediately, or you may want your payments spread out over a long period of time. The point is, each set of goals and objectives will determine different methods of collection and payment. To maximize your profit, your goals and objectives must be clearly defined.

PROFIT GUIDE: DEFINE YOUR GOALS AND OBJECTIVES

Once you have clearly defined your goals and objectives, you can proceed to use the collection management system. The first step requires that you "fit" the action of the collection system (for both the project and company) into the goals and objectives that have been clearly defined. This is not a particularly easy task, as you will see in the following pages. But don't despair—you will master the secrets of collection management just as you have the others.

Depending on your goals and objectives, the results from company and project collection strategies can be drastically different. Instead of attempting to presuppose what your goals and objectives may be, it will be a greater help to you to learn how to build your own collection management system; then, as your goals and objectives change during your successful business career, you will be able to develop and tailor your collection management system to meet your individual needs.

HOW COLLECTION MANAGEMENT RELATES TO THE PROFIT EQUATION

It is important to understand the relationship of collection management to the profit equation. The primary objective of the *company* collection management system is to maximize break-even company payment and profit payment.

The function of the *project* collection management system, on the other hand, is to maximize break-even project payment, change order payment, and contract payment.

In other words, the primary function of collection management is to collect each factor from the profit equation. As noted in the beginning of Chapter 1, success is based on the following profit equation:

$$\boxed{\text{PROFIT} = \text{FULL PAYMENT}}$$

Let's look at Figure 6.1, which is a duplication of Figure 1.6 in Chapter 1.

Since the primary goal of the collection management system is to maximize the profit equation, company and project objectives that are compatible to realize this goal must be found. Therefore, each part of collection management must be developed into one cohesive system. This means developing the method of collection, the conditions of collection, and the method of payment *before* initiating any collection action.

Figure 6.1: Project and Company Profit Equation

THE PROJECT PROFIT EQUATION

PROFIT = FULL PAYMENT

PROFIT = (BREAK-EVEN PROJECT PAYMENT)

+

(CHANGE ORDER PAYMENT)

+

(CONTRACT PAYMENT)

THE COMPANY PROFIT EQUATION

PROFIT = FULL PAYMENT

PROFIT = (BREAK-EVEN COMPANY PAYMENT)

+

(PROFIT PAYMENT)

FIVE METHODS OF COLLECTION FOR PROJECT PAYMENT

There are five methods commonly used for the collection of project payment: negotiation, mediation, arbitration, litigation, or capitulation. *Negotiation* is the most effective method.

Negotiation

Negotiation provides you with the opportunity to reach an agreement that is of low cost to you and of high benefit to the owner, and vice versa. Negotiation also provides you with maximum control over your evidenciary information. You show only what you feel the other party needs to know. This keeps all your options open. Once you've shown something, you are required to make it available to the other party should you litigate.

Negotiation is most effective because it allows you to establish and to maintain strong business relations. With negotiation, you remain in control of the situation, while only the people directly interested are involved.

In order to establish and maintain strong business relations it is imperative to concentrate everyone's effort, thoughts and discussions on the causes and results of problems and only on the people to the extent of documented actions. Of course this is much easier said than done. Often the people negotiating are the people that were involved in the causes that led everyone to the negotiating table. Therefore, a negotiating team including members that have not been involved in the causes is often necessary.

Five Items of Successful Negotiation

Your negotiating team will help you focus on the critical elements of negotiation, which are (1) know your strengths and weaknesses, (2) factually state your position with verified documentation, (3) clearly understand the opposition's objections to your position, (4) overcome the opposition's objections with brilliant reasoning, and (5) have the patience and fortitude to compromise (let the other person also win).

Let's apply this to a situation in which the owner has caused delays in the timely and productive execution of the contract and refuses to pay the delayed completion damages presented by the contractor because of Estoppeled Schedule Deviations (an expressed

contract document provision that anticipated and provided for
scheduled deviations and precluded the contractor's right of recovery for all contract delays).

Unless the negotiating contractor can convince the owner that
he is legally entitled to recover these impacted damages, both the
owner and the contractor are headed for court or the contractor is
going to wind up with serious losses.

Here is where an experienced negotiating team is worth their
weight in gold. Often these expressed contract provisions that
preclude the contractor's right of recovery are perceived by the
contractor as the final word. In other words, there is no legal way to
recover damages in this situation. This perception can be wrong!
By focusing the discussions on the "interference" that caused the
delays, the negotiating team will have found a brilliant reason—and
a powerful and compelling legal reason—to be used and understood by everyone to reach an equitable agreement. After all, would
anyone take a contract that said "I can and will do anything I can to
make sure you lose money"? Of course not, this is diametrically
opposed to the legal doctrine of good faith, but that is exactly the
connotation of the owner's interference. By negotiating the cause
and not the results, the contractor's right of recovery is established
and the team can move on to settlement.

Mediation

Mediation is the next best choice after negotiation. In fact, some
negotiators use mediation as a negotiating tool. Mediation is a
process in which all parties submit their dispute to an impartial
third person, the mediator. The mediator then prepares a confidential set of findings for each party, pointing out each party's weak
points. The mediator also includes a recommendation for dollar
settlement on an issue-by-issue basis. Such things as the realistic
cost in time and money of arbitration or litigation should also be
pointed out in the mediator's report. Essentially, the idea behind
mediation is to establish what the probable results of an arbitration
would be and to explain why. The primary benefits of mediation are
that it narrows complex issues and limits the amount of time and
resources that the company must divert toward legal matters.

There is an increasing amount of interest in mediation. Within
a ten-month span (from 1984 to 1985), the American Arbitration
Association administered more than 70 commercial mediations,

with claims ranging from $2,000 to $8.3 million.[1] But these figures are only a portion of the disputes in the construction industry. One specialty contractors' association recently completed a survey among only 6,000 contractors that indicated the existence of recovery claims in excess of $200 million in just one year.[2] This volume (which was only 1 percent of all contractors nationwide), when projected out over the entire construction industry, indicates an enormous amount of litigation each year.

The growing popularity of mediation is further indicated by the appearance of mediation clauses in more and more contract documents. Such contract document clauses may take the form of permitting the parties only to mediate, or they may be a combination of mediation and arbitration, commonly referred to as a "med/arb" clause. One large contracting source, the Metropolitan Atlanta Rapid Transit Authority (MARTA), offers mediation as an option for settling disputes in its initial letter to all new contractors.

Despite its popularity, there are some major disadvantages to mediation. To mediate, you must circulate information that may have to be produced later if the dispute is litigated. In addition, and most important, mediation forces a loss of control in the negotiating process via the bringing in of a disinterested third party. Even though I have used mediation to success, I have never been able to find a truly "disinterested" third party. A mediator who starts out as impartial does not always stay that way for very long. Unless the mediator can find major weaknesses in either party's position, matters tend to go right back to where they were before, but with a "tainted" mediator.

Arbitration and Litigation

Arbitration and *litigation* are the least desirable methods of collection. Arbitration is extremely expensive and seldom provides an opportunity for a "second chance" (which is provided by litigation) in the form of an appeal. Arbitration is a process whereby two or more people settle a dispute. The arbitrators are mutually agreed upon by both parties to the dispute. Furthermore, the proceedings

---

[1]George Friedman, "Mediation: An Alternative to Litigation?" in *Specifying Engineer*, June 1985.
[2]National Electrical Contractor's Association, *Guide to Electrical Contractors' Claims Management*, Volume III (Washington, D.C.: NECA, 1980).

are not restricted by "courtroom" rules. Arbitration (as well as litigation) possesses the "hidden cost" of customer ill will.

It is important to consider "hidden costs" that arise from any form of arbitration or litigation. *Where* the claim is to be adjudicated can be a hidden cost if the project is not in the contractor's home town. In a court of law, there are court costs as well as attorney's fees. With arbitration, you have all these costs *plus* the payment of a fee based on the amount in dispute. A $12 million claim may require a $20,000 filing fee.

Furthermore, court cases and arbitration can be an emotional experience, dragging out the entire affair. Why suffer when negotiation is the answer? A good negotiating team will get the job done fast and build customer good will. That means receiving full payment and possibly your next big contract.

In the case of impacted damages, a lawyer and a claims consultant will save you valuable time in the preparation and negotiation of your claim. The more time they save you and the quicker the settlement is made, the smaller your costs.

Capitulation

As for *capitulation,* our final category, need I say anything? Avoid it. You certainly don't want to forego collecting profits that are rightfully due to you.

> THE NEGOTIATION
>
> All too often negotiators end up like the proverbial sisters who argued over an orange. When they finally agreed to divide the orange in half, the first sister ate her half and threw away the peel, while the other threw away the fruit and used the peel from her half to bake a pie.[3]

Remember, the purpose of negotiation is for all parties involved to arrive at a fair and equitable agreement. This will require all parties to work together to examine the problem of how to satisfy their collective interests. Before any realistic settlement can be reached, entitlement and quantum must exist.

---

[3]From GETTING TO YES by Roger Fisher and Wiliam Ury. Copyright © 1981 by Roger Fisher and William Ury. Reprinted by permission of Houghton Mifflin Company.

THE IMPORTANCE OF PROVING ENTITLEMENT AND QUANTUM

As you learned in Chapter 3, *Entitlement* is your right to something, and *quantum* is "how much money." Obviously, you are not going to get far talking quantum until everyone has agreed to your entitlement.

The importance of a well-prepared invoice cannot be overstressed. You must first identify and invoice your profit from a closed-loop information and control system among the field, office, and owner. This will provide on-time payment of the original contract payment and all authorized change orders. But, most important, it provides substantiated billing and entitlement for those items that affect project break-even.

A classic example of entitlement with no proof of quantum is the newspaper story that reports a case in which someone has won but the court awarded the victim only $10 in damages.

FOUR CONDITIONS OF COLLECTION NECESSARY TO ACHIEVE BREAK-EVEN

Time and again I have seen negotiators "leave money on the table" or even fail to reach an agreement because they did not realize what conditions had to exist before an agreement could be made. The collection of break-even payment requires four fundamental conditions to be met after you have billed the owner:

1. THE OWNER MUST HAVE REASON TO PAY YOUR INVOICE EARLY.[4]
2. THE OWNER MUST BELIEVE YOU ARE ENTITLED TO THE PAYMENT OF YOUR INVOICE.
3. THE OWNER MUST KNOW YOUR INVOICE IS CORRECT.
4. THE OWNER MUST HAVE THE MONEY AVAILABLE TO PAY YOUR INVOICE.

Let's take a closer look at these conditions.

Condition Number One: Reasons to Pay Early

Be flexible in your negotiations but always be aware that your recovery rights include civil court or arbitration. Use them only

[4]Gerard I. Nierenberg, *The Art of Negotiating* (New York: Hawthorn Books, Inc., 1968).

when necessary. Too many contractors tend to stick their heads in the sand when they are negotiating. Successful negotiating means having an open mind, not an empty one. Make sure that you provide the owner with reasons to pay early. Any good lawyer will tell you that over 90 percent of all lawsuits are settled on the courthouse steps. Delaying decisions to invoke your rights of recovery will only delay the settlement of your claim. It is also the major cause of claims dragging on for two or three years when they should have been settled in 30 days.

Once billing has been made, it is imperative to take every step available to protect your rights of recovery. It is reasonable to expect that billings of large, complex amounts may take extended periods of time to be fully understood, processed, and financed. For this reason, a contractor should *never* sign away his lien rights until he has received full payment. This is the reason lien rights exist. As a matter of fact, lien rights are so unique that they are normally available to the construction industry exclusively.

Another right of recovery includes beneficial occupancy of the owner. Most contracts do not provide for the owner's beneficial occupancy *until* the project is complete and acceptable to the owner. This means that full payment be made as well as the "punch list" being completed and acceptance received. Realize immediately that these are powerful rights of recovery that should be exercised. Exercise your lien rights before expiration if you have not been paid. This will provide the owner with a reason to pay early. The more reasons you can provide for the owner to pay early, the better.

How to Deal with Late Payment: A Case Example

The right to deny the owner beneficial occupancy is often critical. It can be a major motivating force that can swiftly bring all negotiations to a successful conclusion. I remember when I had just completed a large incinerator plant for a major city and my superintendent could not receive acceptance, no matter how hard he tried to please the owner. As soon as he finished each punch list, he was given a new and longer one. Not only was this annoying (and expensive) to continue working on a project that was already completed, but the entire retainage was being held up. This cost big bucks. Interestingly enough, the city was at the same time operating the plant quite successfully. By keeping my superintendent and men on the site, it seemed as though the city had found itself a free maintenance staff.

After careful review of the contract specifications, I called a meeting and my superintendent shut down the plant, much to the consternation of the city. The purpose of this meeting with all the involved parties was (1) to determine what was left to be done in order to receive acceptance, (2) to agree on a schedule of when this work would be done, and (3) to schedule inspection and the owner's acceptance of the plant *before* the owner's beneficial occupancy. After all, if the facility is not acceptable, then it should not yet be operational, which means that the *contractor* is still the effective "owner" of the plant.

Needless to say, the city's operating and engineering people were not wearing smiles. But after they realized that we were going to put whatever they wanted on the punch list (as long as it was legitimate) and immediately schedule the work to be done, they agreed that this was the best approach. I should add that a large ceremony followed their acceptance of the plant, with all the city officials telling the public what a fine plant they now had and how happy they were with the contractors. And they were sincere! In fact, we did a great deal of maintenance work in that very same plant under a *separate* contract.

Condition Number Two: Proof of Entitlement

The owner must believe that you are entitled to the payment you have invoiced. This means that the owner must know of your entitlement as soon as possible. You should inform him as your claims arise. Liken this to your son or daughter asking, "Can I use the car tonight?" or "Can I use the car next Saturday?" Which would you prefer? People need time to schedule changes into their planning. The owner must know of the claim, know of the causes, and know how you are keeping track of the costs. The earlier you do this, the less time it will take to receive payment after you have submitted your invoice. The sooner you inform the owner, the stronger your credibility as a professional will be when your invoice is reviewed.

Condition Number Three: The Invoice Must Be Correct

Your invoice must be processed by the owner to make sure it is correct, which means you should be available to answer all of his questions, providing him with whatever additional back-up material he needs to substantiate your invoice (such as union wage rates and equipment rental rates). Remember, these things may be familiar to you, but they may be completely foreign to the owner. In fact, he'll most likely be shocked when he finds out how much you pay for labor and equipment rental. I once flew to California on the "red-eye express" to present a recovery claim report to a client and then spent the next seven days on the coast answering questions and supplying various supporting data that he requested. I remember how surprised he was by the price of an 80-ton crane. Finally, at the end of the seventh day, full payment was made and I was on the plane home with check in hand.

Condition Number Four: The Owner Must Have the Money

The fact that the owner may not have the money available to pay the invoice is often overlooked by many contractors. Finding out if the owner has the money to pay is generally not a difficult task. What's the easiest way to find out? Ask.

After you have given the owner sufficient time to review your invoice and have provided him with whatever substantiation he has requested and you still do not receive payment, *ask* if he has the funds available to pay. Just keep this in mind: If you keep your attention and effort (and even your hostilities) focused on the *claim* and not on the *people* involved, you will often enlist the aid of all concerned to solve the problem. If you want to get anywhere, the owner must perceive you to be responsive to his problems. Psychologists refer to this as cognitive dissidence. It is a powerful tool for settlements. The inability of the owner to pay is just a fact of life. If you find this to be the problem, you have just become a banker as well as a builder and an insurance company. You are in a strong position to work out a mutually beneficial financing arrangement.

Remember, it is the contractor who normally provides the bond (not the owner), so choose your clients as carefully as they choose you.

METHODS OF PAYMENT TO CHOOSE FROM

Payment can be made in various ways. Therefore, you have to know how you want to be paid. In some instances, it may be to the contractor's advantage to defer payment. For example, a contractor may reduce his invoice in order to win a lucrative maintenance contract. A subcontractor may reduce his billing to receive another contract that is similar to the recently completed project with the same contractor. This not only ensures more work, but it will also allow the "sub" to capitalize on what he and his men have just learned on the project recently completed.

This is often an attractive alternative for many subcontractors with only technical management expertise. These subs often do 80 percent of their work for only one or two general contractors. If this is your present situation, then you have a serious problem. You're making yourself vulnerable to the fortunes of your general contractors. One thing is certain, you need all your profit, which in this case means increasing your marketing efforts in order to broaden your customer base, *fast!* Otherwise, you will never experience any real growth.

Also remember, many of the items that affect *your* project break-even also affect *other* contractors' break-even. It is to your advantage to keep track of this and to join with other contractors when collecting your invoice. In Chapter 3 you saw the case example of an actual invoice and documentation that was originally prepared to accompany a general contractor's claim to the owner. Since the general contractor later decided it was to his advantage to settle the claim and then negotiate with the owner separately, it made the collection of the claim all that much faster, easier, and more profitable.

In general, the owner should do his best to acknowledge each situation as it arises and to settle each claim as it arises. Sticking your head in the sand and hoping your problem will go away will only exacerbate the situation and work to the advantage of the contractor.

The contractor should do his best to delay bringing a claim to a conclusion until it has passed from everyone's mind. It is easier to argue the effects of not having access to the first floor when you are working on the tenth. Timing and presentation are critical. The longer the owner waits before settling a claim, the more money the contractor will collect. However, the more a contractor bills, the harder it is to collect.

Lawyer and claim consultants are valuable investments. The earlier they are involved, the sooner proper documentation systems are put into place, responsibility agreed upon, and realistic payments made.

In the settlement of a claim, the construction company should seriously evaluate its business plan relevant to the profit equation. If the possibility exists (which it often does) of obtaining another contract (during negotiations) that will generate profit by being properly scheduled, it should be seriously considered. This will often allow the contractor to "trade a straw hat for an overcoat," so to speak. In other words, it is possible for the contractor to take a contract at 10 percent less than his competition and still make a profit (remember proper break-even scheduling?). Using this knowledge in negotiations of a claim is a sure-fire way of getting the next big contract.

PROFIT GUIDE: YOU MUST KNOW AND USE COMPANY BREAK-EVEN SCHEDULE ANALYSIS

You no doubt have seen contractors who are performing a contract behind schedule and over budget only to find the same contractor start on another contract for the same owner. This is the way it is done. This contractor has proven his entitlement and quantum, his willingness to negotiate, and, most important, his knowledge of negotiating by *using the profit equation.*

> Let us begin anew, remembering on both sides that civility is not a sign of weakness, that sincerity is always subject to proof. Let us never negotiate out of fear. But let us never fear to negotiate.
>
> —*John F. Kennedy*

SUMMARY

Effective collection management maximizes break-even company payment and profit payment for growth and profit. It is the management of the method of collection of all invoices, the conditions of collection, and the optimum method of payment.

You have learned the secret and importance of substantiating entitlement and quantum as the base of all methods of collection. You have also learned the five methods of collection: negotiation, mediation, arbitration, litigation, and capitulation. Negotiation is the best alternative, and mediation is second best. The other three alternatives should be avoided.

In addition, the importance of protecting your right of recovery has been illustrated in the case of the late payment. Also, the importance of the method of payment has been focused to show how the next big contract can be obtained from the one you are now working on. This has been augmented by the use of the company break-even schedule.

Thus far you have learned the secrets of why contractors lose money (Chapter 1), how to identify risk (Chapter 2), how to quantify risk (Chapter 3), how to win the contracts you want (Chapter 4), how to maximize profit (Chapter 5), and here in Chapter 6, how to collect your hard-earned profits.

In the final chapter (Chapter 7), you will learn how to guarantee those big profits time after time with positive action management using the information and Control System.

How to Establish a Complete Information and Control System to Guarantee Growth and Profits

GETTING READY FOR A PLAN OF ACTION

Up to this point all four elements of profit management have been discussed: risk, bid, money, and collection management. You've learned the groundwork and studied, in detail, each of these elements to develop a strong understanding of profit management. Now that you (1) understand the techniques of project control from risk management based on the concept of the contractor as an insurance company, (2) have a grasp on company growth via bid management (which maps your potential for growth or profits), (3) have the ability to maximize the use of all cash received for growth and profit through money management, and (4) have clarified collection management so that you will collect the rewards from your hard work, you are now ready for a *plan of action!*

What do you have to do to guarantee growth and big profits? You must implement a comprehensive *information and control system* (ICS), which governs your project schedule and business plan. The information and control system is your comprehensive management action plan.

HOW THE INFORMATION AND CONTROL SYSTEM WORKS

Chapter 1 introduced the "Construction Management Model" (which is again presented in Figure 7.1). However, this time around we have made a slight change. It is now presented as the "Construction Management *Action* Model."

Along with this title change, there are other changes as well. Notice an important addition to this model—the box labeled "The Information and Control System."

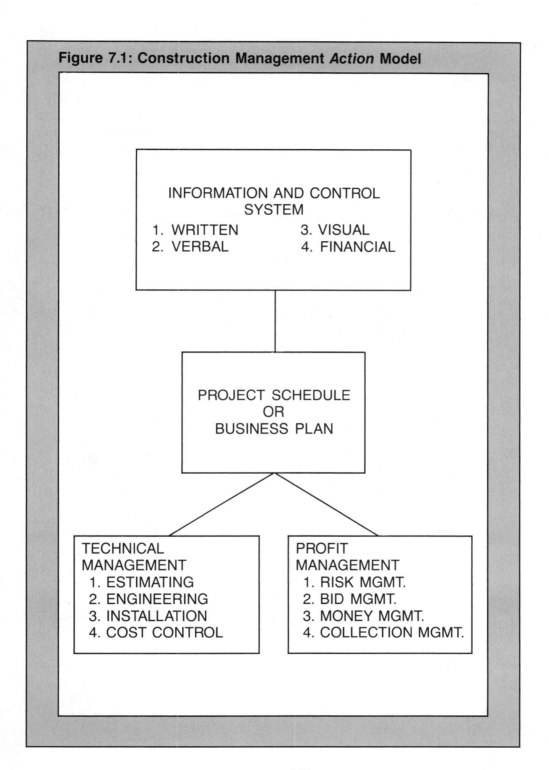

Figure 7.1: Construction Management *Action* Model

INFORMATION AND CONTROL SYSTEM
1. WRITTEN
2. VERBAL
3. VISUAL
4. FINANCIAL

PROJECT SCHEDULE
OR
BUSINESS PLAN

TECHNICAL MANAGEMENT
1. ESTIMATING
2. ENGINEERING
3. INSTALLATION
4. COST CONTROL

PROFIT MANAGEMENT
1. RISK MGMT.
2. BID MGMT.
3. MONEY MGMT.
4. COLLECTION MGMT.

The Information and Control System is a network of various channels of communication and a system of checks and balances that manages the entire project schedule or business plan. These channels are written, verbal, visual, and financial information and control. In order for our information and control system to be most effective, each one of these channels must be founded on the principles of communication and accountability.

HOW COMMUNICATION AND ACCOUNTABILITY DETERMINE PROFIT

Communication is the process of transferring knowledge or information onto others. Without transferring this knowledge or information onto someone else, you have no communication. Your goal is to maintain and to strengthen effective and open lines of communication. Without effective and open communication, you can never guarantee, much less manage, big profits.

PROFIT GUIDE: EFFECTIVE COMMUNICATION MEANS PROFIT

This should be easy enough to understand. However, it is often very difficult to achieve. A contractor must be a strong and effective communicator. The successful ones are. If you think about it, communicating ideas to others is basically what contracting is all about. Just keep this in mind: You can't do it alone. Contracting is a team effort. You depend on others to complete a project.

PROFIT GUIDE: CONTRACTING IS TEAMWORK

There are two things that you should always keep in mind. First, people have different self-serving interests. Second, never assume that others already know what you are talking about. Don't ever forget this. If you forget all else from this chapter, don't let it be these two items.

Remember That People Have Their Own Self-serving Interests

Everyone has different self-serving interests. You. Your clients. Your lawyer. Even your partner (if you have one). We're all individuals. However, it is your responsibility as a contractor to "quarterback" the construction project for everyone's benefit. Contracting is a team effort, and you need someone to take charge.

Have you ever noticed how construction project meetings sound like the planning of the Tower of Babel? If you've never been to one of these meetings, I'll fill you in. There are a group of people consisting of the owner, a few general contractors, a few more subcontractors, architect/engineers, suppliers, lawyers, and the list goes on and on. These people sit around a huge table, talking. They talk and talk and talk. But they never get anywhere. Total chaos. Why? Because everyone is talking a different "language." Sure, they're all speaking English, but they're not *communicating* because each one is speaking from his own self-serving interest (and each one is also putting forth his particular form of trade jargon, which further complicates matters). There is no common "language" of interest.

You can dissect the individual interests of one of these "Tower of Babel" meetings as follows:

The owner is primarily interested in getting the facility completed so that he can move in and assume operations as soon as possible for his economic profit. Everyone else in the room perceives him as the one with the checkbook, who wants to save every penny he can building a $100 per square foot facility for $50 per square foot.

The owner thinks of the architect/engineer as a "genius," the one who can give him everything he wants and needs. On the other hand, the contractor couldn't disagree more with this opinion. The contractor sees the architect/engineer as one who is powerless or who refuses to dictate the methods or manner of performance of the work. Instead, he is the one person who will interfere and impede progress the most by failing to make decisions within the necessary time specified.

The equipment suppliers are interested only in being paid as soon as possible and in limiting their product liability as much as possible. The rest is of no concern to them.

The contractor's (general or sub) underlying interest is to make sure that he does not lose from all the risks he has assumed. As for the others, they look at the contractor as the "worker." He is *needed* by everyone to perform the work according to the plans and specifications within the time specified, but nobody would trade places with him because of the risk involved.

Everyone has his own self-serving interest. Everyone is looking out for number one. Realizing and understanding this basic truth is an important step toward becoming an effective communicator and a successful contractor.

Don't Assume Others Know What You Are Talking About

Many communicators wrongly assume that others already know what they are talking about. What you *think* you are saying and what is *actually* being heard can be (and often are) worlds apart.

I once attended a seminar on communications that dealt with this very subject. The speaker demonstrated this important point in an amusing manner. He called three prominent individuals from the audience onto the stage. The stage was then divided by a screen. The three individuals were seated on one side of the screen, while on the other side, there hung a common shirt. The speaker explained that he would be on the side of the screen with the shirt and the three men would be on the other side, unable to see the speaker. All they had to do was to instruct him, one at a time, as to how to put on the shirt. Well, you can imagine what happened. The results were hilarious. Not one of these men could properly instruct the speaker as to how to put the shirt on correctly. The speaker was following every instruction, but the results were disastrous. Sleeves were buttoned to the collar and so forth. The speaker followed each instruction quite literally, taking nothing for granted.

This simple demonstration dramatically illustrated how we assume that the other person already knows what we are talking about. To communicate effectively, we must take nothing for granted!

The "Control" of the Information and Control System Is Accountability

In addition to communication, an information and control system is also founded on accountability. *Accountability* is being responsible for one's actions. This is the system that checks to be sure that your objectives and goals are being met. This must be a closed-loop system to make sure that instructions have been understood and are being carried out correctly.

Accountability is the "control" part of the information and control system. It must be built into all areas of performance. Accountability standards that monitor are the manager's way of knowing when (and what) corrective action must be taken. Just as the captain of a ship monitors his ship's position by taking longitude and latitude "fixes" to determine if he is on course or if steering changes are required, you must also have a similar system for your contracting firm.

A model of such a closed-loop system of control (accountability) is illustrated in Figure 7.2.

In previous chapters you discovered the vital need for clearly defined goals (which are supplied via the project schedule or the company business plan). You also know of the vital need for a system that can determine when these goals are not being realized. You have learned the benefits of "management of exceptions," how it reduces great quantities of numbers to a manageable few and identifies serious negative variations that require your immediate attention.

"Management of Exceptions": The "Control" Part of the System

The "control" part of your information and control system relies on "management of exceptions." The closed-loop system in Figure 7.2

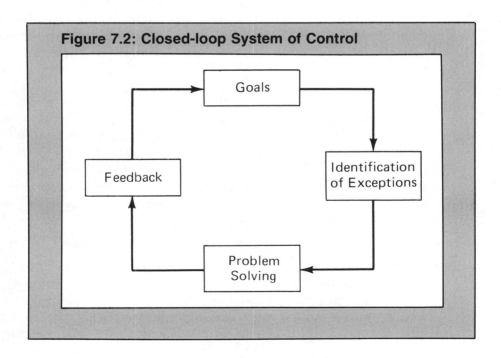

Figure 7.2: Closed-loop System of Control

demonstrates that, first, goals must be clearly defined; second, all exceptions (negative variations to preplanned profit) must be identified; third, corrective action (problem solving) must then be taken; and fourth, all results of corrective action must be monitored (feedback) to be sure that you are back on your course line to preplanned profit. Clearly, this is accountability.

PROFIT GUIDE: WITH COMMUNICATION AND ACCOUN-
TABILITY YOU HAVE ACTION

Everyone involved in the construction process must understand that no deal is a good deal unless everyone makes money. Every project must have a working information and control system that correctly imparts knowledge to everyone. This is one of the big secrets to guarantee big profits for everyone.

FOUR KEY CHANNELS OF INFORMATION FLOW AND CONTROL

The information and control system guarantees profits by providing the information necessary to mitigate all damages from risks contracted for and to recover payment for all damages from risks not contracted for. Again, the key work here is "information." No one can control or recover damages unless he has complete and up-to-date information. Although the contractor must depend on others to take appropriate action to stop damages from items not contracted for, this can be done only if the others are informed of the damages (whether they are realized or potential damages).

The information and control system serves also as a means of communicating with the owner: a "hotline." Virtually every construction contract contains provisions that require one to notify the owner when certain situations occur. Normally, it is mandatory for the contractor to notify the owner within a stipulated period of time. Even if your contract does not contain such a provision, by law you are expected to notify the owner. The law expects you to mitigate all damages as much as possible.

PROFIT GUIDE: THE OWNER MUST BE INFORMED

In order to have an effective information system, you must have *information flow.* Figure 7.3 illustrates information flow. Such an information system should begin in the field at the project site. The foreman's reports must document all situations that are to be followed up in the office to the owner. They also document

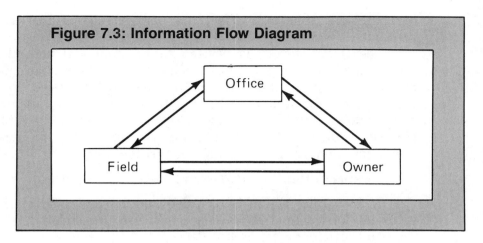

Figure 7.3: Information Flow Diagram

feedback from both the owner and the field. The list of sources of impacted damages is the basis for a constant interchange of information among field, office, and owner.

The fundamental secret is to know what is occurring and to make everyone aware of it as soon as possible. Does this require printed forms, photographs, and accounting? It certainly does! Imagine a project where the owner is in California, the architect/ engineer is in Pennsylvania, the contractor is in Illinois, and the project site is in Indiana. Obviously there are information and control requirements necessary for this project that cannot be ignored. If they are, losses are sure to result.

There are four channels within our network of information and control: written, verbal, visual, and financial. Each one of these channels is essential for a complete and effective information control system. Let's take a closer look at these channels to better understand why they are essential and how to use each of them most effectively.

Written Information and Control

If you review the list of the sources of impacted damages (which negatively affect project break-even point), you see that personnel in the office must be notified of each occurrence and that the appropriate costs must be tracked and then billed to the owner. Likewise, it is also required that personnel in the field be notified of conditions that will affect the performance of the original contract.

The first category is written information and control, and appropriately so. Written information is one of the most basic means of communicating. It is also one of the most effective. Written information immediately satisfies both prerequisites of communication and accountability. In fact, the "control" half of the information and control system relies almost exclusively on written documentation. Everything must be written down!

PROFIT GUIDE: DOCUMENT EVERYTHING IN WRITING

Written information is recorded and disseminated via many different forms. Businesses commonly use preprinted forms for ease and efficiency. Figures 7.4 through 7.12 are useful forms for this purpose. Although they are by no means the only answer, they work. You can customize or improve on them as desired to best suit the needs of your operation. This may include designing additional forms that you and your employees feel comfortable with. The purpose of these forms is to enhance and strengthen effective communication. Therefore, be sure to use forms that you *and* your employees feel comfortable with. Make them interesting. I've seen forms that would take a Ph.D. to fill out. Keep it simple.

It is also important that you add your company name and logo at the top of each form and have them professionally reproduced. Everyone who receives and uses your forms will tacitly judge the professionalism of your organization by what you send. The adage, "You have to look good to do good" certainly applies to everything you use in building your ICS.

In Chapter 3 you learned the importance of identifying and tracking those damages that negatively affect the project break-even payment and how this was accomplished by preparing documentation throughout the course of the project. The following forms can be used to ensure that confirmation of critical information will exist in everyone's files. They will provide you with valuable documentation of your understanding of what happened. And they will help close "the loop" (with other principals in the construction process) in your IC system. They will also help establish the professional status you deserve.

They are the part of your system that checks to see if thoughts, understandings, directions, and orders (agreed upon with other principals) are followed through. Telephone conversations can be easily documented (Figure 7.4), and all parties involved will have had the opportunity to respond (in writing) to your understanding of what was said and what was agreed upon.

In addition, drawings, schedules, and reports can be easily documented and sent out with the Letter of Transmittal form (Figure 7.5). This form quickly tells the recipients what you are sending and what action they are to take with the attached materials.

The Work Order (Figure 7.6) will clarify many cloudy and costly situations. Particularly the ones when your superintendent or foreman is told, "Do this extra work and I will settle up with your boss later." I am sure your attorney has told you, "Don't do any additional work to the contract without a signed work order." Sometimes this can be easier said than done. I am sure you will find that having a stack of these forms on the job will go a long way in solving this problem. People hesitate arguing against SOP (standard operating procedure), and supervisors love to use it as an answer to any objection. Also, make sure these forms have consecutive numbers and are assigned to a particular project. This will ensure that none are lost.

The Quotation Request (Figure 7.7) provides two control functions (1) documentation of the price of materials and equipment used on the project and (2) a basis of price evaluation for the purchasing department. Often invoices of materials from suppliers are difficult to read, and many materials that are used on a project are used from your own inventory. The Quotation Request establishes and documents current market prices that you used in your bid for the materials on a particular project. Even if the materials are to be used from your inventory, suppliers will be happy to fill out the pricing on the Quotation Request for these materials. Your purchasing department will have many uses for the Quotation Request. They can use it as the basis of comparing price, substituted products, shipping dates, method of shipment by weight, and quantities in stock at the project site.

The Certified Receipt is a method of tracking tools and equipment used on a particular project. The form has three copies that are clearly stamped in bold letters on each copy. The office copy (Figure 7.8) is to be sent immediately to the project manager at the home office as soon as the tools or equipment are assigned to workers. The record copy (Figure 7.9) is to be retained at the project and is the superintendent's record of who has what. The employee copy (Figure 7.10) is for the worker receiving the tools or equipment.

The Certified Receipt has both internal and external company advantages. Internally, three primary benefits are (1) responsibility for costly items is acknowledged in writing, (2) deficiencies or excess in the types and quantities of tools and equipment become apparent to both the project manager and the superintendent, and (3) potential theft problems are signaled to your supervisor. I have always found trade unions most cooperative with this procedure. But when individual workers refuse to follow the procedure, it is prudent to immediately find out what the problem is, otherwise things may start to disappear.

Externally, the Certified Receipt is invaluable in documenting the type of tools and equipment used and the length of time they were required. You will use this information in calculating cartage and rental costs. It will also clarify SID item 15, Unavailability of Adequate Tools and Equipment. These are the unforeseen tools and equipment that are required and that delay work and affect everyone's schedule. It is the use of equipment not originally planned for that can cause special procurement problems and, if impossible to obtain, will require alternative methods for performing the work. As you have seen in previous chapters this will produce a loss of productivity, greatly affecting the crew's perception of how the project is being managed.

The Foreman's Weekly Progress Report (Figure 7.11) is a confidential report from the project foreman to the project manager. It tabulates the number of men on the job, the weather conditions on a daily basis, and his perception and opinion of what is going on. The manpower tabulation on the project will assist the project manager in updating his work schedules.

Weather conditions will clarify SID item 2, Environmental Conditions. With this information, you will be able to calculate the effects of temperature, humidity, wind, rain, snow and sleet, freezing rain, temperature extremes, dense fog, ground freeze, drying conditions, temperature inversions, and flooding on worker productivity.

The foreman's perception of what is going on should address many SID items such as item 5—Site Obstructions, item 6—Out-of-Sequence Work, item 7—Reassignment of Manpower, item 8—Manpower Unavailability, to name a few. The foreman should be provided the reference checklist of SIDs (shown in Figure 7.12, as well as in more detail in Chapter 1) of those items that will impact his performance. This will also provide a common language for everyone involved with defined meaning, as well as a valuable checklist to close your control loop.

Figure 7.13 shows a foreman's field report with a matrix for identification of the applicable items to be cataloged and followed in the office. Those in the field must be instructed as to what to look for so that they may best collect the information.

A time sheet signed by the foreman that shows a waste of twenty hours due to delays and that is accompanied by an attached photograph showing the cause of the delay is extremely valuable for substantiating your invoice years later. Without this documentation, the burden of proof is on you. The amount of effort required to initiate such a system is insignificant when compared to the difficulties faced when depending on the mercy of the court to believe accounting numbers. I have never found such a system to add any great additional cost (other than the cost of the photographs). As a matter of fact, I actually use these very photographs to obtain more business!

Always keep in mind that you are responsible for the mitigation of all costs. This means spending as little of the owner's money as possible. Keep the owner updated in writing, explaining the situation as you find it. Really work on his behalf.

Verbal Information and Control

Verbal information is the most basic form of communication. It is also the most unreliable. An effective information and control system hinges on your ability to control one of the most deadly instruments in any business: the telephone!

Telephone conversations and other verbal discussions must be followed up in writing. What appears unimportant at the time often proves to be of paramount importance at a later date. People conveniently forget. Figure 7.4 is one way of making the job easier. It can even be printed on EDP paper with carbon copy characteristics. They need only be filled out by hand, popped into an envelope, and sent to the parties concerned. Also, be sure to keep a copy of this form in your job file.

Remember, information and control means communication and accountability. Once you channel the information (such as via a telephone conversation or foreman's field report form), you must then document the control (confirm the phone conversation in writing and keep a copy of the form) in order to control it. Document everything!

Figure 7.4: Telephone Confirmation

DATE: _____

TO:

Telephone Confirmation
or Conference

Project No.

PROJECT:

Sheet _____ of _____

Gentlemen:

The following data was discussed on the subject project:

Because this information and these decisions are so important to the success of the project, we are herewith transmit-
ting copies to you for your confirmation and record. Unless
notified immediately that corrections or changes are necessary, we shall assume this information to be final and base
our designs thereon.

Very truly yours,

By: _____

Deerfield Consultants and Associates, Inc., Chicago, IL, Ft. Lauderdale, FL,
1975, 1980, 1985.

Figure 7.5: Letter of Transmittal

LETTER OF TRANSMITTAL

TO:

_____

_____

_____

DATE:	JOB NO.
ATTENTION:	
RE:	

Gentlemen:

We are sending you:

__Attached   __Under separate cover via _____the following:
__Shop Drawings __   __Prints   __Plans   __Samples   __Specifications
__Copy of Letter __   __Change Order   _____

COPIES	NO.	DATE	DESCRIPTION

These are transmitted as checked below:

__For approval __Approved as submitted __Resubmit __copies for approval
__For your use __Approved as noted   __Submit   __copies for distribution
__As requested __Returned for corrections __Return   __corrected prints
__For review and comments   _____
__For bids due _____ 19___   __Prints returned after loan to us

REMARKS: _____

_____

_____

_____

_____

_____

Copy to: _____ Signed: _____

Industrial Environmental Controls, Inc., Chicago, IL, 1970, 1975, 1980.

Figure 7.6: Work Order

JOB NUMBER	CUSTOMER ORDER NO.	DATE

NAME OF JOB

LOCATION _____

THIS IS YOUR AUTHORITY
TO _____

Your
Company's
Name
Here

BILL TO _____

DATE	NAME	HOURS		QTY.	MATERIAL	PRICE	
		REG.	O/T			UNIT	TOTAL

AUTHORIZED BY	COMPLETION APPROVED	
		BY

Figure 7.7: Quotation Request

Your Company's Name Here

CONFIDENTIAL

Page _____ of _____

Inquiry Code _____

ATTENTION:

Gentlemen:

You are invited to provide your quotation on the listed equipment.

QUANTITY	DESCRIPTION, MANUFACTURER, AND CATALOG NUMBER	WEIGHT	UNIT COST	TOTAL PRICE	

We wish to thank you for your courteous consideration of our company.

_____
PURCHASING AGENT

Deerfield Consultants and Associates, Inc., Chicago, IL, Ft. Lauderdale, FL, 1975, 1980, 1985.

Figure 7.8: Certified Receipt: Office Copy

CERTIFIED RECEIPT

Your
Company's
Logo here

_____
DATE

THE FOLLOWING TOOLS AND/OR EQUIPMENT HAVE BEEN RE-
CEIVED BY THE UNDERSIGNED FOR CONSTRUCTION USE AND
ARE TO BE RETURNED ON PROJECT COMPLETION OR COMPANY
REQUEST:

_____
_____
_____
_____
_____

The undersigned will be held responsible for all of the above tools
and/or equipment not returned.

_____   _____
SUPERVISOR   RECEIVING EMPLOYEE

CERTIFIED RECEIPT

Your
Company's
Logo here

_____
DATE

THE FOLLOWING TOOLS AND/OR EQUIPMENT HAVE BEEN RE-
CEIVED BY THE UNDERSIGNED FOR CONSTRUCTION USE AND
ARE TO BE RETURNED ON PROJECT COMPLETION OR COMPANY
REQUEST:

_____
_____
_____
_____
_____

The undersigned will be held responsible for all of the above tools
and/or equipment not returned.

_____   _____
SUPERVISOR   RECEIVING EMPLOYEE

Industrial Environmental Controls, Inc., Chicago, IL, 1970, 1975, 1980.

CERTIFIED RECEIPT

Your
Company's
Logo here

_____
DATE

THE FOLLOWING TOOLS AND/OR EQUIPMENT HAVE BEEN RE-
CEIVED BY THE UNDERSIGNED FOR CONSTRUCTION USE AND
ARE TO BE RETURNED ON PROJECT COMPLETION OR COMPANY
REQUEST:

_____

_____

_____

_____

_____

The undersigned will be held responsible for all of the above tools
and/or equipment not returned.

_____   _____
SUPERVISOR   RECEIVING EMPLOYEE

CERTIFIED RECEIPT

Your
Company's
Logo here

_____
DATE

THE FOLLOWING TOOLS AND/OR EQUIPMENT HAVE BEEN RE-
CEIVED BY THE UNDERSIGNED FOR CONSTRUCTION USE AND
ARE TO BE RETURNED ON PROJECT COMPLETION OR COMPANY
REQUEST:

_____

_____

_____

_____

_____

The undersigned will be held responsible for all of the above tools
and/or equipment not returned.

_____   _____
SUPERVISOR   RECEIVING EMPLOYEE

Industrial Environmental Controls, Inc., Chicago, IL, 1970, 1975, 1980.

Figure 7.10: Certified Receipt: Employee Copy

CERTIFIED RECEIPT

Your
Company's
Logo here

_____
DATE

THE FOLLOWING TOOLS AND/OR EQUIPMENT HAVE BEEN RE-
CEIVED BY THE UNDERSIGNED FOR CONSTRUCTION USE AND
ARE TO BE RETURNED ON PROJECT COMPLETION OR COMPANY
REQUEST:

_____
_____
_____
_____
_____

The undersigned will be held responsible for all of the above tools
and/or equipment not returned.

_____   _____
SUPERVISOR   RECEIVING EMPLOYEE

CERTIFIED RECEIPT

Your
Company's
Logo here

_____
DATE

THE FOLLOWING TOOLS AND/OR EQUIPMENT HAVE BEEN RE-
CEIVED BY THE UNDERSIGNED FOR CONSTRUCTION USE AND
ARE TO BE RETURNED ON PROJECT COMPLETION OR COMPANY
REQUEST:

_____
_____
_____
_____
_____

The undersigned will be held responsible for all of the above tools
and/or equipment not returned.

_____   _____
SUPERVISOR   RECEIVING EMPLOYEE

Industrial Environmental Controls, Inc., Chicago, IL, 1970, 1975, 1980.

Figure 7.11: Foreman's Weekly Progress Report

C O N F I D E N T I A L
FOREMAN'S WEEKLY PROGRESS
REPORT   PAGE _____ OF _____

. . . .

NUMBER OF MEN _____
WEATHER _____

_____ _____ _____ _____
DAY   MONTH DATE   YEAR
DESCRIPTION:

_____
_____
_____
_____
_____

. . . .

NUMBER OF MEN _____
WEATHER _____

_____ _____ _____ _____
DAY   MONTH DATE   YEAR
DESCRIPTION:

_____
_____
_____
_____
_____

. . . .

NUMBER OF MEN _____
WEATHER _____

_____ _____ _____ _____
DAY   MONTH DATE   YEAR
DESCRIPTION:

_____
_____
_____
_____
_____

. . . .

NUMBER OF MEN _____
WEATHER _____

_____ _____ _____ _____
DAY   MONTH DATE   YEAR
DESCRIPTION:

_____
_____
_____
_____
_____

. . . .

DATE _____ **FOREMAN** _____

Industrial Environmental Controls, Inc., Chicago, IL, 1970, 1975, 1980.

Figure 7.12: Quick-Reference Checklist of 111 Sources of Impacted Damages (SIDs)

- ☐ 1. DELAYED COMPLETION
- ☐ 2. ENVIRONMENTAL CONDITIONS
- ☐ 3. UNFORESEEABLE DELAYS
- ☐ 4. SITE ACCESS
- ☐ 5. SITE OBSTRUCTIONS
- ☐ 6. OUT-OF-SEQUENCE WORK
- ☐ 7. REASSIGNMENT OF MANPOWER
- ☐ 8. MANPOWER UNAVAILABILITY
- ☐ 9. LEARNING CURVE
- ☐ 10. STACKING OF TRADES
- ☐ 11. INTERRUPTED UTILITIES
- ☐ 12. ATTITUDE AND MORALE
- ☐ 13. SABOTAGE
- ☐ 14. EQUIPMENT THEFT AND VANDALISM
- ☐ 15. UNAVAILABILITY OF ADEQUATE TOOLS AND EQUIPMENT
- ☐ 16. MATERIAL THEFT AND VANDALISM
- ☐ 17. VANDALISM TO STRUCTURES
- ☐ 18. NEW WORK DAMAGE
- ☐ 19. DILUTION OF SUPERVISION
- ☐ 20. JOINT OCCUPANCY
- ☐ 21. BENEFICIAL OCCUPANCY
- ☐ 22. RIPPLE
- ☐ 23. ACCELERATION
- ☐ 24. PROJECT EXPANSION
- ☐ 25. INTERRUPTED BUSINESS
- ☐ 26. CONTRACT ORGANIZATION
- ☐ 27. PROJECT ORGANIZATION
- ☐ 28. CREW SIZE
- ☐ 29. EXTERNAL SUPERVISION
- ☐ 30. INTERNAL SUPERVISION

Figure 7.12: Quick-Reference Checklist of 111 Sources of Impacted Damages (SIDs) *(continued)*

- ☐ 31. NONWORKING SUPERVISION
- ☐ 32. WORKING SUPERVISION
- ☐ 33. START-UP SUPERVISION
- ☐ 34. PREINSPECTION
- ☐ 35. WORKING INSPECTION
- ☐ 36. PUNCH LIST
- ☐ 37. FINAL INSPECTION
- ☐ 38. SCHEDULE STABILITY
- ☐ 39. DESIGN STABILITY
- ☐ 40. PERFORMANCE SPECIFICATIONS
- ☐ 41. DETAIL DRAWINGS
- ☐ 42. AS-BUILT DRAWINGS
- ☐ 43. OPERATING MANUALS
- ☐ 44. MAINTENANCE MANUALS
- ☐ 45. REPAIR MANUALS
- ☐ 46. ADDENDUMS
- ☐ 47. REVISIONS
- ☐ 48. APPROVALS
- ☐ 49. START-UP
- ☐ 50. STIPULATED PRICE CHANGES
- ☐ 51. UNILATERAL CHANGES
- ☐ 52. TIME AND MATERIAL CHANGES
- ☐ 53. CONSTRUCTIVE OR UNAUTHORIZED CHANGES
- ☐ 54. UNIT-PRICE CHANGES
- ☐ 55. CHANGES IN CODES AND REGULATIONS
- ☐ 56. CONCEALED CONDITIONS
- ☐ 57. DEFECTIVE PERFORMANCE
- ☐ 58. ERRORS AND OMISSIONS
- ☐ 59. DEFECTIVE PLANS AND SPECIFICATIONS

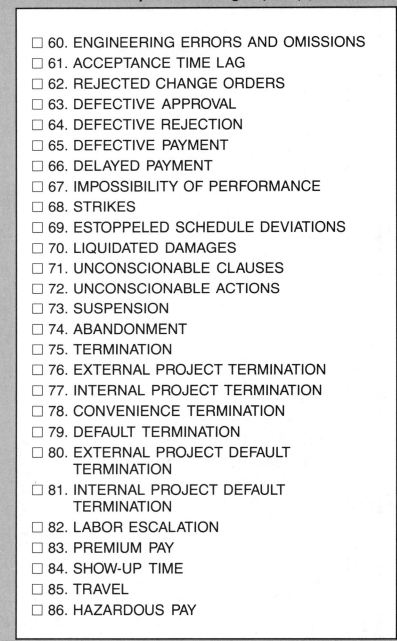

Figure 7.12: Quick-Reference Checklist of 111 Sources of Impacted Damages (SIDs) *(continued)*

- ☐ 60. ENGINEERING ERRORS AND OMISSIONS
- ☐ 61. ACCEPTANCE TIME LAG
- ☐ 62. REJECTED CHANGE ORDERS
- ☐ 63. DEFECTIVE APPROVAL
- ☐ 64. DEFECTIVE REJECTION
- ☐ 65. DEFECTIVE PAYMENT
- ☐ 66. DELAYED PAYMENT
- ☐ 67. IMPOSSIBILITY OF PERFORMANCE
- ☐ 68. STRIKES
- ☐ 69. ESTOPPELED SCHEDULE DEVIATIONS
- ☐ 70. LIQUIDATED DAMAGES
- ☐ 71. UNCONSCIONABLE CLAUSES
- ☐ 72. UNCONSCIONABLE ACTIONS
- ☐ 73. SUSPENSION
- ☐ 74. ABANDONMENT
- ☐ 75. TERMINATION
- ☐ 76. EXTERNAL PROJECT TERMINATION
- ☐ 77. INTERNAL PROJECT TERMINATION
- ☐ 78. CONVENIENCE TERMINATION
- ☐ 79. DEFAULT TERMINATION
- ☐ 80. EXTERNAL PROJECT DEFAULT TERMINATION
- ☐ 81. INTERNAL PROJECT DEFAULT TERMINATION
- ☐ 82. LABOR ESCALATION
- ☐ 83. PREMIUM PAY
- ☐ 84. SHOW-UP TIME
- ☐ 85. TRAVEL
- ☐ 86. HAZARDOUS PAY

☐ 87. OVERTIME

☐ 88. SHIFT WORK

☐ 89. MATERIAL PROCUREMENT

☐ 90. FBO

☐ 91. MATERIAL ESCALATION

☐ 92. MATERIAL STORAGE

☐ 93. REMOVAL OF DEBRIS

☐ 94. TOOL RENTAL

☐ 95. MACHINERY RENTAL

☐ 96. FREIGHT

☐ 97. CARTAGE

☐ 98. INSURANCE

☐ 99. COMMERCIAL INSURANCE

☐ 100. SELF-INSURANCE

☐ 101. WARRANTY RISKS AND COSTS

☐ 102. INTEREST

☐ 103. FINANCING

☐ 104. TAXES

☐ 105. CONTRACT AWARD COSTS

☐ 106. START-UP COSTS

☐ 107. SHUT-DOWN COSTS

☐ 108. EXTENDED DIRECT JOB EXPENSES

☐ 109. EXTENDED MAIN OFFICE OVERHEAD

☐ 110. ANTICIPATED PROFITS

☐ 111. CLAIM RECOVERY AND SETTLEMENT COSTS

Deerfield Consultants and Associates, Inc., Chicago IL, Ft. Lauderdale, FL. 1975, 1980, 1985.

Figure 7.13: Foreman's Field Report

DESCRIPTION OF WORK OR CODING

Foreman _____

Project _____

Contract No. _____

Date _____

	NAME	CLASS						HOURS				TOTAL HOURS	RATE	TOTAL AMT		

Deerfield Consultants and Associates, Inc., Chicago, IL, Ft. Lauderdale, FL, 1975, 1980, 1985.

Why You Should Document Telephone Conversations

I once received a phone call that ruined my day. After spending several months designing an electrical system for a large manufacturing plant and seeing the project nearing completion, it happened. The phone rang. It was the superintendent at the job site. They were ready to connect the electrical service switchgear to the incoming local power company service, but they did not match. Connection was impossible. The plant had been built with 4 wire 208 volt service and the power company had 3 wire 480 volt service available on the "pole," which they intended to provide. Needless to say, a flurry of activity followed, resulting in a big meeting with everyone (including the fellow from the local power company). The representative from the local power company insisted that he had notified us by phone before we started design that they would provide 3 wire 480 volt electrical service. What was our reaction to that statement? You guessed it. No one at the meeting could remember any such telephone conversation. But I learned. You can bet that that was the last time I did not confirm all telephone conversations in writing.

**PROFIT GUIDE: CONFIRM ALL TELEPHONE CONVERSATIONS
IN WRITING**

Verbal information and control are not limited merely to phone conversations and meetings. Recording verbal information is also an excellent means of achieving information and control. Many contractors tell me that these ideas may work in the office but it won't work in the field.

"My foreman divorced paper and pencil fifteen years ago," they say. "Do we fire the foreman because he won't fill out our forms?"

Remember, you need the information but you also need that foreman and the benefit of his experience. Just as you made sure the forms here were compatible with your employees at the office, you must also do the same for your headstrong foreman. As the man said, "There are many roads to Rome." Does this mean redesigning your forms every time you hire a new foreman? Of course not.

Chances are that the foreman will never be satisfied with any forms. He hates to write, remember? But you need that information!

Suppose you give the foreman a tape recorder so that he can give you the information verbally without even picking up a pencil? He could simply go down a checklist everyday, verbally on tape. It's simple. It's convenient. But most of all, it works! With the recordings, you not only get the information, but you also have accountability (not to mention a happy foreman, because all foremen love to tell jokes, and you'll hear them all on tape). A recording is a form of tangible documentation that lasts forever.

Visual Information and Control

Our third channel for an effective information and control system is visual information and control. Show them what you want to say! Today, visual communication is at its peak. Everyone realizes the power of the image and the importance of its lasting effects.

How to Monitor Progress on Videotape

I developed a process called Cinprom™ (which is an acronym for CINematography PROject Management).[1] Here's how it works. Video cameras are set up at the construction site at consistent physical locations that are compatible with the nature and progress of the project. Then, every day footage is taken, recording the day-to-day progress of the project, documenting the entire project on videotape. This tape is then edited by our own in-house production company to produce a comprehensive progress-monitoring film.

Perhaps the most important benefit of Cinprom™ is that the videotapes provide for truly educated communications among owner, architect/engineer, manufacturer, and contractor. Visual information loses little in translation. It also makes for more meaningful and friendlier business relations, along with smoother labor relations as well.

Cinprom™ is a way of working smarter, not harder. With it, comprehensive project supervision is possible. Unforeseen schedule conflicts that often produce physical difficulties and obstructions can be eliminated. Fewer delays occur, increasing productivity. Areas of responsibility are clearly defined.

Cinprom™ also allows a project manager to monitor job progress easily on several projects on a timely basis in an environ-

[1]Leonard Brunotte, "Cinematography Project Management," in *Power Engineering*, Jan. 1980.

ment (back at the office) that is far from the confusion of the job site. When you consider the acclimation period of visiting a job site, along with the time it takes to travel to and from a job, how many jobs can a project manager really handle productively? The ease and comprehensive nature of the videotapes will no doubt increase his productivity more than any other system.

In addition to the immediate on-site benefits of video documentation, there are many fringe benefits that may prove useful in the long run. A video that documents all jobsite operations would be an invaluable evidenciary instrument for realistic settlement of any claim recovery. Second, the footage can be edited into an ideal training film for operating or maintenance personnel. Any post-production or in-house video service could produce such a video from the jobsite tapes, adding graphics, instructional footage, and narration at a cost nominal in comparison with the cost of hiring a production company to come in and shoot original footage. Furthermore, a public or customer relations' film could also be produced from the tapes. The future benefits of such a video could also be used by the owner, manufacturer, and architect/engineer as well as the contractor himself.

Visual information and control satisfies both prerequisites for complete information and control: you have communication and accountability. You can use videotapes to communicate your ideas and/or problems to others rapidly, easily, and efficiently while holding an effective form of documenting this same information.

Financial Information and Control

The fourth and final channel is financial information and control. This channel entails the recording and presentation of financial (numerical) data and information using accounting principles.

In addition to the normal direct cost accounting system kept by all companies (which is only used to keep track of how much in taxes you owe), a Segmented Absorption Accounting System is absolutely necessary for intelligent company management decisions. A good indication of how useful the standard direct cost accounting Profit and Loss Statement is for running a business is to consider its availability and usefulness.

As for availability, when I ask a client to see these statements, they are either six months old or buried in some file drawer that normally takes the client twenty minutes to find.

As for usefulness, there has been a great deal of debate concerning the inability of businessmen to read financial statements. This is unwarranted and misdirected. The problem is not that the businessman cannot read financial statements, but that the statements he receives from his accountant are totally inadequate for management decisions. They are useless.

How to Use a Segmented Absorption Accounting System

The function of an accountant is (in most cases) to manage the company's tax liability, not to provide an accounting management system. Instead, a Segmented Absorption Accounting System should be utilized to provide this needed information. The problem is not that businessmen cannot read financial statements, but that most do not receive the information in the proper format. The reason for this is that they do not know what this proper format is or should be.

This format confusion is not caused by any fault or inadequacy of the accountant. On the contrary, it is the responsibility of the businessman (contractor) to realize what the function and capabilities of the accountant are and to implement a Segmented Absorption Accounting System.

A *Segmented Absorption Accounting System* numerically separates each project and generates a clear financial picture of the amount each project is contributing toward company fixed expenses. Although this enables management to obtain an accurate overall operational financial picture, it is seriously lacking in the detail necessary for day-to-day project decisions. For this reason, various types of job cost control systems have been developed with varying degrees of success. Many of these systems are managed "in house" because of the critical need for timely information required for intelligent decision making.

These decisions demand that all financial information be reduced to as few numbers as possible. If this is not done, you may find yourself conveniently visiting the job site or playing golf. The mind can deal with only so many variables before it becomes saturated and unconsciously turns to something else. This is not what we want! One successful method of reducing all financial information to more manageable amounts is the *Daily Operating*

Control sheet (commonly called the DOC sheet). The DOC sheet is a summary of numbers.

The Daily Operating Control Sheet Concept

DOC sheets are successful in reducing financial information into a summary, but they are unable to track items that cause impacted damages. As you have seen in Chapter 5 on money management, DOC sheets currently in use merely reduce numbers to summaries of cost and expense items that show positive and negative variations from dollar amounts that have been previously budgeted. Even when the previously budgeted items have profit amounts allocated in each item, the end result is that management is *only* considering positive or negative variation from bid *estimated* items. The DOC sheet concept is effective in tracking profit, but it can "see" only budgeted or estimated items.

In other words, the items that affect losses are not even listed on a "chart of accounts." Therefore, as far as any job cost control system is concerned, they do not exist. This is another example of the uniqueness of the construction business. What works in many other businesses is not enough for construction. A DOC sheet is needed that focuses on *impacted damages* as well as on bid estimated or profit items.

The items that negatively impact project break-even must be tracked in dollar value on a continuous basis. The fewer the numbers, the better.

This is best accomplished by making a project DOC sheet that itemizes each source of impacted damages, showing the total negative dollar value of losses. Figure 7.14 presents a sample DOC sheet that accomplishes this.

With this information tabulated on a weekly basis, the contractor is able to take appropriate action. What type of action would *you* take if your project manager handed you this DOC sheet on Monday morning? Or, better yet, what action *could* you take if you were receiving this information? Of course, the costs that are caused internally—those due to the fault of the contractor—can be quickly corrected. And those that qualify as externally caused require immediate action with the involved parties.

Figure 7.14: DOC Sheet

"PROJECT A"

	CAUSES OF DAMAGES	
Item	*Internal*	*External*
Stacking of Trades	($ 1,515)	$ (0)
Equipment Rental	(5,779)	(15,425)
Learning Curve	(9,677)	(23,689)
	($16,971)	($39,114)

THE PROJECT SCHEDULE

Everything relates to the *project schedule*. The project schedule documents your goals. The decision to use one type of schedule versus another is normally decided upon by the complexity of the project. One type of scheduling, PERT (Program Evaluation Research Tank), was developed for complex projects such as the U.S. Navy Fleet Ballistic Missile Program. Other types of scheduling include CPM (Critical Path Method) and the good old bar graph.

The Critical Path Method of Scheduling

The schedules mentioned here provide the sequence of work, the amount of work, and the completion time. A distinctive feature of CPM is that it enables tasks to be performed systematically and separately so that the contractor does not have to monitor and evaluate the sequence of operations, time requirements, and procurement simultaneously.

There is no magic or mystery to CPM. Extensive mathematics or elaborate equipment is not required to use CPM either. The only prerequisites are a knowledge of grammar school arithmetic and a good understanding of the construction process. Amazingly, many contractors avoid working with schedules, particularly subcontractors. One reason for this is that the project schedule is often general and complex. These two conditions represent a paradox that can exist at the same time. This happens when the schedule is made by someone who does not gather all the information needed, thus finding himself with large periods of undefined time.

This commonly occurs when the architect/engineer is unfamiliar with a particular piece of equipment and/or phase of the project he is designing, especially when learning enough about it in order to schedule it in detail would mean spending more time and money than he is being paid for the entire project design. Or, this can occur when the project is on a "fast track," which means that engineering and construction will be going on at the same time. The cost-effective alternative that is normally taken in these cases is to call in the manufacturer to write a performance specification and "block out" the schedule time required for construction. This approach is also adopted by the general contractor who is unfamiliar with the equipment, leaving the "real" schedule to be developed by the specialty subcontractor if a schedule is ever made.

I recall when electrostatic precipitators were first being used on incinerator plants around the country. Many of the architect/engineers whom I was working with were old hands at designing incinerator plants. But they hardly knew how to spell "electrostatic precipitator," much less know what the required job functions were for erection. So, more often than not, there would be a big square on the contract drawings located between the furnace and smokestack with the notation: "Electrostatic Precipitator—See Contract Specifications, Section IV." There may be some advantages to this for the specialty subcontractor who is familiar with this equipment; however, there is also one big disadvantage. There is no realistic time schedule.

When to Use a Bar Graph

As you learned in Chapter 4, the contractor must take the time to work out a schedule. This is best started with a bar graph. The bar graph is used because it is easily understood by everyone and because it breaks the project down into understandable and manageable tasks (which are needed even if a CPM schedule is required). The bar graph serves as an effective tool for smaller job segments. It is well accepted in the field at the job site and is a good way of sending information back and forth between the job site and office. In fact, one method of scheduling that works well for me and one that you may seriously want to consider is what I call the *Critical Bar Method (CBM)*. This is effective because the bar chart is so familiar in the field to the workers due to its years in use. Sticking with it has obvious advantages.

The CBM schedule considers in-depth and displays (1) the various job functions or tasks to be performed, (2) the calendar dates during which the tasks are to be performed, (3) the duration of the tasks, (4) the sequence in which the job tasks are to be performed, (5) the tasks that must be completed in order to complete other tasks productively, (6) the calendar dates on which materials and equipment must be on the job site, and (7) the manpower required on weekly basis.

Figure 7.15 below illustrates how this is accomplished with a sample CBM schedule.

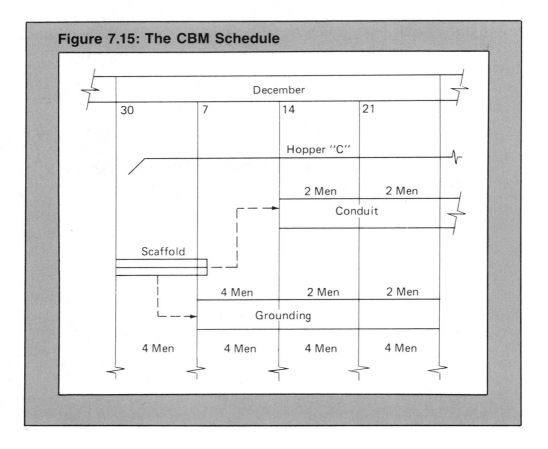

Figure 7.15: The CBM Schedule

The dashed lines with directional arrows indicate which tasks should be finished in order to proceed in a productive manner, producing the best results. The CBM schedule can also be color-coded for easy reference. For instance, the total elapsed time to date of issue could be colored blue and the current progress on respective tasks could be colored red. The CBM works well for individual job segments; however, if complexity dictates, an overall CPM must also be made.

Remember, the project schedule is the "game plan" to a successful project. Don't be afraid that it will be used against you. Without it, everything can and will be used against you. Once the schedule has been made and submitted, it must be continually kept updated. This provides a frame of reference, allowing you to foresee and to keep track of occurrences that impact the project. It will also lead you to the causes of lost profits, whether they are self-inflicted or not.

THE COMPANY'S BUSINESS PLAN AND ITS IMPACT ON GROWTH AND PROFIT

You've seen how the information and control system relates to the project schedule; now let's consider the company *business plan* and its impact on company growth and profit. Remember, the business plan documents your goals.

One important use, discussed previously, is the business plan's value in obtaining a clear picture of the company's break-even position for intelligent management decisions relevant to bidding and negotiating fixed-price contracts.

By knowing company break-even for various amounts of sales revenue, you can implement growth strategies with a balance between fixed-price contract and negotiated sales volume, thereby reducing your dependence on any one client.

In other words, an information and control system will allow you to determine a "course line" for the year and then monitor it for performance. Think of it this way. If you were going to pilot a boat from the United States to Ireland, the first thing you would do is draw a course line. Then, as you were underway, you would periodically take your latitude and longitude to determine your position, then make whatever steering adjustments were necessary to return to the predetermined course line. You have seen, thus far, how important this is for time period profit planning (refer to Figure 1.7). The information and control system shows you in what time periods you are below break-even so that you can take appropriate action to ensure your profit; this can be accomplished by increasing sales, reducing costs, or a combination of the two.

Another important use of the information and control system is its ability to control costs and expenses. This is a necessary and fundamental condition needed to implement company growth strategies. What often looks like an intuitively sound decision may often be the wrong decision. The boat captain analogy fits here also. Imagine that you are in a dense fog and you cannot see where you are going. You should rely only on your compass, not your intuition. The following case example is an effective way of understanding this.

DEALING WITH DECREASED SALES: A CASE EXAMPLE

Suppose you are faced with a situation where your sales are dropping off even though your competition is doing the same or a little more volume than you. Obviously, you need to increase your sales with greater market penetration. The intuitive choice would be to cut overhead to become more competitive. But this is wrong! Let's find out why.

For the purposes of this illustration let's assume your company's Profit and Loss Statement can be broken down into percentages that look something like Figure 7.16.

Now let's see what could happen if you were to follow your intuition and cut overhead to become more competitive so that you might obtain more work. Then let's see what you really should do in order to increase your market penetration effectively.

If you decide to cut back on overhead, the most intuitive places to make the cuts are in supervision, accounting, or equipment. Once you have done this, it is reasonable to assume that material and direct labor costs are going to increase because the items that you have cut back are the items that are controlling these costs.

Although there may be other increases, let's see what happens to the competitive position with only material and labor being affected. Let's assume nominal increases: 2 percent for material and 4 percent for direct labor. Of course, you must deduct something for the cuts you have made. Let's see what happens with only a 2

Figure 7.16: "Current Profit and Loss Statement"

CURRENT PROFIT AND LOSS STATEMENT

Item	Current
Material	38%
Direct Labor	24%
Indirect Labor	16%
Overhead	12%
SUBTOTAL	90%
PROFIT	10%
SELL/BID PRICE......................	100%

percent cut in indirect labor (supervision) and 1 percent for overhead (let's assume this is accounting and you put off your plans to buy a computer). Compare the results of these cuts with the original Profit and Loss Statement in Figure 7.17 (see p. 284).

Look what happened to profit. It went down by 3 percent (from 10 percent to 7 percent). This certainly is not what you had planned. After all, you are in this business to make a *profit*. To add insult to injury, not only did your profit go down, but your selling or bid price remained exactly the same. You are no more competitive than you were to start with. You have literally lost money. That's what can happen when you follow your intuition and not your compass...the information and control system.

Well, what should you do? You need market penetration to increase sales. This means that you must lower your bid price (as shown in Chapter 4 on bid management) and at least maintain your profit percentage. You have to increase control of costs. If decreasing supervision, accounting, and equipment allows your costs to increase, then the reverse should also be true—that increased control will decrease costs.

Let's see what happens when you increase these items of control: overhead and indirect labor. Assume that an increase in

Figure 7.17: Intuitive Action to Increase Sales

Item	Current	Intuitive Cuts
Material	38%	40%
Direct Labor	24%	28%
Indirect Labor	16%	14%
Overhead	12%	11%
SUBTOTAL	90%	93%
PROFIT	10%	7%
SELL/BID PRICE.............	100%	100%

indirect labor of 2 percent and overhead of 1 percent produces material and labor control of 36 percent and 20 percent respectively. This means that if you increase control you will realize a nominal 2 percent reduction in material expenditures and 4 percent in labor.

Figure 7.18 compares the original (or current) situation to the previous intuitive choice to cut overhead and indirect labor.

This looks more like what you want. Your competitive position has been increased by lowering your bid by 3 percent and you have maintained your profit percentage of 10 percent. This was accomplished by increasing control of costs.

PROFIT GUIDE: INCREASED CONTROL INCREASES SALES

Since this works for market penetration, will it also work if you don't need market penetration and just want to increase your profits? Yes! Let's chart it out so you can be sure. Figure 7.19 illustrates the new market penetration and profit increase.

Now you have a 13 percent profit instead of 10 percent from the same increased control of costs (bid price was held constant).

So far you have seen that an effective company information and control system can (1) increase sales volume by reducing the selling price in time periods when you are at or above break-even, (2) increase profits by knowing when you are at break-even and

Figure 7.18: Market Penetration

Item	Current	Intuitive Cuts	Market Increase
Material	38%	40%	36%
Direct Labor	24%	28%	20%
Indirect Labor	16%	14%	18%
Overhead	12%	11%	13%
SUBTOTAL	90%	93%	87%
PROFIT	10%	7%	10%
SELL/BID PRICE.	100%	100%	97%

Figure 7.19: Market Penetration and Profit Increase

Item	Current	Cuts	Market Increase	Profit Increase
Material	38%	40%	36%	36%
Direct Labor	24%	28%	20%	20%
Indirect Labor	16%	14%	18%	18%
Overhead	12%	11%	13%	13%
SUBTOTAL	90%	93%	87%	87%
PROFIT	10%	7%	10%	13%
SELL/BID PRICE	100%	100%	97%	100%

performing projects in those time periods, (3) increase profits by cutting costs in time periods when you are below break-even, and (4) increase market penetration or increase your profits by cutting controllable costs by strengthening the information and control system.

TIPS ON IMPLEMENTING A COMPUTERIZED INFORMATION AND CONTROL SYSTEM

If a good information and control system can do all this, then what can a stronger one do? This is one of those cases that if "some" is good, then "more" is even better. The results you have been looking at so far can be obtained easily with manual systems that have accountability. In other words, it is quite realistic to be able to control your company within the parameters that have been discussed with manual bookkeeping and accounting systems that have preplanned profit built into them.

However, suppose you want to move on and get into the areas of super market penetration and bigger profits. Such a move would require that you make indirect labor and overhead economies. I know I said that you needed *more* indirect labor and overhead to properly control costs, not less. This is true. However, if you expect to obtain more market penetration and bigger profits, something must be cut. You have already cut controllable costs. What else is there? Cuts in indirect labor and overhead are the only answer.

Interestingly enough, cuts in indirect labor and overhead are possible with the development of labor-saving devices. To be effective, you must be able to make these cuts without increasing labor or material cost. In other words, you need the same control but with more efficiency. One such device that has the greatest current impact is the *computer*.

Before you begin to explore the benefits of an information and control system enhanced by a computer, it is imperative that you realize that an automatic system is no better than the manual system on which it is based.

PROFIT GUIDE: A COMPUTER IS USELESS WITHOUT A GOOD MANUAL SYSTEM

Time after time clients with no working manual information and control system tell me that what they need is a computer. This may be true, but for all the wrong reasons. They believe that somehow the computer will teach them what they don't know. Yet this is not possible—the computer is a machine. It's only a tool, a highly efficient and productive one, but a tool nonetheless. You must first have a good manual information and control system before you even consider buying a computer for more efficiency.

The next step is to find someone to computerize your *working* manual system. This means finding a computer programmer. But remember, the programmer comes *after* the system, not before. If not, you will wind up with a system that the programmer has designed. Quite simply, you have just allowed some computer programmer to design the control of your business. Now if the programmer also happens to be a technical and profit management expert, fine. But more often than not, the programmer is going to be just that...a programmer. You'll be destined for trouble. This probably accounts for all the computers I see in contractor's offices that do nothing more than gather dust.

Let's assume you have a strong manual system and a technical wizard for a programmer. Before you run to your local computer store, you should first determine if a computer is going to be cost effective. In other words, can you afford to buy one? The average leasing cost (for the size computer needed by a majority of contractors) is currently around $1,500 a month. This includes all the software and peripheral equipment you need. To find out if you can afford such a computer, you should start by analyzing the market penetration and profit results you can expect.

In Figure 7.19 you saw that you could either increase your market penetration by lowering your bid by 3 percent (at a 10 percent profit), or increase your profit by 3 percent (without changing your bid) with a good information and control system. Now let's chart what happens to market penetration if you reduce indirect labor by 3 percent to 15 percent and overhead by 3 percent to 10 percent. This information is illustrated in Figure 7.20.

Now you have reduced your selling price by 9 percent and maintained a 10 percent profit. Will this allow you to obtain enough additional business to pay for the computerized information and control system? How much additional business is needed at your 10 percent profit to pay the $1,500 a month for the computer? The answer is that you will need $180,000 in additional business at 10 percent profit to pay for the computer. Will a 9 percent cut in your selling price generate the $180,000 in additional business? You decide. It may help you to consider that if you were doing $1 million in sales *before* you bought your new computer, the $180,000 is only a 5.6 percent increase in sales. That sounds reasonable.

Now that you know what a computerized information and control system can do to increase sales with "super" market

Figure 7.20: *Super* Market Penetration

Item	Current	Intuitive Cuts	Market Increase	Super Market Increase
Material	38%	40%	36%	36%
Direct Labor	24%	28%	20%	20%
Indirect Labor	16%	14%	18%	15%
Overhead	12%	11%	13%	10%
SUBTOTAL.......	90%	93%	87%	81%
PROFIT	10%	7%	10%	10%
SELL/BID PRICE .	100%	100%	97%	91%

penetration, the next step is to consider what a computer can do to increase your profits when you don't need "super" market penetration. Figure 7.21 makes this comparison.

Figure 7.21: Greater Profit Increases

Item	Current	Intuitive Cuts	Profit Increase	Greater Profit Increase
Material	38%	40%	36%	36%
Direct Labor	24%	28%	20%	20%
Indirect Labor	16%	14%	18%	15%
Overhead	12%	11%	13%	10%
SUBTOTAL.......	90%	93%	87%	81%
PROFIT	10%	7%	13%	19%
SELL/BID PRICE .	100%	100%	100%	100%

Now your profits have increased from 9 percent to 19 percent. Will this increase pay for the computerized information and control system? You have to do $200,000 in business at a 9 percent increase in profit to pay for it! If you were doing $1 million before the computer, the 9 percent would make an additional $72,000 *after* it was paid for.

Experience dictates that you would at times need some form of market penetration and at other times be able to take advantage of the opportunity to increase your profit. Therefore, a computerized information and control system based on a good working manual system will greatly increase your competitive position and company financial strength with increased profits. This will give you independence from any or all clients and will enable you to realize real growth strategies.

SUMMARY

In this chapter, you have learned the secret of guaranteeing growth and big profits by establishing a complete information and control system that efficiently manages your project schedule and business plan. You have learned that the information and control system must conform to the principles of communication and accountability.

You have also learned that the information and control system is actually a network of four channels of communication: written, verbal, visual, and financial. In addition, you have learned that the "control" half of the system relies on a closed-loop control system, which allows for the workings of "management of exceptions."

You have discovered how the information and control system governs your project schedule and company business plan, which relies on four elements of profit management to realize preplanned goals of growth and profit. You have also seen the construction management action model, which synthesizes all of the secrets from each chapter into a comprehensive whole.

In conclusion, you have now discovered the secrets of successful contracting—construction profit management.

Construction Profit Management is company preplanned profit and growth that maximizes the benefits to the owners (common stockholders) at the lowest possible risk. It consists of risk, bid, money, and collection management, which executes the goals set by the company business plan and project schedule governed by the information and control system.

Construction Profit Management increases profit while simultaneously decreasing construction costs by enhancing the total operating performance and leadership effectiveness of those involved in the construction process.

Construction Profit Management provides a system of educated communication, establishing a common language of business between each and every principal in the construction process: contractor, field supervisor, architect, engineer, attorney, accountant, insurer, financier, manufacturer, supplier, developer, and building owner.

Construction Profit Management has one primary objective: to receive full payment for constructing the highest quality project in the shortest possible time at the lowest possible cost.

—*Leonard Brunotte*

Profit Management Directory

CHAPTER 1

PROFIT GUIDES:

PROFIT = FULL PAYMENT
YOU MUST BE ABLE TO IDENTIFY BREAK-EVEN
YOU MUST SCHEDULE COMPANY BREAK-EVEN
"WHEN" DETERMINES "HOW" WORK IS DONE

PROFIT AIDS:

KNOW YOUR STRENGTHS AND WEAKNESSES
KNOW YOUR MARKET OPPORTUNITIES
KNOW YOUR TRADING AREA
KNOW YOUR MARKET POSITION
PRICING IS BASED ON THE DEMAND CURVE
THE EXTERNAL MARKET AFFECTS PROFITS
YOU MUST KNOW WHICH CONTRACT TO WIN
EXPENSE AS A PERCENTAGE MAXIMIZES GROWTH
EXPENSE AS A CONSTANT DOLLAR VALUE MAXIMIZES
  PROFIT
FIXED EXPENSES ARE NOT FIXED
FIXED EXPENSES DETERMINE PROFITS
REDUCING YOUR SELLING PRICE WILL INCREASE PROFITS
TECHNICAL AND FUNDAMENTAL ANALYSIS IS MARKET
  TIMING

PROFIT AIDS:

CHAPTER 5

PROFIT GUIDES:

ASSETS AND LIABILITIES ARE MONEY

PLANNED ACTION IS PREPLANNED PROFIT
PROFIT MUST BE YOUR FIRST ITEM OF EXPENSE
COMMON STOCKHOLDERS ARE OWNERS
YOU MUST CONSIDER TIME
FIRST, KNOW WHEN THE MONEY IS REQUIRED
NEXT, KNOW HOW MUCH MONEY IS REQUIRED
NO PROJECT SCHEDULES MEANS NO CASH AND NO PROFIT
CASH IS NOT PROFIT
CASH IS FUEL
YOU MUST KNOW AND USE THE CORRECT TOOLS
YOU MUST "CRUNCH NUMBERS"
RATIOS CRUNCH NUMBERS
YOU MUST KNOW WHY A RATIO IS OUT OF LINE
KNOW WHY A TREND IS OUT OF LINE
FINANCIAL TRENDS ARE INDICATORS OF THINGS TO COME
INCOME STATEMENTS ARE HISTORY
USE YOUR OWN PAST EXPERIENCE
GOOD DECISIONS REQUIRE TREND ANALYSIS
YOU MUST KNOW WHEN AND WHERE TO TAKE ACTION
BUDGETS PROVIDE PROFITABILITY WITH ACCOUNTABILITY
BUDGET VARIATIONS CREATE ACTION
NO CASH FLOW PROJECTIONS MEANS FINANCIAL TROUBLE
YOU MUST KNOW YOUR FUTURE FINANCIAL NEEDS
POSITIVE CASH FLOW IS EXCESS CASH
NEGATIVE CASH FLOW MEANS FINANCIAL TROUBLE
CONTRACT PARTIAL PAYMENTS CAN WORK FOR YOU
YOU MUST INVOICE TO BE PAID
YOU MUST COLLECT OVERHEAD AND PROFIT ON TIME
SCHEDULES ARE CONTRACTS
REVISED SCHEDULES REQUIRE REVISED PARTIAL PAYMENTS
KNOW YOUR INSURANCE RATE
USE THE CORRECT INSURANCE RATE
VERIFY YOUR INSURANCE RATES IN ADVANCE
DO NOT FORGET OVERHEAD AND PROFIT

EXTRA WORK CAN MEAN NO PROFIT
ALL COSTS OF EXTRA WORK MUST BE BILLED
BEFORE DECIDING, ASK "WHAT IF...?"
CHOOSE THE CORRECT SOURCE OF FINANCE
KNOW YOUR NET RETURN
CONSIDER ALL FACTORS
YOU MUST KNOW AND USE ROI
KNOW AND CONTROL ROI
CONTROL MEANS PROFIT

PROFIT AIDS:

PROFIT OPPORTUNITY EXAMPLES:

CASE I: MAKING PARTIAL PAYMENTS WORK FOR YOU

CASE II: POSITIVE CASH FLOW AND REAL COSTS

CASE III: "WHAT IF...?" AND INTEREST LEVERAGE

CASE IV: "WHAT IF...?" AND ROI

CHAPTER 6

PROFIT GUIDES:

DEFINE YOUR GOALS AND OBJECTIVES

YOU MUST KNOW AND USE COMPANY BREAK-EVEN SCHEDULE ANALYSIS

PROFIT OPPORTUNITY EXAMPLES:

HOW TO DEAL WITH LATE PAYMENT: A CASE EXAMPLE

PROFIT AIDS:

Figure 6.1   Project and Company Profit Equation

CHAPTER 7

PROFIT GUIDES:

EFFECTIVE COMMUNICATION MEANS PROFIT
CONTRACTING IS TEAMWORK
WITH COMMUNICATION AND ACCOUNTABILITY YOU HAVE
   ACTION
THE OWNER MUST BE INFORMED
DOCUMENT EVERYTHING IN WRITING
CONFIRM ALL TELEPHONE CONVERSATIONS IN WRITING
INCREASED CONTROL INCREASES SALES
A COMPUTER IS USELESS WITHOUT A GOOD MANUAL
   SYSTEM

PROFIT AIDS:

PROFIT OPPORTUNITY EXAMPLES:

DEALING WITH DECREASED SALES: A CASE EXAMPLE

Glossary

ABANDONMENT: Termination of all field work before the contract is completed.

ACCELERATION: Shortening the overall project schedule on one or more subcontractor's schedule.

ACCEPTANCE TIME LAG: The time between when a physical change in the work is required to when it is authorized and planned for in the project schedule.

ACCOUNTABILITY: Being responsible for one's actions.

ADDENDUMS: Additions or deletions made by the owner to the original contract specifications, normally before construction begins.

AECR: Assumed Expense of Contracted Risk. The dollars, similar to an insurance premium, required to protect the contractor against those risks of impacted damages he has accepted in the project contract documents.

AEPR: Assumed Expense of Project Risk. The dollars, similar to an insurance premium, required to protect the owner against those risks of impacted damages he has accepted in the project. In the case of the owner these risks are the ones he is left with, those that have not been accepted by his contractors.

ANTICIPATED PROFITS: The amount of profit originally expected from the base contract and provided for in the contractor's bid. This includes provisions for anticipated profits of impacted damage when incurred ("profits of float time" and "profits of new time").

APPROVALS: Owner's acceptance of materials and equipment to be used in the construction of the project.

AS-BUILT DRAWINGS: Modified original contract drawings that delineate all deviations from the original drawings made during construction.

ASSETS: All things of value owned by the company. Tangible things or intangible rights that constitute the resources of a company.

ATTITUDE AND MORALE: The general perception of workers and supervisors on the project relevant to whether they believe it is a well-run project and one they are proud to be working on.

AVERAGE PROFIT: Total net income for one year divided by total net sales for the same period of time.

BALANCE SHEET: A financial catalog of assets, liabilities, and owner's equity, stating the financial health of a company at a specific point in time.

BASE MAN-HOUR RATE: The amount of money paid in wages before all deductions or additions of any working benefits.

BENEFICIAL OCCUPANCY: Being forced to work in close proximity with the owner's personnel because he has moved in and taken over part or all of the project for his own use.

BID DOCUMENTS: All information furnished to the contractor by the owner and governing authorities. All information furnished to the owner and governing authorities by the contractor.

BID MANAGEMENT: The second element of a profit management system. The determination of strategies to carry out company goals and objectives and the development and implementation of tactics to actualize these strategies.

BREAK-EVEN ANALYSIS: A numerical evaluation of profit and loss that determines the amount of existing profit or loss at a specific point in time relative to known fixed expenses.

BREAK-EVEN POINT: A point in time, money, or sales where all fixed expenses have been paid.

BREAK-EVEN SCHEDULE ANALYSIS: A financial evaluation of the break-even position relative to time periods and sales volume. The evaluation determines the amount of sales below or above the break-even point for each time period.

BREAK-EVEN SCHEDULING: A financial chart of the break-even position relative to time periods and sales volume.

BUDGET: An explicit allocation of financial resources.

BUSINESS PLAN: Overall organizational strategy of a contracting firm consisting of the basic goals and objectives of the organization, the major programs of actions, and the allocation of resources needed to achieve these goals.

CARTAGE: The total costs for the transportation of tools and materials from manufacturer, supplier, or warehouse to the project site by other than commercial carrier.

CASH FLOW PROJECTION: A statement of the cash required relative to time. This is the total difference between cash inflow and outflow, relative to time.

CBM: Critical Bar Method. A method of project scheduling.

CHANGES IN CODES AND REGULATIONS: Changes in various regulatory codes and regulations that occur after the awarding of the contract.

CINPROM™: CINematography PROject Management. A method of visual project management.

CLAIM RECOVERY AND SETTLEMENT COSTS: All expenses incurred by the claimant while pursuing payment.

COLLECTION MANAGEMENT: The fourth element of a profit management system. The management of the method of collection of all invoices, the conditions of collection, and the optimum method of payment.

COMMERCIAL INSURANCE: Third party insurance. Pertains to who is the insurer and to whom the premium is paid. Insurance coverage provided by a third party (the insurer) for a stipulated premium paid by the insuree.

COMMON STOCKHOLDER BENEFITS: To receive the highest return on total stockholder's equity, at the lowest possible risk for growth and profit.

COMMUNICATION: The process of transferring knowledge or information onto others.

COMPANY BREAK-EVEN POINT: The point in time and money where the company's fixed expenses are paid for and the company starts to make money.

COMPANY BREAK-EVEN SCHEDULE: A financial chart of the company's break-even position relative to time periods and sales volume.

COMPANY BREAK-EVEN SCHEDULE ANALYSIS: A financial evaluation of the break-even position relative to fiscal calendar time periods and sales volume. The evaluation determines the amount of sales below or above the break-even point for each time period.

COMPANY PROFIT EQUATION: Profit equal to full payment. Full payment consists of two factors: break-even company payment and profit payment. Therefore, profit is equal to full payment, which in turn is equal to break-even company payment and profit payment.

CONCEALED CONDITIONS: Conditions that were not recognized when the contract was awarded but proved to be at variance with contract documents at a later date.

CONSTRUCTION FUNDAMENTAL ANALYSIS: Used in bid management. Evaluation of the social needs and the anticipated type and quantity of contracts that will be awarded.

CONSTRUCTION MANAGEMENT: A system that efficiently manages a contract or firm.

CONSTRUCTION PROFIT MANAGEMENT: Company preplanned profit and growth that maximizes the benefits to the owners (common stockholders) at the lowest possible risk. It consists of risk, bid, money, and collection management, which executes the goals set by the company business plan and project schedule governed by the information and control system.

CONSTRUCTION TECHNICAL ANALYSIS: Used in bid management. Evaluation of the type and quantity of contracts currently being awarded in the marketplace.

CONSTRUCTIVE OR UNAUTHORIZED CHANGES: Changes in work necessary to proceed with the project schedule.

CONTRACT: A promise to perform a specific task at a particular time for a specified consideration.

CONTRACT AWARD COSTS: Costs incurred by the owner or contractor in bidding and obtaining or awarding the final contract.

CONTRACT DOCUMENTS: All bid documents, drawings, specifications, addendums, revisions, correspondence, and written contract on which the contractor has based his contract bid price.

CONTRACT DRAWINGS: Drawings furnished by the owner or contractor that define the scope of work to be performed by the contractor. Those drawings are made part of the original contract.

CONTRACT ORGANIZATION: The organization of project responsibility delineated in the contract.

CONTRACT SPECIFICATIONS: Written description furnished by the owner or contractor that defines the scope of work to be performed by the contractor. Also describes type of materials to be furnished by the contractors. These specifications are made part of the original contract.

CONTRACTING COMPANY: A firm that performs more than one contract over an extended period of time.

CONTRACTOR: Earns income by performing one contract.

CONTRIBUTION MARGIN: The remaining total dollars available to pay off fixed expense and preplanned profit after deducting all variable costs.

CONVENIENCE TERMINATION: Termination of the contract for the sole convenience of the owner.

COST PLUS CONTRACT: A contract whereby the beneficiary of the contract assumes all risk of contract performance and pays all costs to perform the contract plus a stipulated monetary amount for profit.

COST PLUS PRICING: What management *thinks* it needs for overhead and what it would *like* for profit, as opposed to preplanned profit and growth based on pricing developed with the tools of bid management.

COSTS: Those dollars spent for materials and services that can be traced directly to the building of the project.

CPM: Critical Path Method. A method of project scheduling.

CREW SIZE: The number of workers per supervisor. Crew size is often determined by the amount of supervision available on a project or the type of work to be performed.

CURRENT ASSETS: All company resources that are expected to be realized in cash within one year.

CURRENT LIABILITIES: All company debts that are expected to be paid with current assets. Thus, current liabilities are expected to be paid within one year.

DEFAULT TERMINATION: Termination of the contractor's work at the project site by the owners physically taking control of the contractor's work, tools, and materials.

DEFECTIVE APPROVAL: The owner's refusal to approve adequate substitutes for specified materials or methods when specified materials are unattainable or specified methods are impossible.

DEFECTIVE PAYMENT: Any deviation from the terms of payment of the original contract documents.

DEFECTIVE PERFORMANCE: Any fault or error by company personnel that is not in accordance with the project plans and specifications.

DEFECTIVE PLANS AND SPECIFICATIONS: Term applied to a project completed correctly by a contractor from plans and specifications that he has altered to correct any defective portions of those plans and specifications.

DEFECTIVE REJECTION: Owner's rejection of work or material that requires the contractor to rework what has already been installed in accordance with the contract documents.

DELAYED COMPLETION: The extension of the original contract time schedule, requiring work to be performed in "new time."

DELAYED PAYMENT: Owner's late payment for correct work performed and invoiced by the contractor.

DEMAND CURVE: The relationship of the amount of contracts won to the award price.

DESIGN STABILITY: The state-of-the-art architectural and engineering development of the project to be constructed.

DETAIL DRAWINGS: How-to drawings required to manufacture and install equipment and material.

DILUTION OF SUPERVISION: Decrease of supervision productivity due to a diversion of supervision from the original contract work to other matters.

DIRECT COST ACCOUNTING: A system of accounting designed to provide tax liability information. Has limited management value.

DIRECT INTERFERENCE: Any overt occurrence that delays the timely and productive completion of the contract.

DOC: Daily Operating Control sheet. A tool for daily management operations.

EBIT: Earnings before interest and taxes are deducted.

ENGINEERING ERRORS AND OMISSIONS: Term applied to a project completed incorrectly by a contractor from defective plans and specifications as a result of engineering errors and omissions.

ENTITLEMENT: The legal right to some amount of monetary consideration.

ENVIRONMENTAL CONDITIONS: The effects on worker productivity of temperature, humidity, wind, rain, snow and sleet, freezing rain, temperature extremes, dense fog, ground freeze, drying conditions, temperature inversions, and flooding.

EPR: Expense of Project Risk. Is the amount of dollars, similar to an insurance premium, chargeable to impacted damages. It is the total amount of project impact damage liability divided between the principals involved in the project.

EQUIPMENT THEFT AND VANDALISM: Unauthorized removal or destruction of equipment and tools stored on the project site.

ERRORS AND OMISSIONS: Work that is incomplete, poorly completed, or not completed at all.

ESTOPPELED SCHEDULE DEVIATIONS: Expressed contract document provisions that anticipate and provide for schedule deviations, limit or preclude the contractor's right of recovery, or provide no reasonable basis to expect the contractor to complete the work in a fixed period of time.

EXPENSES: Those dollars spent on company operations that are incurred if no projects are performed.

EXTENDED DIRECT JOB EXPENSES: Additional jobsite expenses incurred due to schedule delays.

EXTENDED MAIN OFFICE OVERHEAD: Additional main office expenses incurred due to schedule delays.

EXTERNAL PROJECT DEFAULT TERMINATION: The owner's termination of the contractor's project site work.

EXTERNAL PROJECT TERMINATION: A point in time when all project site work is completed in accordance with the contract documents.

EXTERNAL SUPERVISION: The supervisory personnel required at the project site for the safe and productive execution of the contract work.

EXTERNALLY CAUSED DAMAGES: Damages caused by outside factors beyond the control of the contractor.

EXTRA: Work required in addition to the original contract drawings and specifications.

FAST TRACK: Project site work commencing before contract drawings and specifications are complete.

FBO: Materials that are Furnished By Others.

FINAL INSPECTION: Determination of the correctness of material and equipment installed with conformity to as-built drawings that the owner has approved.

FINANCING: Charges incurred for working capital to benefit work beyond the scope of the contract documents.

FIXED EXPENSE: Those dollars spent for items that must be paid whether sales revenue is realized or not.

FIXED-PRICE CONTRACT: States that the beneficiary of the contract assumes partial or no risk in the performance of the contract and pays one stipulated monetary amount.

FLOAT TIME: The difference in time between the budgeted completion time originally planned on and the actual ahead-of-schedule completion time.

FREIGHT: Total costs for the transportation of tools and materials from the manufacturer, supplier, or warehouse to the project site by commercial carrier.

FRONT-END LOADING: Contract partial payments that provide the contractor the majority of his overhead and profit before the completion of the first half of the contract.

GENERAL SERVICE ADMINISTRATION (GSA): The construction contracting authority of the U.S. government.

HAZARDOUS PAY: Premium payment to workers for work performed in hazardous conditions.

ICS: Information and control system. The information and control system is a network of various channels of communication and a system of checks and balances that manages the entire project schedule or business plan.

IMPACTED DAMAGES: Losses from the originally scheduled time period in which the job should have been completed and the additional losses incurred as the job is extended into and completed in a new time period or periods.

IMPOSSIBILITY OF PERFORMANCE: When performance as specified in the contract documents which cannot be completed by any contractor.

INCOME STATEMENT: A financial catalog of costs, expenses, and taxes, stating the financial operations over a period of time.

INDIRECT INTERFERENCE: Any covert occurrence that delays the timely and productive completion of the contract.

INFORMATION AND CONTROL SYSTEM: A network of various channels of communication and a system of checks and balances that manages the entire project schedule or business plan.

INFORMATION FLOW: The written, verbal, and visual interchange of information between field, office, and owner.

INSURANCE: All insurance related to the project and its activities, such as Worker's Compensation, hospitalization, bonding, and special policies.

INTEREST: The cost of borrowing money to finance the contractor's labor and material costs.

INTEREST LEVERAGE: (1) To secure funds at a fixed rate of interest and invest them at a rate of return greater than the fixed rate paid for them, and (2) Maximize interest leverage for the highest possible return on common stockholders' equity.

INTERFERENCE: Any overt or covert occurrence that delays the timely and productive completion of a contract.

INTERNAL PROJECT DEFAULT TERMINATION: The owner's termination of required project work being done by the contractor's internal project management and support office personnel caused by the contractor's failure to proceed with the diligence to ensure completion of the contract within the time specified in the contract documents.

INTERNAL PROJECT TERMINATION: A point in time when all project work required by the contract of the contractor's management and support office personnel is complete.

INTERNAL SUPERVISION: The supervisory personnel required to coordinate activities between all principals involved in the project: owner, architect, engineer, manufacturer, supplier, inspector, subcontractor, external supervision, support office personnel, and so forth.

INTERNALLY CAUSED DAMAGES: Damages caused by the contractor himself.

INTERRUPTED BUSINESS: The stoppage of normal business by one or more of the principals involved in the project.

INTERRUPTED UTILITIES: The unplanned interruption of utilities at the project site, which are required for the productive execution of the contract work. These utilities include electricity, heat, light, air, and water.

JOINT OCCUPANCY: When work area is occupied by another organization performing tasks not stipulated in the original bid documents.

LABOR ESCALATION: The increase in hourly wage rates relevant to the wage rate anticipated in the project bid.

LEARNING CURVE: The time required to become familiar with the work, supervision, other workers' habits and abilities, types of tools available, where tools are stored, procedures regarding working, and safety are all factors of the learning curve.

LETTER OF TRANSMITTAL: A letter or preprinted form that accompanies and describes the data being sent and the action the sender expects the recipient to perform.

LIABILITIES: All debts of a company. All things of value owed by the company. Tangible things or services that constitute the debts of a company.

LIQUIDATED DAMAGES: A specified amount of dollars required to be paid to the owner by the contractor for each day the contractor takes to complete the project in addition to the time allotted in the original project schedule.

LONG-TERM ASSETS: All company resources that are set aside in special funds or investments.

LONG-TERM LIABILITIES: All long-term debts of a company. They are expected to be paid in a period of time in excess of one year.

MACHINERY RENTAL: The commercial rental rate for all machinery used on a project.

MAINTENANCE MANUALS: Written instructions from manufacturers and engineers on the correct procedures for maintenance of the equipment installed by the contractor.

MANAGEMENT ACTION: A system whereby management takes positive action to exceptions to preplanned profit and growth. The action is in accordance with a clear and concise business plan and project schedule. Governed by a responsible and accountable information and control system.

MANAGEMENT BY REACTION: All effort put into "the problem of the day." No system of identifying losses.

MANAGEMENT OF EXCEPTIONS: A system whereby management knows and acts upon negative variations to preplanned profit.

MANPOWER UNAVAILABILITY: The unavailability of qualified and productive workers, which necessitates retaining less productive workers in order to maintain sufficient manpower to meet original schedule.

MARGIN: The amount of money earned in excess of break-even on an individual project.

MARKET PENETRATION: The share of the total available market, measured in number of clients, dollars per client, and total dollar volume.

MARKET TIMING: Knowing when to start developing internal company expertise in a newly emerging type of construction project. Founded on construction, technical, and fundamental analysis.

MATERIAL ESCALATION: The increase in the price of materials between the time of order and the time of payment.

MATERIAL PROCUREMENT: All work and costs associated with the purchase of materials.

MATERIAL STORAGE: All storage of materials, either on the job site or in an off-site warehouse.

MATERIAL THEFT AND VANDALISM: Unauthorized removal or destruction of material stored at the project site.

MONEY MANAGEMENT: The third element of a profit management system. The management of all assets and liabilities for maximum stockholder benefit.

NEGATIVE CASH FLOW: The lack of enough cash to pay all costs and expenses during the execution of a contract.

NEW TIME: The time required to complete a project that was not planned for in the original contract schedule.

NEW WORK DAMAGE: The costs incurred to restore completed work to its original condition because of unintentional damage done by others.

NONWORKING SUPERVISION: Project site supervisory personnel who do not perform work with "tools." Complete time is spent supervising other workers.

OPERATING LEVERAGE: Determines the percentage increase (or decrease) in profit caused by a percentage increase (or decrease) in sales. The formula is

$$\text{Operating Leverage} = \frac{\text{Contribution Margin}}{\text{Profit}}$$

OPERATING MANUALS: Written instructions from manufacturers and engineers on the correct procedures for operating the equipment installed by the contractor.

OUT-OF-SEQUENCE WORK: Work that does not follow a logical path to produce maximum productivity.

OVERTIME: The time worked "beyond" that of a normal workday in the area where the project is being built.

PARTIAL PAYMENT: Contract payments for labor and material during the progress of the contract.

PERFORMANCE SPECIFICATIONS: Contract specifications written by the owner that specify only the end result of the project acceptable to the owner.

PERT: Program evaluation research tank. A method of project scheduling.

POSITIVE CASH FLOW: The excess of cash after the payment of all costs and expenses during the execution of a contract.

PREINSPECTION: Determination of the correctness of material and equipment prior to installation.

PREMIUM PAY: Any payment to workers in addition to the "going" rate or union agreement.

PREPLANNED PROFIT: Providing a total dollar amount as the first item of expense.

PROFIT EQUATION: Profit is equal to full payment.

PROFIT MANAGEMENT: Risk management, bid management, money management, and collection management. (See Construction Profit Management.)

PROFIT OF A COMPANY: The amount of net income realized by a company at the end of its fiscal year.

PROFIT OF A PROJECT: The amount of money originally anticipated in the contractor's bid as "margin."

PROFIT OF FLOAT TIME: The amount of money that is saved by reducing the original scheduled construction time.

PROFIT OF IMPACTED DAMAGES: The amount of money that is added to float time losses and new time losses.

PROFIT OF INDUSTRY AVERAGES: The average profit of construction companies, including the worst performing companies and the best performing companies.

PROFIT OF NEW TIME: The amount of money that is added to all costs and expenses to complete a project in a time period beyond the completion date specified in the original construction schedule.

PROFIT PAYMENT: Year-end earnings in excess of company break-even point.

PROJECT BREAK-EVEN POINT: The point in time and money where the project starts to make money.

PROJECT BREAK-EVEN SCHEDULE: A financial chart of the project's break-even position relative to contract time periods and contract dollar amount.

PROJECT BREAK-EVEN SCHEDULE ANALYSIS: A financial evaluation of the break-even position relative to project calendar time periods and contract dollar amount. The evaluation determines the amount of sales below or above the break-even point for each time period.

PROJECT EXPANSION: The increase of the amount of man-hours required to perform the original contract.

PROJECT FIXED EXPENSE: The total monetary amount required to execute one project without profit.

PROJECT ORGANIZATION: The organization of project responsibility and authority.

PROJECT SCHEDULE: The "game plan" for completing an individual project on time and on budget.

PUNCH LIST: A list of all items of work not in conformance with the original contract drawings.

QUANTUM: The amount of monetary consideration.

RATIO ANALYSIS: A numerical comparison of the proportional relationship between two quantities.

REASSIGNMENT OF MANPOWER: The changing of the job assignments of the crew or individual workers once they have been hired, trained, and scheduled.

RECOVERY CLAIM: Invoice (consisting of a substantiating four-part report) for the costs of all recoverable impacted damages.

REJECTED CHANGE ORDERS: Owner-requested engineering work and cost estimates of changes in the original work that is subsequently rejected or ignored.

REMOVAL OF DEBRIS: The removal of debris from the job site, such as equipment packing materials.

REPAIR MANUALS: Written instructions from manufacturers and contractors on the correct procedures for repair of the equipment installed by the contractor.

RETAINAGE: A dollar amount that is withheld by the owner from each project partial payment made to the contractor.

REVISIONS: Improvements made by the owner to the original contract drawings either before or after construction begins.

RIGHTS OF RECOVERY: Those rights that provide an owner reasons to pay a recovery claim early.

RIPPLE: The direct effect of change orders or delays from one contractor to the schedule or sequence of work of another contractor.

RISK MANAGEMENT: The first element of a profit management system. Risk management is knowing what the contract risks are, knowing how they can be controlled, and taking action to effectively control the risks that fall upon the contractor's shoulders.

ROI: Return On Investment (of owner's equity):

$$ROI = \frac{Total\ Net\ Income}{Total\ Owner's\ Equity}$$

$$ROI = \quad Average\ Profit \times Turnover$$

$$ROI = \frac{Total\ Net\ Income}{Net\ Sales} \times \frac{Net\ Sales}{Total\ Owner\ Equity}$$

ROI OF EQUIPMENT: Return On Investment of owner's equity invested in equipment:

$$ROI\ (of\ Equipment) = \frac{Total\ Net\ Income}{Net\ Sales} \times \frac{Net\ Sales}{Equipment}$$

SABOTAGE: Intentional damage done to job site material and equipment.

SCHEDULE STABILITY: The amount of time variation that is reasonably expected in the original project construction schedule.

SEGMENTED ABSORPTION ACCOUNTING: Financial management tool. Numerically separates each project and generates a clear financial picture of the amount each project is contributing toward company fixed expenses.

SELF-INSURANCE: First or second party insurance. Pertains to who is the insurer and to whom the premium is paid. Insurance coverage provided by the insuree. The insurer and the insuree are one and the same.

SEMIVARIABLE COST: Income statement items that have both variable-cost and fixed-expense components.

SHIFT WORK: When more than one eight-hour working period per day is utilized on a project.

SHOW-UP TIME: Compensation for workers who "show up" for canceled work.

SHUT-DOWN COSTS: All costs associated with stopping a project.

SIDs: Sources of Impacted Damages; occurrences that negatively affect project break-even.

SITE ACCESS: Security regulations necessary to obtain clearances for workers or other special conditions required to enter the work area that can cause additional expenses.

SITE OBSTRUCTIONS: Anything that physically prohibits workers from proceeding with their work.

STACKING OF TRADES: Multiple crews of different trades working in a confined area, thus reducing the ability of working in an orderly and efficient manner.

START-UP: Placing the equipment installed by the contractor in working operation.

START-UP COSTS: All costs associated with "commencing work" on a project.

START-UP SUPERVISION: Supervision necessary during the time of placing the installed equipment in working operation.

STEP CURVE: The graphic depiction of how there can suddenly be a tremendous amount of work and then absolutely no work.

STIPULATED PRICE CHANGES: A fixed-price change that is provided for in the original contract documents.

STRIKES: Direct and indirect labor strikes that affect the timely execution of the contract.

SUSPENSION: Suspension of any part of the contract work for a period of time.

TAXES: The obligation to federal and state governing authorities relevant to labor and material.

T_e: Time used to perform the originally scheduled task ahead of schedule.

TECHNICAL MANAGEMENT: Estimating and engineering capabilities applied to labor, material installation techniques, and cost control.

TERMINATION: A point in time when all work is completed in accordance with the contract documents.

TIME-AND-MATERIAL CHANGES: Owner-authorized changes that are paid on a time-and-material basis.

TOOL RENTAL: The commercial rental rate for all tools used on a project.

TRADING AREA: The geographical area in which a company performs the majority of their projects.

TRAVEL: Payment to workers for their travel expenses.

TREND ANALYSIS: A comparison of the proportional relationship between two quantities relative to time.

T_s: Time scheduled in the original project schedule.

TURNOVER: The proportional relationship between net sales revenue and owner's equity available to be used in performing total sales. The number of times owner's equity equals net sales revenue in one year.

UNAVAILABILITY OF ADEQUATE TOOLS AND EQUIPMENT: Unforeseen tools and equipment that are required at a project site.

UNCONSCIONABLE ACTIONS: Actions taken by others that any reasonable person would consider outrageous.

UNCONSCIONABLE CLAUSES: Clauses in the contract documents that do not provide for both parties' benefit or protection.

UNFORESEEABLE DELAYS: All project delays beyond the contractor's control.

UNILATERAL CHANGES: An authorization in the original contract documents that gives the owner the right to direct the contractor to proceed with a change prior to an agreement on price and time extensions.

UNIT-PRICE CHANGES: Changes authorized by the owner based on unit prices provided by the contractor in his bid.

VANDALISM TO STRUCTURES: Intentional damage done to material and work already performed and installed at the project site.

VARIABLE COSTS: Those dollars spent for materials and services that can be traced directly to the building of the project.

WARRANTY RISKS AND COSTS: Warranties provided by the contractor and manufacturers.

WORK ORDER: Written confirmation of a request for work in addition to the original contract.

WORK WITH TOOLS: The process of installing material and labor, also referred to as "swinging the tools."

WORKING INSPECTION: Determination of the correctness of material and equipment installed with conformity to original contract drawings and specifications during the progress of the project.

WORKING SUPERVISION: Project site supervisory personnel who supervise other workers and also work with "tools."

Index

Rejected change orders, 33, 70
Removal of debris, 36, 77
Rental:
  machinery, 36, 77
  tool, 36, 77
Repair manuals, 31, 65
Return on investment (ROI), 183
  case study of, 218-20, 222-27
  how to maintain and control, 219-20
  risk management and, 226-27
Revisions, 31, 66
Risk management:
  contracts and, 45-54
  how it works, 42-43
  profit and, 43-45
  return on investment and, 226-27
Ripple, 29, 59

S

Sabotage, 28, 57
Schedule stability, 30, 63
Self-insurance, 36, 78
Semivariable expenses, 9-10
Settlement costs and claim recovery, 37, 80
Shift work, 35, 76
Show-up time, 35, 75
Shut-down costs, 37, 80
Site access, 27, 55
Site obstructions, 27, 55, 258
Sources of impacted damages (SIDs), 189,
    212, 213
  abandonment, 34, 73
  acceleration, 29, 59
  acceptance time lag, 33, 70
  addendums, 31, 65-66
  anticipated profits, 37, 80
  approvals, 31, 66
  as-built drawings, 31, 64
  attitude and morale, 28, 57
  beneficial occupancy, 29, 58
  cartage, 36, 77-78
  changes in codes and regulations, 32, 68
  claim recovery and settlement costs, 37, 80
  commercial insurance, 36, 78
  concealed conditions, 32, 68-69
  constructive or unauthorized changes,
    32, 67-68
  contract award costs, 37, 79
  contract organization, 29, 59-60
  convenience termination, 34, 74
  crew size, 29, 60
  default termination, 34, 74

Sources of impacted damages (SIDs)
    (cont'd.)
  defective approval, 33, 70
  defective payment, 33, 71
  defective performance, 32, 69
  defective plans and specifications, 32, 69
  defective rejection, 33, 70-71
  delayed completion, 27, 54
  delayed payment, 33, 71
  design stability, 30, 63-64
  detail drawings, 31, 64
  dilution of supervision, 28, 58
  engineering errors and omissions, 32, 70
  environmental conditions, 27, 54-55, 258
  equipment theft and vandalism, 28, 57
  errors and omissions, 32, 69
  estoppeled schedule deviations, 33, 71-72
  extended direct job expenses, 37, 80
  extended main office overhead, 37, 80
  external project default
    termination, 34, 74
  external project termination, 34, 73
  external supervision, 29, 60-61
  FBO, 35, 76
  final inspection, 30, 63
  financing, 37, 79
  foreman and checklist of, 258-59
  freight, 36, 77
  hazardous pay, 35, 75
  impossibility of performance, 33, 71
  insurance, 36, 78
  interest, 37, 79
  internal project default
    termination, 35, 74
  internal project termination, 34, 73-74
  internal supervision, 29, 61
  interrupted business, 29, 59
  interrupted utilities, 28, 56-57
  joint occupancy, 28, 58
  labor escalation, 35, 75
  learning curve, 27, 56
  liquidated damages, 33, 72
  machinery rental, 36, 77
  maintenance manuals, 31, 65
  manpower unavailability, 27, 56, 258
  material escalation, 36, 76
  material procurement, 35, 76
  material storage, 36, 76-77
  material theft and vandalism, 28, 57-58
  new work damage, 28, 58
  nonworking supervision, 30, 61
  operating manuals, 31, 65
  out-of-sequence work, 27, 55, 258